£2.50

GW00566810

No Shining Armour

A PLATFORM BOOK

No Shining Armour

Edward Milne

JOHN CALDER
LONDON

First published in Great Britain 1976 by
John Calder (Publishers) Ltd.,
18 Brewer Street, London W1R 4AS.

ISBN 0 7145 3501 X casebound
     0 7145 3514 1 paperback

Typeset in 11 on 12 point Plantin by
Woolaston Parker Ltd., Leicester

Printed in England by
Compton Offset Ltd.,
Frome, Somerset.

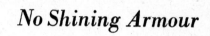

No Shining Armour

Chapter One

My grandmother's home was in an Aberdeen tenement, where she lived until her death, and it is my earliest childhood recollection. It was there that the workaday existence of one of the great cities of the world whirled around me in the period during and after the Great War of 1914–18 and where I found myself again in September 1939 at the start of the Second World War. Reared and nurtured in that turbulent atmosphere, one did not need lessons in political economy to understand the need for social change of a world in turmoil.

Six large families were reared and nurtured in that stone-staired granite building at 53 Spring Garden. My grandfather was a docker, living with all the uncertainty of employment that the calling implied, and my earliest memories, strange in the light of my involvement some forty odd years later with Blyth and its people, were of reading or having read to me the shipping notes that gave details of coal movements from that Northumberland port, which would provide much needed employment for my grandfather and his mates on the Aberdeen dockside, who might well have been hanging around the harbour entrance at the time waiting for work to turn up. For me good news meant sweets or pocket money on the Saturday evening, so the names of coal boats like the *Thrift*, *Ferryhill*, *Redhall*, *Spray* and others had a ring of glory to them, and their coming and going provided me with my first lessons in economic theory. My mother's parents and family lived in that Aberdeen tenement, but my father sprang from the same stock, born and bred in the Liberal Radical tradition of North East Scotland and moving, inevitably, from there to the policies, programmes and sometime evangelical messages preached by Smillie,

Hardie, John Wheatley, Maxton and a host of others. In those days coming from a farming community often meant having to seek work in the city; my grandfather had to take up employment at the Corporation gas works. Because of this, I was in contact with both town and country.

To-day's economic upsurge, arising from the discovery of oil and gas in the North Sea is hardly likely to have more impact on the lives of people in that area than the effect of the 1914–18 war through which my parents and grandparents lived. I am not sure when political ideas first entered my mind, but my hatred of war, its waste and its horror, is easy to trace. Two years after I was born in another Aberdeen tenement, 32 St. Clair Street, my father was badly wounded at the battle of Beaumont Hamel in France, suffering in the decade that followed a series of major operations which left him with a permanent disability and continuing ill health. So it was not surprising that I, the eldest of four sons, who from around the age of five to twelve or thirteen, who had to watch father departing periodically for hospitals in Edinburgh and Glasgow, with all the attendant struggles with authority about pensions, unemployment benefit and other associated matters, should turn to questioning the kind of society in which we lived.

The industrial unrest of the 1920s has provided many an economic historian with his material. I was ten years old when the General Strike of 1926 hit a disturbed and troubled Britain. Just as I wondered why my father, reared in the North East of Scotland, should have had his health shattered in a conflict with men of his own kind with whom he had no quarrel in a far-off-land, so the appearance of colliery bands in the streets of Aberdeen appealing for help, financial and otherwise, for the wives and children of men living in colliery villages in Scotland and North East England, appeared to my boyhood mind to have an air of unreality about it. Living at that time in Bedford Road near the great Kittybrewster Goods Station I was roped in, by no means unwillingly, to distribute leaflets for the National Union of Railwaymen.

On the Friday that the Strike was called off, I was collecting bread from a Co-operative van and the dark pain of that news I remember vividly. The days of excitement, even hope, which had led me to think a new era was dawning were finished, but the foreboding had started. The elation of strike activity gave way to a dull apathy. Talk of recession, high unemployment and hard times meant nothing new to the ordinary folk in that corner of North East Scotland that had already endured so much in the past. But Britain moved ahead. Apparent normality returned to the industrial field, and the Labour Party was returned with Ramsay McDonald as Premier at the general election of 1st June 1929. Victory at the polls was the political answer to the general election defeat of 1926 and the bitter period that followed. Again for the working class there was a glow of hope throughout Britain. Labour was at the helm, McDonald was in Downing Street and political democracy seemed to be ahead. 'Just wait and see what can and will be done': such was the mood of expectancy as Britain moved towards the nineteen thirties. But in 1931, so often compared to the Britain of 1974, there was impending slump, world recession, high unemployment, and a coalition government. Around me, in the homes of both my grandparents, there was an air of depression and defeat aroused by the sense of betrayal. McDonald had become a nasty word and another stage in the country's post-first world war history had arrived, or was it the run up to world war No. 2? Father was still being moved backwards and forwards to hospitals in Glasgow and Edinburgh, times were hard but not noticeably so, for all around us in the streets we knew, people were living the same sort of lives, facing the same sort of problems. Nations do not indulge in war, or preparation for war, with the attendant aftermath of boom and slump, without feeling the draught, and in some cases gale-force winds.

Due to the Aberdeen habit of 'flittin' each quarter, families moved from tenement to tenement and this in our case meant being at three schools before the age of eleven, George Street, Kittybrewster and Sunnybank. Education in Aberdeen was of a high standard and I was fortunate enough to get a scholarship to Robert Gordon's College at 11 years of age. This was not the result of any outstanding academic merit, for there were hundreds who could equally have qualified in the school. Nevertheless I went gratefully to Gordon's College and as in my previous schools I felt particular gratitude for the teachers I came to know there, who helped me to think for myself and get the maximum value and enjoyment from reading. Where I might have gone from Gordon's no one knows, for father, who had managed in the intervals between treatment at home and visits to hospitals in the South to acquire a small confectionery and grocery shop in the town for the now seemingly ridiculous price of £25, fell seriously ill and had to be removed to hospital. No more college. I was in charge of a shop, plunged in at the deep end. My entry into the distributive trade was to lead me into varied fields, and ultimately to Parliament.

One other factor in my political apprenticeship in Aberdeen remains an abiding memory and guided me to a large extent in my Parliamentary life, at Constituency level and in the House of Commons. Just after being returned in the 1929 election, Frank Rose, the member for North Aberdeen, died and his successor chosen to fight the by-election for Labour was Wedgwood Benn, father of the present controversial Tony Benn. Benn was returned to Parliament and became Secretary of State for India in the McDonald administration. The by-election fought by Benn in Aberdeen was the first occasion on which the Communist Party had fought a Labour candidate since its formation after the First World War.

On the day of his election to Parliament, Benn toured the constituency and told his audiences that now he was returned as MP, all his constituents, no matter how they voted, were his responsibility and could bring their problems to him. It was a point I was to use later in my own speech following election to Parliament in 1960 for the Blyth Constituency.

Labour was swamped in the landslide election of 1931. McDonald, Snowdon and others had decided to form a Coalition Government, a National Government as it was styled. The feel of economic and financial collapse was in the air, for Britain and the world had entered the 1930s, the era of mass unemployment, rearmament, the rise of Hitler and the Second World War. Although I had helped in the General Strike and in the North Aberdeen by-election and others around that period, I did not join the Labour Party until 1934. That year I attended my first meeting of the Greyfriars Ward Labour Party, in the

North Aberdeen Constituency, where the prospective Labour candidate was then Garro Jones, later to become Lord Trefgarne and a Minister in the 1945 Attlee Administration. But I was never happy in the Labour Party, although the comradeship was warm and friendly, and the political discussions interesting and enlivening. My instinct, and my heart was with the Maxton-led Independent Labour Party. The war clouds were looming ahead, the tragedy of Spain and the Labour Party Conference decision to support the Government policy of non-intervention, made in 1936 in Edinburgh, which meant no arms or assistance were sent to Republican Spain, led to my resigning from the Labour Party in 1937 and joining the ILP.

The war clouds were gathering on the horizon: Chamberlain was in conflict with Eden, his Foreign Secretary, who resigned in 1938, mainly because the Prime Minister was carrying on negotiations and discussions with Hitler without consulting Eden on the issues. Chamberlain and Czechoslovakia, and the deal with Hitler is a story in itself, but war was made more certain by the machinations of Britain's Prime Minister and those around him in Government then, than by any other cause.

September 3rd 1939 was one of the rare occasions when the House of Commons has met on a Sunday. World War Two had started. Arthur Greenwood, speaking for the Labour Party on that fateful Sunday morning, looked ahead to a distant peace when he said, 'Once the gunfire ceases and the roll of the war drums dies away, when dictatorships have disappeared for ever, there will emerge from the smoking ruins of the struggle, a new order of society.' But a long time was to pass before the guns were quiet, and in many ways we still await the beneficial changes he prophesied. The decision I took to refuse conscription, and my marriage in 1939, were both linked with my feelings about the era that had ended, and a war that had begun with the peace of 1918. David Low's marvellously prophetic cartoon, showing the war leaders leaving the Hall of Mirrors at Versailles at the end of the peace conference, watched by a small child from behind a pillar bearing the caption 1940, predicted almost to the day the beginning of the next war, and expressed vividly my feelings.

The early days of the war had a phony reality about them, but

Dunkirk, saturation bombing and a long conflict lay ahead. Churchill became Prime Minister and the course of history was altered. Churchill himself, in 1938, had laid the responsibility for the coming war and our unpreparedness for it, in the following words (Hansard 5th Oct 1938): 'When I think of the fair hopes of a long peace which still lay before Europe at the beginning of 1933, when Herr Hitler first obtained power, and of all the opportunities of arresting the growth of the Nazi power which have been neglected or squandered, I cannot believe that a parallel exists in the whole course of history. So far as this country is concerned, the responsibility must rest with those who have the undisputed control of our political affairs. They neither prevented Germany from rearming, nor did they rearm themselves in time. They quarrelled with Italy without saving Ethiopia. They exploited and discredited the vast institutions of the League of Nations, and they neglected to make alliances and combinations which might have repaired previous errors, and thus they left us in the hour of trial without adequate national defence or effective international security.'

Churchill of course was not himself entirely blameless in estimating the dangers ahead, nor the military action needed. His support for Hitler and Mussolini is instanced in his *Great Contemporaries:* 'Thus the world lives on, hopes on, that Hitler will emerge a gentler figure in a happier age;' or his reference that if he had been an Italian, he would have been a fascist. His military judgement cannot stand up to the examination of history either, when one recollects that during the Russian attack on Finland he stated, in a broadcast to the nation, 'Mankind owes a debt of gratitude to little Finland. The inefficiency and ineptitude of the Red Army, and the Red Air Force, have been exposed for ever in the Finnish snows.'

It is therefore not surprising that Nye Bevan in the same debate, pointed out to Churchill, and to the House of Commons, the full import of the Churchill appointment, not only to the nation but to the guilty men who had misled us in the thirties. Bevan finished the quotation and said, with a sweep of his arm across the Chamber, 'Those are the people Churchill will lead back to power. There they are. Those are the guilty men, all of them.' Again Bevan's gift of prophesy was revealed, for when the war ended, it was the memory of that speech at the war's beginning that persuaded the nation and many Labour Party leaders, that Churchill the warleader was not the person to lead us in the different but even more important days of the peace that followed. It echoed the sentiments expressed by the miners' leader, Jim Bowman, when post-war problems were being discussed: 'We have passed the phase in this war when slogans and appeals are of any use. The speech of the Prime Minister in the House of Commons, in the recent coal debate, was one of the greatest disservices to the mining industry . . . Men in the coalfields have seen, as result of the statement by the Prime Minister, that anything which involves major political changes cannot be done during this war, and the capitalists are now crawling out of their funkholes and claiming their position for the post-war world.'

I had to appear before a tribunal in Aberdeen as the result of my refusal to accept military service. This took place after the fall of Belgium, with all the atmosphere of hostility which the military situation engendered. My statement was based on my boyhood experiences and the political knowledge gained over the years. Wars solved nothing. We had seen, in the streets of Aberdeen following the first world war, the heroes of Mons and Passchendaele selling bootlaces and playing barrel organs for a living, the same men who had been promised homes fit for heroes to live in, citizens of the richest empire the world had ever seen. I cited my own personal experiences, shared by most of my generation, which resulted from my father's war wounds in 1917. But no exemption or objection to war on political or moral grounds was acceptable as conscientious objection, the grounds had to be religious. The same attitude prevailed when I appeared at the High Court in Edinburgh before the Appelate Tribunal. Some weeks after the Edinburgh hearing, I was ordered to appear for medical examination but did not do so. A summons to appear at the Sheriff Court, on the charge of failing to submit for medical examination, was served on me, and from the Court hearing I was ordered to be taken for medical examination.

On arrival at the Medical Examination Centre, I was greeted in friendly fashion by all concerned, and a doctor, who had known my father from his war wound treatment days, appealed to me to give up my objection to military service, pointing out that I could be assured of a good career in the Forces. My discussion with Dr Connon was cordial and friendly, I pointed out to him that the experience of my parents' generation in the holocaust of the Great War, and the political, economic and moral factors which flowed from it, had made up my mind for me. My role was to oppose the war, take no part in it whatsoever, and make certain that in no way would I benefit from the activities of that period. I was very conscious that many who posed as the greatest patriots and supporters of the war had themselves not been in the forefront of the move to enlist for military service. I also reminded the good doctor of the judgement of Maynard Keynes, writing in *The Economic Consequences of the Peace*, who described the Parliament of the 1918 General Election as being composed of 'hard-faced business-men who looked as if they had done well out of the war.' The medical examination was completed and it proved a complete anti-climax to the arguments and discussions that had gone before, because I was classified Grade 3 because of a heart condition, a relic of a childhood bout of rheumatic fever, which had in no way affected my work or my activities since I was eleven years old.

I was still helping in the family shop, but fate intervened in a number of ways, and the next fifteen months were to bring bewildering changes for my wife and myself. The Scottish Council of the ILP decided to fight a by-election in Central Edinburgh at the end of 1941 with Tom Taylor (who later became President of the Scottish Co-operative Wholesale Society and moved to the House of Lords in the nineteen-sixties as Lord Taylor of Gryffe) as the candidate. The Aberdeen branch of the ILP sent me to Edinburgh to help in the campaign, in which the Conservative candidate was returned. There was no official Labour candidate because of the war-time electoral truce. The ILP were assisted in their campaign by most of their leading Scottish figures, and in the course of both indoor and outside propaganda activity, I shared a host of electioneering activities with John McNair, then General Secretary of the ILP and its National Chairman, Jimmie Maxton, who as a member of parliament for Bridgeton, Glasgow, was easily the best-loved political figure it has ever been my lot to meet. Another lovable character who took part in the Central Edinburgh contest was Sir Hugh Roberton, of Orpheus Choir fame, the Scottish choir whose singing has brought so much joy to all parts of the globe. Hugh Roberton has the most delightful speaking voice of any orator I have ever heard, and for sheer spellbinding oratory, Jimmie Maxton was in a class by himself. In my view, only Nye Bevan came within reach of the Clydeside rebel.

Following the election, I continued my political activity and my studies with the National Council of Labour Colleges, which was later to become the Trade Union Congress Educational Department, which I had been attending since joining the Labour Party in 1934. I went to work for a short time in the Co-operative grocery department in Forres in Morayshire. The countrywide travels of my wife and I had started, for we had not long settled in Forres when I was offered a post in Stirlingshire with the Dunblane Co-operative Society, and whilst in that area I was granted a scholarship to a Summer School being held in Bangor University in North Wales. No sooner had we unpacked in Dunblane from Forres, than a post with the National Council of Labour Colleges fell vacant in Birmingham. I was successful in being appointed to it, so the Milnes again headed southwards to the Midland cities of England, and I became responsible for the political and economic educational facilities of the Trade Union and Labour Movement, in the counties of Warwick, Worcester, Stafford and Shropshire. From the moment in September 1942 when we arrived in Birmingham, my wife and I took to the city. Coventry and Birmingham were already torn and bleeding from the wounds of war, but the years ahead were to prove challenging, exciting and interesting.

The story of working class educational activity in the Midlands during the Second World War, and its impact on the wider Labour and Trade Union movement, with the ultimate success of Labour in 1945, the first socialist government with complete Parliamentary power in Britain, is part of history. The Conservatives had dominated Birmingham, England's Second City and the stronghold of the Chamberlains for generations; it was represented in the pre-war era by a solid bloc of 12 Tory

MPs. The product and symbol of this midlands metropolis in the nineteen-thirties was conservatism, but changes were afoot. The most varied collection of work-people seen anywhere in the world had poured, both before and during the war, into Birmingham. They came from all parts of the British Isles, from those areas of the world that would later become the Commonwealth, and the source of so much of the city's post-war influx as well. Refugees from the European tyrannies that had produced the war, all races, all religions gathered together as an impetus from the greatest struggle mankind had ever known, and they brought their political philosophies and theories with them. In our years in Birmingham, we saw the war ending and the nation move to victory. What kind of world we would have here at the end of the conflict, and what form and shape it would take, were discussed and hammered out in the Forces, in the factories, in the mines and mills of this great industrial complex. If I had to nominate the most capable and competent debating forum I have known, including the House of Commons, it would be the Birmingham Trades Council's monthly meetings during the war and immediate post-war era. My activities in the West Midlands area brought me into contact with trades, professions and callings I had never known, the Miners of North Staffordshire, Cannock Chase and Warwickshire, the workers of the most famous Potteries in the world, the foundries and factories of the Black Country, the car plants and the munition factories of Birmingham, Coventry and the surrounding area, into which humanity, drawn from all the corners of the earth, was crowded.

1945 brought victory and its problems. In addition to my official duties with the NCLC, I was actively helping the ILP in my spare time in its propaganda work in the West Midlands. The ILP, in the period of the political truce between Labour and the Tories, was enjoying something of a political hey-day. From 1941, ILP candidates, along with Commonwealth Party and other organisations, were securing big votes at by-elections. Arthur Eaton at Bilston, and Bob Edwards, national chairman of the ILP at Newport, almost pulled off astonishing victories against coalition candidates who had the support of both Attlee and Churchill behind them. The ILP had selected some thirty to forty candidates in readiness for the post-war election, and I was invited to contest the seat for them against L. S. Amery in the Sparkbrook division of Birmingham. In 1945 Amery was defeated by Alderman Percy Shurmer, the Labour Candidate, in a series of Labour victories that swept the City.

The victory over Germany revived talks in Britain of a coalition Government to face the rigours of the post-war world. It was obvious from the talk, in the cities, towns, and villages of war-beleagured Britain, and in the various battle-fronts scattered round the world, that there was no desire or intention to return to the pre-war Britain. The words of Arthur Greenwood in that far-away Sunday of September 1939, which followed Chamberlain's declaration that this country was now at war with Germany, took on a prophetic note. He had predicted that 'from the smoking ruins of the struggle, a new order of society' would emerge. Whatever may have happened subsequently, there is no doubt that the Deputy Leader of the Labour party, at the outbreak of the war, had predicted what the mood of a determined war-weary people would be at the cessation of hostilities.

The uncertainty whether Labour would or would not go it alone in the first post-war General Election was resolved at the Labour Party Conference held at Blackpool in the June of 1945. At that Conference, with fiery Ellen Wilkinson, Jarrow's MP, in the Chair, there was no doubt that it was no longer a practical proposition to follow the nation's war time leader, Winston Churchill, into the years of peace. The 1945 General Election would be fought on party lines.

Chapter Two

The hush of peace on an eager, expectant world was accompanied by a clamour from the people of Britain for social change. A war against tyranny in Europe was now extended to those groups which had dominated and dictated events in Britain in the years between the two world wars. The war in Europe had ended. The war against Japan, Hiroshima and Nagasaki, still lay ahead, as did the General Election. The events of those hectic months have filled many volumes. Britain was to take a journey into hope and to turn its back on the hungry thirties. The nation, united in war, was to strive for the same conditions in peacetime.

Churchill called a General Election and Labour picked up the gauntlet. Amazing scenes were witnessed in Britain. Churchill stumped the country but the reaction to him, particularly in the Midland cities of England was mixed. He had been a great war leader, but the nation had doubts about his ability to move into the equally turbulent years of peace.

Labour's decision to fight for power in the 1945 General Election posed a dilemma for those of us in the Independent Labour Party. Should we fight the seats we had intended to fight, stay on the sidelines and watch the battle as spectators, or should we join, or in some cases rejoin, the Labour Party in its election campaign in order to help lay the foundations of a new Britain in the wake of the most disastrous war in history? I had no doubt about my own decision. I was the first ILPer to return to the Labour Party. Writing in the Town Crier, Birmingham Labour's official newspaper, I said: The battle for a new Britain is on. Attlee and the Labour Party in *Let Us Face the Future* have pinpointed the hopes and aspirations of

Britain's people in their desire to build a new Jerusalem in our green and pleasant land. To turn the disillusionment of the aftermath of the First World War into the glowing dawn of a national resurgence in the second half of the 20th Century I was returning to a Labour Party that should be given the responsibility for the Britain of to-morrow.

In Birmingham and throughout the country the election was vigorously fought. Churchill toured the industrial areas, but his war-time glamour had dimmed. Labour scored a sensational victory. In Birmingham, the 100% Tory representation disappeared and Labour won ten of the thirteen seats, narrowly failing to take King's Heath from Sir Patrick Hannon by a mere 800 votes, in a seat held in the 1935 General Election by a majority of 40,000.

There was an unusual situation in the 1945 General Election, in that there was a three-week gap between polling day and the count to enable the ballot boxes from the battle areas of the Second World War to reach home. I had gone on holiday following the election campaign to the little Worcestershire village of Acton Beauchamp on the borders of Hereford and Worcester. With me were my wife and daughter Edna. On the day on which the results were declared, I cycled to nearby Bromyard to pick up the papers with the details of Labour's victory. Sitting in a restaurant and drinking coffee, it was amusing to observe the dismay amongst the farming fraternity and others, which hung heavy in the air and formed the topic of every conversation. 'Was it really true that we now had a Labour Government?' were the enquiries made by tweedily dressed ladies in doom-laden tones. The disaster of Labour's victory, or so it seemed in this Tory stronghold of Midland Britain would strike deep and hard. Travelling back from Bromyard in the summer sunshine, I stopped to rest and read on the slopes of the Malvern Hills overlooking Hereford and Worcester. It was a sentimental occasion. For the first time in British history, there was a Labour Government with power. All this and the future was ours. The Labour Manifesto *Let Us Face the Future* was now to be the blueprint for a new Jerusalem, the Britain of our dreams lay just ahead. The days of neglect were over for the people who produced the wealth of Britain. It was heady stuff. I cycled home across the beautiful, sunbathed countryside in a euphoric mood. I little realised the struggles that lay ahead within the Labour Movement, or that the victory of 1945 and Labour's accession to power was to become for many of us the dream that died.

Attlee as Prime Minister led a powerful team. People like Bevin, Dalton, Ellen Wilkinson, Morrison and a host of others, had served a grim apprenticeship in Churchill's War Cabinet and were well equipped to take over the tasks that lay ahead. Labour's new Prime Minister created an intriguing situation by appointing Nye Bevan, one of the party's outstanding war-time rebels, to the key post of Minister of Health. Labour was pledged to carry out the proposals of Lord Beveridge for a National Health Service. The years from 1945 were tremendous indeed. For possibly the first time in British history, a Government was returned which began to carry out the programme on which it had fought the election, not that usual an occurrence in British political life. It was a challenging, heart-warming period in which to live. But pitfalls lay ahead and 1947, with the harshest winter for a century, saw a close-down of industry and soaring unemployment. But despite this, solid progress in many fields was being made, with housing, health and the social services, all in Nye Bevan's area of control, making an impact on the lives of the ordinary folk of Britain.

Then the Attlee administration ran into problems on a personal basis. Corruption, during the war and in the post-war period, was at a minimum, and Labour was stunned when the Prime Minister set up a Tribunal of Enquiry to examine the activities of a Junior Minister, Sydney Stanley, a London financier and entrepreneur, who subsequently had to resign from Parliament. But the storms were weathered. By the time of the 1950 General Election campaign, which Labour was to win by 6 seats in a fiercely fought contest, the country had come to recognise the splendid job done by Attlee and his team, and even in the 1951 election, when Churchill was returned to the Premiership and the Tories to power, Labour still commanded the majority of votes cast and recorded the highest poll in its history, a total never since surpassed in any subsequent election. The post war era, at least the Labour Government's part in it, was over. The victory of 1945, the return of Labour to power and all the bright hopes it engendered were now stilled and silent. The future, at least for the time being lay cradled in other hands.

One of the contributory factors in the 1951 situation was the resignation of Wilson, Freeman and Nye Bevan from Attlee's administration in the April of that year. The continuing battles within the Cabinet and the Labour Movement throughout the country about re-armament, steel production and national-isation, the retreat from the basic principles of the Health Service, and a number of other matters which had boiled and bubbled for some time, suddenly erupted. The three Ministers resigned. Wilson at that time was President of the Board of Trade. The edifice built on the 1945 victory, indeed all the hopes and aspirations of generations was toppling. All sorts of reasons were advanced for the collapse: the weariness of Attlee and his top Ministers, who not only had borne the burden of the post-war Government, but had been the pillars of Churchill's coalition government in the years of war; there was also con-jecture about Wilson's position at the Board of Trade, and issues which had caused raised eye-brows at the Lynskey Tribunal were attributed to his resignation rather than the political reasons being advanced in all quarters.

The Churchill victory of 1951 was to keep the Tories in power till the end of 1964 and the defeat of the Douglas-Home Government. An era that not only gave the premiership back to Churchill but straddled the reigns of Eden, Macmillan and Douglas-Home, seemed like 13 wasted years to many of Britain's people, years in which the 'never had it so good' philosophy held sway. It was a period in which private wealth was to accompany public squalor in the cut-back on Government expenditure on homes, hospitals and schools, and during which Britain's economy laid the roots of the difficulties ahead, some of the consequences of which were to blow Wilson's 1966 Government completely off course.

The 1951 resignations had some relationships to myself. Following the departure of Nye Bevan, Alf Robens became Attlee's Minister of Labour, an appointment which was to lead him to the chairmanship of the Coal Board and out of the

21

Labour Party. I was to follow Robens at Blyth in 1960 when he took up the Coal Board appointment. At the time the resignations took place, I was in Paris with a TUC delegation visiting a Summer School arranged by the International Federation of Free Trade Unions to study the structure and purpose of the Coal and Steel Community which was being formed there at the time. The trade union movements of some 24 countries were represented, including most of the European nations and a strong delegation from America. The seminars were heavily slanted in favour of the idea of a Coal and Steel Community, later to lead to the European Economic Community. As delegates we sat for some of the time at the feet of Monnet and Schuman, the architects of the Common Market. I was more impressed by the approach of Jean Johaux to this subject, the veteran French Socialist and those around him. This led me eventually to oppose Britain's entry into the European Economic Community, which incurred the wrath of John Silkin, Labour's Chief Whip when I voted in 1967 against the attempts of Harold Wilson to take Britain into Common Market membership. At a time when membership of the Market was recently the subject of a national referendum, it is interesting to recall that Parliament, on May 10th 1967, voted in favour of 482 to 62 against joining, and that Attlee's Labour Government, with Wilson at the Board of Trade, had decided in 1951 not to join the Coal and Steel Community, because it would curtail the freedom of Britain's management of her newly nationalised Coal and Steel industries.

1951 was a vital year for me in many ways. Towards the end of it, I was advised by Alan Birch the USDAW General Secretary and chairman of the TUC Economic Committee to apply for full-time employment with the Union. Up to that time I had been reluctant to do so. As a family we did not like the prospect of leaving Birmingham. My wife and I had grown to love this sprawling industrial city, our three girls had been born there, and much of my political activity was centred on it. I had been on the short list for the Kings Norton Division in 1950, but was beaten by a past Lord Mayor for the candidature. I was a member of the Board of Management of the Ten Acres and Stirchley Co-operative Society, one of Birmingham's two Co-operatives, chairman of the USDAW branch at Stirchley, the Kings Norton Divisional Labour Party and senior vice-president of the Birmingham Borough Labour Party. I was delegated by many bodies at that time to attend both the National Labour Party Conference and the Trades Union Congress. Despite these contacts with and our love for the city, we accepted the appointment and the opportunities for change and challenge which they presented, and set out to return to Scotland in 1952 as Central Scotland Area Officer of the Union for a period that was to span nearly a decade and lead to Blyth and Parliament.

Then came 1955 and the General Election. I was asked by the Union to act as agent for a colleague, Davie Connell, in the Edinburgh Pentlands constituency that was held by Lord John Hope with a comfortable majority. The 1955 General Election was easily won by the Tories, who also kept Pentlands. Eden was confirmed as Prime Minister—Suez lay ahead! But the long arm of chance reached out for me again within months of the 1955 General Election when Britain's representative to the United Nations, Hector McNeill, Minister of State and MP for Greenock, died suddenly in New York. David Connell, my colleague at Pentlands was nominated for the vacancy, but was killed in a car crash on his way to being interviewed by representatives of the constituency party. I was elected to succeed him on the Union's Parliamentary panel. Some eight months later I was selected to be the candidate for the Rutherglen constituency of Lanarkshire. The area covered by Rutherglen lay on Glasgow's doorstep, was highly marginal and held by Brooman-White with the narrow margin of 2,100 votes. It was a winnable seat, but Brooman-White was a good constituency member who had fought Maxton at Bridgton in the 1945 General Election, and he possessed an organisational machine of top calibre.

The run up to the 1959 election was accompanied by much organisational activity and Labour hopes in Rutherglen ran high, while a bright prospect for my own constituency naturally raised optimism for the return of a Labour Government. In fact Rutherglen was a barometer constituency, always held by the party forming the Government of the day. Gaitskell had followed Attlee as the Labour leader, and Eden's departure after Suez left Macmillan at the Tory helm with his now infamous slogan of 'You have never had it so good.' The 1959 election was a disappointing one for Labour. Gaitskell's dreams of becoming Prime Minister were shattered, and a number of Labour hopefuls who had eagerly anticipated Cabinet posts in the wake of a Labour victory, like Robens, Chetwynd and others were bitterly disappointed. Robens left Labour's ranks to become chairman of the NCB and Chetwynd, aided by Ted Short, was appointed head of the newly formed Northern Economic Development Council some months later.

I was naturally disappointed with the General Election results and more so with my own. Although reducing the Tory majority from 2,100 to 1,500 in an election which brought only five Labour gains, four of them in Scotland, it was not enough to get me to Westminster or secure the return of a Labour Government to power in Britain.

So the 1959 General Election meant back to a trade union job, work which I thoroughly enjoyed, while continuing my activities on the Labour Party Scottish Executive on which I was a representative of my Union, USDAW. Many people in Rutherglen wished me to continue my candidature in that constituency, but I decided to wait a little to see how matters developed in the months ahead. One matter that was raised on the Scottish Executive after the General Election defeat, was a proposal, which was peddled behind the scenes by Labour's Regional Secretary, to employ a public relations firm to improve the image of the Labour Party in Scotland and in the North-East of England. To some of us on the Scottish Executive this was a little surprising, for Labour had fared rather better in Scotland and in the North-East in the 1959 General Election than in most of the rest of the country. Only a small section of the executive opposed the idea. The opinion of a group, which comprised John Pollock from Ayrshire, who is now General Secretary of the Educational Institute of Scotland, Willie Fraser from Aberdeen, Jack Irvine of the Scottish Steelworkers, and myself, was that political parties and political activists did not need the help of public relations men to further their interests or proclaim their policies. At the time we considered

24

the issue as being only of academic interest and confined to meetings of the Scottish Labour Party. Little did I realise that this suggestion to employ public relations firms would lead to a major clash with Labour's National Agent Reg Underhill and other members of the Party's National Executive Council, including Andrew Cunningham, the North-East boss of the General and Municipal Workers Union, and to my losing my Union candidature and my seat in Parliament. Neither did I know that the public relations firms in question were financially involved with Dan Smith.

The question of public relations and the business interests of MPs was also to become an issue in the North-East, with the disclosure that Gordon Bagier, the Member for Sunderland South had worked for a firm of consultants employed by the Government of the Greek colonels. Ted Short is, at the time of writing, engaged in an exercise to set up a system under which MPs will have to declare their outside interests and name the firms who engage them to promote those interests, but as is not unknown when Short is dealing with matters of this kind, decisions seem to take a long time to come. Often, of course, MPs accept appointments or allow their names to be used by a company for a fee without much knowledge of its activities. This, in my view, undesirable practice can often put an MP at risk. He can only blame himself if, by association, it is assumed that he approves of or participates in the company's policies and activities.

So the pattern began to emerge. In June 1960, I was on holiday from work and in our home at Falkirk in Stirlingshire had got up to make the morning cup of tea. I went downstairs to collect the then *Manchester Guardian*. Its front page lead story was an exclusive on Alf Robens' impending appointment to succeed Sir James Bowman, the well respected leader of Northumberland's miners, as Chairman of the National Coal Board. Returning to give my wife and daughters their morning cup of tea, I remarked jocularly, 'This is it this time.' Alf Robens was like myself a member of the Union's Parliamentary panel, and in the event of his resignation I was the automatic choice as the Union's nominee for the Blyth vacancy, which would occur in the event of Robens going to the Coal Board.

Robens, the previous Saturday, as MP for Blyth, had been a guest at the Northumberland Miners' Picnic. This has been the traditional gathering of the county's mining folk ever since the days when such an event was held to enable miners to get together, thus defeating the anti-assembly laws which prevented them from combining with their fellow workers. It has always been a joyous, happy and carefree family occasion, hallowed by tradition and cut deep into the folk-lore of this corner of North-East England. Although Robens made great play after his appointment was announced about consulting his agent at Blyth before taking on the job, and his intention to let Hugh Gaitskell and other Labour leaders know before intimating his decision, the story had a ring of unreality about it, as far as I was concerned.

In an article dealing with the career of Robens, the *New Statesman* of 24th January 1975 had this to say:

> After being out of political office for ten years he was suddenly summoned by R. A. Butler and, on Macmillan's instructions, offered the NCB together with a peerage. Although he was a prominent member of the shadow cabinet, he accepted the offer with such alacrity that his leader Hugh Gaitskell, first heard of it in a 'splash' story in the *Guardian*.

No Labour leader was more disappointed at the party's failure to win the 1959 General Election and no one sought after office more. No one was so less well-equipped to bear the heat and burden of opposition in the five years ahead than Robens. Strong signs of his displeasure, and his lack of acceptance of any situation away from the trappings of power, was instanced by his acceptance of the post of Labour Relations Adviser to Atomic Power Construction Ltd. The appointment, stated by the *Blyth News* to carry a salary of £1,000 (the salary of an MP at that time was £1,750), was bitterly attacked by trade unionists, including the General Secretary of the Steelworkers Union. Robens was also heavily criticised at the USDAW Annual Delegates Meeting and throughout the branches of the union. In the constituency the executive committee had a number of meetings, but matters appeared to have been smoothed over. The *Blyth News* of 21st January 1960 had this to say:

> Mr Robens denied this week that his appointment as Labour Relations Adviser to Atomic Power Construction Ltd would clash in any way with his parliamentary duties. It is understood that union representatives strongly expressed their disapproval of Robens' acceptance of the offer. Some members believed that any time the MP has to spare from his parliamentary duties would be better spent in attending to the affairs of his constituency, particularly the position of those miners in the division who face the prospects of redundancy.
>
> It is believed there is a feeling among the Party EC that Mr Robens should have been in contact with his constituency before giving consideration to the appointment and that opinion is divided on whether he was justified in accepting.

It is interesting to reflect that the furore of his appointment to a firm practising private enterprise did not prevent the then Blyth MP returning to his constituency to declaim against private profit. The text of his speeches during the week-end prior to this announcement, being already known and agreed to by Robens, has an hypocritical sound. Talking to the Blyth Labour Party Women's Federation, he said:

> I am in favour of public ownership, would like to see common ownership of wealth, but like Christianity this would not come all at once. Public ownership was better than wealth in private hands making private profit. There were still many social ills to cure and work in the Labour Party held out the key of golden opportunity to adventure for youth.

All this, in the aftermath of the Labour election defeat and in the run up to his moving into the business field and eventually the chairmanship of the National Coal Board, did not diminish Robens' prospects in the battle to be No. Two in the Labour Party to Hugh Gaitskell. What the attitude of the then Honourable Member for Blyth would have been if he could have looked into the future and foreseen that both Nye Bevan and Hugh

27

Gaitskell would no longer be with us at the next General Election is an interesting question. A strangely sycophantic article in the *Blyth News* in February 1960 put the claims for Robens.

> The position of Robens in Labour's hierarchy has been advanced several notches during the past week and now that they have studied Mr Wilson's speech last Wednesday in which he publicly rebuked Mr Gaitskell for getting his priorities wrong, they are more critical than in their first reaction. It is not that they disagree with his argument, rather they feel he was getting his priorities wrong in not making loyalty his first consideration, and when it comes to loyalty their thoughts turn naturally to Mr Robens. Among the stalwarts of the Party not only is his loyalty a strong point but also his common sense approach to political problems which appeal more directly to them than Mr Wilson's intellectual tactics. It looks as if Mr Wilson will have to watch his step if he is to continue to be regarded as the Third Man.

But the NCB appointment had still to come. A new world lay ahead in the years between the wrangles over party leadership and the 1964 General Election, and the Premiership of the Rt. Hon. Harold Wilson.

The *Guardian* splash story was duly confirmed. Robens was to take over the chairmanship of the National Coal Board in February 1961 and act as Deputy Chairman from September 1960 till then. When Robens left the House of Commons in September, this created a vacancy at Blyth and the Executive Council of USDAW confirmed my nomination for the Blyth seat. There was naturally great controversy over Robens' successor, and several defeated Labour MPs from the 1959 General Election had already put out feelers for the position, but no action was taken officially until Len Williams, later Sir, the General Secretary of the Labour Party, visited Blyth to meet the Constituency Party Executive Committee on 21st July 1960.

A month earlier, the Labour Movement had been stunned and saddened by the death of Nye Bevan. He was a legend in the Party and his stature enhanced it to an extent which few of the labour and trade union leaders of his day would care to admit, so often had they been the subject of scathing attacks from Bevan for failing to live up to the programmes and the policies they proclaimed on public platforms. Typical of his forthright approach to the attitudes of his party was expressed in a speech at Manchester in 1956, when he accused the party leaders of secret dealings in the Commons. He was reported in the *Daily Mirror* as saying, 'The rank and file do not get to know what decisions are reached, and members are not allowed to say. That is a travesty of democracy. If the speeches of Labour MPs on the Commons floor did not agree with what had been decided at a private meeting upstairs, they were threatened with expulsion. The electorate did not know how their representatives voted at these secret meetings.' The same sort of thing was happening in local authorities, he suggested. Nye Bevan had opened his attack by stating that he was not interested in being the leader of any party just for the sake of being leader. 'If the Labour Party is not going to be a Socialist Party I don't want to lead it.'

Although the Labour party has thrown up other sincere and brilliant figures since the war, nobody in political understanding, intellectual sophistication and selfless honesty and loyalty to an ideal has matched Bevan. He had his faults and was often carried away by the emotion of his own rhetoric, but he was nevertheless a titan, who understood only too well the way that familiarity with power corrupts. The constant shifting of Harold Wilson on a whole range of policies can only be explained by his love of power and determination to remain in government. We have seen the measures that Nixon did not hesitate to employ to remain president. In every country, one finds a willingness to betray party ideals, and Wilson, although once regarded as a Bevanite, has politically, regularly put the pursuit and retention of power in front of principle. He is not interested in being out of power. He has been aided in this by a clique of similarly-minded Labour politicians, who ruthlessly try to eliminate anything that stands in their way, often including their own principles and policies of the previous year. I was one victim of that ruthlessness, and in 1974 there was no Nye Bevan to expose the betrayal of Labour principles, which is one subject of this book.

No matter what the yardstick or measurement used, Nye Bevan was an outstanding political figure and parliamentarian: I did not enter Parliament soon enough to make judgement on a personal basis, but this has been confirmed hundreds of times over in conversation with those with whom he lived and worked. Bevan had always said that to be successful in politics one had to be loved and hated at the same time and that in the political arena one very often won and lost on the same issues and the same decisions. But at the time of his death a mood of sympathy and affection swept across the country. Nothing quite comparable has happened in our lifetime. It must also be remembered that although Nye Bevan was an outstanding Minister of Health in the Attlee administration, he had only occupied office for six of his thirty-one years in Parliament. In that period he had clashed, not only with his Party and its leaders, but with leading figures in the other Governments, and in the war-time coalition of Churchill. Michael Foot in his summing up of the Bevan career got closest to the real man:

When he died, no formal or forced note was heard. The nation expressed its sense of loss unfeignedly, spontaneously, without restraint. What could be the meaning of it all?

For Socialists, for those of us who heard him talk and speak and argue, and who shared his political aspirations, he was the man who did more than many others of his time to keep alive the idea of democratic socialism. With him it never lost its power as a revolutionary creed. Others might define it as well or serve it as faithfully, but no one else could give it his vibrant and audacious quality and make it the most ambitious and intelligent and civilized of modern philosophies. He was, as the Speaker of the Indian Parliament had said in introducing him to its members during a visit in 1957, a man of passion and compassion; but only his closest friends could know that to the full. The feeling which surged towards him in those months of 1960 cannot be easily explained. For it was not confined to his political friends or his own party and it burst all banks and frontiers. It was, perhaps, a sense of national guilt, a belief that he had been cheated of his destiny, that some part of his greatness had been shamefully thrown away;

an awareness that he had had much to say to our perplexed, polluted world, and that we had listened only fitfully. What the nation mourned was the tragedy which mixed with the brilliance and the genius, and what it did in expiation was to acknowledge his unique place in our history. (From *Aneurin Bevan* by Michael Foot, Vol. 2, page 659.)

So two of Labour's leaders had gone their separate ways. I could not help but reflect at that time, and afterwards in retrospect, for the death of Hugh Gaitskell lay unknown and ahead of us, how much of human history is due to chance, and wish that the powerful, but in many ways different, characters of Bevan and Gaitskell had forged the political weapons to take Britain into the new era that lay ahead. Instead the leadership, at both Government and local authority level, was to dip to a new low after those tragic months.

In some ways the death of Nye Bevan added a new dimension to the struggle for the Blyth succession. In meeting many of my Blyth constituents, the theme or conversation veered regularly to the difference in approach and attitude of Bevan and Robens. They felt that in their former member they had had someone who was only prepared to be in, and work for the Labour movement, as long as it suited his own particular aims and ambitions. Not much had been seen of Robens in the Constituency since the 1959 General Election, and the criticism which had lingered since his industrial relations appointment lingered on. It was felt that the appointment should not have been accepted from a Conservative Prime Minister. Some NUM critics expressed opposition to the choice of the new chairman and claimed that he would be used by the Tories to shatter a nationalised industry. But local NUM opinion was expressed by Robert Main, Secretary of the Northumberland Area of the National Union of Mineworkers. Main declared he had too much faith in Robens to believe he would be a party to any such plan. He knew that he would keep the miners' interests in mind. Robens himself had this to say of his appointment in *Blyth News*. 'Money does not enter into my appointment. I like to live a modest life and what you get as a Member of Parliament is ample.' (At that time an MP's salary was £1,750 and Chairman of the Coal Board's was £10,000.) He regarded it as one of the jobs of the Chairman of the Coal Board to go to the Government at the moment it was decided that a particular pit was to be closed in the future and to tell them that so many jobs would be wanted in the area by that time. 'It is my general view,' he is quoted as saying, 'that a British mining industry operating at something like 200 million tons per year produced and sold was about right.' He went on to say, 'I will never rest content while we go on burning oil in power stations.' He regarded it as the chairman's job to decide when was the right time for oil and nuclear energy to fit into the pattern. A further promise that was made by Robens on his appointment to the NCB top job was to bring new industries into areas affected by pit closures. He said, 'I will know well in advance which areas are likely to be affected by redundancy, and will be able to provide alternative employment to enable men to change their jobs without changing their homes.' And, 'I am not going to the NCB to conduct the funeral rites of a great industry.'

The interesting outcome from all this welter of talk and promises was reflected in a number of ways. In regard to alternative employment I was amazed to discover that despite the closure plans which had been set in motion while Robens represented Blyth, no demand had been made for the area to be scheduled as a development district and there was no trace in the columns of Hansard that the MP for Blyth had raised this matter at any time since 1945. Later the Government White Papers on Fuel of 1965 and 1967 were to be the blueprint for a drastic cutting back of the industry and reduction in the manpower employed. It became a situation which, as the next member for the constituency, I had to face in different ways, but it is enough to say, that when Robens left for the Coal Board, some 43,000 miners were employed in the County of Northumberland and by the end of his ten-year stint, as he has called it, the number had dropped to just under 13,000, most of the redundancies having taken place between 1965 and 1969.

But more of that later. The selection conference for Blyth still lay ahead, and its future new member had still to reach the House of Commons. Suffice it to say that Robens was true to form on leaving the Coal Board: just as he had accepted a job outside the House of Commons in private industry whilst still a Labour MP, he now took directorships in the private sector. During his period at the NCB there had been searching enquiries into business relationships between leading members of the NCB and firms with whom the Board had been in contract. The chairman and others were completely exonerated of any improper activity. In May 1973 the Select Committee on Nationalised Industries set up a new sub-committee to inquire into the purchasing of powered roof supports and spares by the National Coal Board. The purchasing of this equipment by the NCB had given rise to disquiet, both within Parliament and outside, at intervals over a period of several years, and a number of enquiries had taken place into different aspects of the subject. It was to lead to the dismissal by the Coal Board of Alan Grimshaw of the Board's Purchasing and Stores Department, under circumstances which certainly related some of the reasons for his being placed on the redundancy list as arising from his frequent demands for an enquiry into the Board's methods of purchasing.

Robens' appointments certainly linked him more closely to the big business tycoons of the City than to his former colleagues of the Parliamentary Party or the constituents at Blyth who he had represented from 1945 to 1960. The firm of *Johnson Mathay*, dealers in bullion, employed him as their chairman, going from Coal Board to gold board, and becoming Chairman of *Vickers*, a director of *The Times* and of the *Bank of England*. Also, while he was a director of *Trust Houses Forte*, he played some part in their resistance to a take-over bid by *Allied Breweries*.

After the visit of Len Williams to the constituency, the battle for the Blyth seat took on a new dimension. After all, with the majority of around 25,000 enjoyed by Robens, the selection conference of the Blyth Constituency Labour Party would choose the next MP, not the electors. As I have already said, the front runners for the vacancy were the displaced MPs from the 1959 Election. Mikardo's name was added to the list of enquirers, but he said that he would not stand against a Trade Union nominee in a trade union seat. The shrewd London cockney, who was later to become chairman of the Parliamentary Labour Party, may have realised that he stood little chance with the hard-headed Northumbrians who would doubt his knowledge or interest in their problems. Another, who was also later to reach the House of Commons, was nominated by the AEU, Ted Garrett of Wallsend. He was soon joined by Arthur Bottomley, defeated in 1959 at Rochester and Chatham, Dennis Howell who had been rejected by his Birmingham constituents, and Arthur Blenkinsop, who had represented Newcastle East from 1945 till the 1959 Election. Jack Davison from Pegswood Colliery near Morpeth, one of the most likeable and most capable of the Northumberland NUM representatives, secured the Mineworkers' support, and with a support of 79 out of over 200 delegates entitled to be present at the selection conference, it was early evident that to secure the seat it was necessary to poll a fairly high early vote. Jackie Davison was under a cloud in the NUM, for he had gone to a selection conference in the Morpeth Constituency and opposed the official candidate and Co-operative nominee, Will Owen, who was nevertheless subsequently elected, only to figure at a later date in a famous Old Bailey trial, where he was charged on indictment and acquitted of selling information to members of the Czech Embassy. Jackie Davison was never really forgiven by the NUM for losing the seat for them, as they saw it. The slightest display of independence can always count on the opposition of the Northumberland NUM hierarchy.

When nominations closed, twelve candidates had been presented for vetting by the Blyth Executive. Local figures nominated were Gilbert Barker, an USDAW Insurance Agent, Ron Hepple, from the NUR, who was later to become my agent, Ald. Curry a former member of the NUR, National Executive and Councillor and later Alderman Fred Smith, chairman of the Blyth Constituency Labour Party. There was some surprise and criticism when the short list was announced. Blenkinsop, Bottomley, Davison, Howell and Milne. No Blyth CLP nominee was included. I think it would have to be admitted that the calibre of nominee that came from within Blyth itself was not really of Parliamentary calibre.

Robens was to intervene in the selection of the candidate in a number of ways, but did so, not for the first time, by saying one thing and acting in another. As reported in the *Blyth News* he stated, 'Choosing a successor is a matter for the local Party and

I would not seek in any way whatever to influence their choice. My relationships with the Party have always been that they are my masters and I am their MP. Blyth was a wonderful constituency. The people are so good, they should have somebody who will serve the constituency absolutely well. Any MP must not only serve his Party but the constituency as a whole.' John Stonehouse, then active in the London Co-operative movement, stated that the Blyth vacancy should get someone of top calibre from The Trade Union or Co-operative movement into the House of Commons and went on to mention Frank Cousins and Jim Peddle, the latter chairman of the Co-operative Party, as the persons he had in mind. It was not surprising for me to hear from some of my trade union colleagues in London that there had been a move to prevent the USDAW executive from nominating me for the Blyth vacancy. Such are the tangled matters involved in the normal Labour Party 'democratic' process of selecting a candidate to represent working people in the British House of Commons.

Following his appointment to the NCB Robens wrote to the USDAW executive requesting leave of absence from the Parliamentary panel. This was not possible under Union rules, but if granted, which it was not, it would have given Robens the opportunity of returning to political life via the Union. At the same time he wrote me to say that there was no-one he wanted to follow him at Blyth more than myself, and would like to arrange a meeting between myself and some of the leading figures in the Constituency Party. This never materialised, and I later heard that he was supporting Bottomley. The difference in his attitude had been determined by the union's refusal to change the rules and allow him to remain on the Parliamentary panel.

However I was well pleased with matters as they stood. I had never been close to Robens in any way and certainly not in the political sense. I discovered his real intentions when visiting a local secretary of the Transport and General Workers Union who asked me if I knew who Robens was working for and when I showed him the letter from Robens, said that he had been approached to support Bottomley from the same quarter. He made one of the most significant remarks of the pre-selection period when he told me that Robens working for Bottomley would mean around forty votes to my advantage. Also, since the vacancy had been announced, I had been receiving sterling help from a close friend and colleague, Tom Hamilton, who was employed at the USDAW Newcastle office. He campaigned untiringly on my behalf, and his knowledge of the area was invaluable in bringing me into touch with the local people, particularly those on the Blyth Constituency Labour Party Management Committee, who were entrusted with the job of making the selection. We moved around the area together, and on occasions I stayed with Tom and his wife at their Seaburn home. It was a great blow when Tom died suddenly in 1963, and an even greater hurt when it became necessary in the closing stages of my spell in Parliament to take legal action against his brothers, Willie, Member of Parliament for West Fife, and Arthur, who is at present an official of USDAW. But more of this in a later chapter.

And so we got to the final stages of the Blyth selection conference to appoint a successor to Robens. Two interesting observations served to lighten the run-up period to the Conference. Ivan Yates, then with the now defunct *Reynolds News*, in plugging the claims of Denis Howell for the seat, described myself as an 'ageing trade union official' (at 44 years of age!). And, on the Sunday immediately prior to the Selection Conference, the *Sunday Express*, in the person of Crossbencher, entered the lists. Gaitskell wants Bottomley, they said, the reason being that left and right in the Party would be united by this choice. 'Roly poly Arthur will replace roly poly Alf,' confidently predicted the columnist. Again, I was told by friends not to worry: a prediction by Crossbencher would possibly mean another ten or twelve votes for me. I campaigned right up till the Thursday of the week of the Conference and then spent the day before the selection with my wife in Berwick; Em had travelled from our home in Falkirk and back in the evening while I was making my way to Blyth and the future. On parting at the station we discussed the possibilities of the next day, conscious that I was very much the outsider in the contest; only Tom Hamilton, amongst all the people who knew about these things, had predicted a Milne victory. I said to Em that whatever the outcome there would be no disappointment that could match our feeling of having just missed out as was experienced when we lost Rutherglen so narrowly in 1959. There could be no greater disappointment than that.

The latest reports from Blyth gave a conference figure of 248 delegates representing 118 organisations affiliated to the Blyth Party, with a NUM delegation of just over 80. The actual attendance turned out to be 204 delegates. I was greatly encouraged at the outset on entering the hall to learn that I was the second choice of a large number of NUM branches, and that the Deputies Union had been mandated that morning to vote Milne. The NUR, another of the big delegations, had decided not to reach a decision until the speeches of the contenders had all been made. I thought the prospects were good, although our USDAW delegation numbered only 24. Five speeches had to be delivered before, at six p.m., we were summoned back into the Locke Hall at Bedlington to hear the result. The figures later revealed that there had been four counts, with Howell dropping out first with only 10 votes; I had led with 69 and Davison, Blenkinsop and Bottomley with 55, 24 and 46 respectively. Blenkinsop was next to go, and then Bottomley, which left Jackie Davison and myself to contest the final division. This produced 63 votes for the NUM nominee (some delegates had left the meeting) and 131 for myself. The decision was given a final unanimous approval by the Conference. Apart from the final speech from myself, the Conference was over. I said, 'One of these occasions when speech making is not very easy. One of my proudest moments. I am sure that I am going to have a really happy association with the district. I shall strive to be a hard-working representative.' Tom Hamilton dashed off to telephone my wife and daughters at Falkirk. It had been arranged that if I lost I would do the 'phoning, and then leave for home. We then adjourned to the home of Mr and Mrs Percival at Hartford to relax and look forward to the by-election.

The by-election campaign was not a happy one. The state of party organisation in the Blyth Constituency was well below average, and having come from highly marginal Rutherglen, where efficiency was at peak pitch, I naturally found it difficult to fit into a 25,000 majority seat where elections were seldom fought in traditional fashion. When arrangements had been completed for the by-election campaign, with the able assistance of Percy Clark from Transport House, I returned to Falkirk for a few days to prepare for the changeover of my union work to another colleague, and for the Labour Party Conference which was due to take place almost immediately at Scarborough, little knowing that this was to be the conference that would send reverberations through the Labour movement for at least another decade. The Campaign for Nuclear Disarmament had been gaining ground, and in a memorable Conference debate, it received the majority support of the Labour Movement. Gaitskell countered in a speech the same evening, with his now famous 'Fight, fight and fight again to save the Party I love.' It was a split of major proportions. The Party was facing a number of by-elections in addition to the one at Blyth, including Nye Bevan's constituency at Ebbw Vale, which was being contested by Michael Foot, defeated in 1959 at Davenport.

From there I went to Blyth and the by-election. I have mentioned the unsatisfactory organisation in the Constituency, but on closer examination it turned out to be even worse than I had anticipated. There were few or no records of local or national elections and no equipment of any standard to match up to the financial assistance that had been given by USDAW over the years ever since Robens was adopted to fight the 1945 General Election. To make matters worse there was deep hostility between the leading officers of the Party. The effect of all this was reflected in the drop in Blyth Party membership in the 1960 Report down to 1,737 or 374 less than in the previous year. This hostility between leading officials of the Party, mostly councillors and aldermen, did not apply to the bulk of rank and file members, or the people of the Constituency generally. As a family we grew to love the warm, friendly people of South-East Northumberland, and this sustained us in the long troubled years at Blyth, because there was in this area the makings of a Labour movement of which Hardie, Smillie and the other pioneers had dreamed, but the people who took control in the North-East of England were of a different calibre. Power was their motivating factor, and the principles of Bob Smillie, who had represented Blyth for a number of years in parliament, to serve not to rule, were trampled underfoot. To anyone with the ambition to climb either through the Trade Union movement or through the Labour Party itself, power could mean many things. Apart from the sense of importance and self-aggrandisement, MPs and Councillors could easily pick up paid directorships, fees and expenses, both from public enterprises and from companies in the private sector contracting for public works, roads, hospitals, schools and housing schemes. One could be a Labour Councillor voting on public expenditure for these schemes and, at the same time, a private contractor making extremely good profits out of the contract. The safe Labour majorities made the position of both MPs and Councillors secure. It was only when Poulson failed to make his business pay that it came to light that not all of these profits were open and above board and that bribes, ranging from free holidays to large sums of money, often decided where the contracts went. Perhaps one day we shall discover how much corruption has cost the tax-payer and the country.

Polling day arrived. There had been much disillusionment and cynicism expressed during the campaign. Often I was greeted with remarks like, 'What big job have they got lined up for you,' and in one or two instances, some old miner standing at the door of his colliery house would shout inside to his wife, 'Come out and see our new MP. You won't see him again till the next election.' The atmosphere was intensified by the impending closures due to take place at a number of collieries, and the lack of job opportunities outside mining. General housing conditions in the area were deplorable, and both the NCB and the local authorities had a heavy responsibility to bear in this matter. This was of course a reflection on the quality of Labour representation in the area. Out of some 90 councillors in the three local authorities comprising the Blyth Constituency, Seaton Valley UDC, Bedlington UDC, and Blyth Borough Council, around 75 to 80 Labour Councillors and Aldermen were regularly returned. Most of the leading council figures in the constituency, when I arrived, had little experience of fighting elections or doing any work to gain the seats they held. It was a sad reflection, when thinking of the bad housing conditions, that the chairman and secretary of the Blyth Constituency Labour Party were both long serving chairmen of their respective local authorities.

Nevertheless the Election campaign had been interesting, and made enjoyable by the friendliness of the people we met, which made up for the committee room atmosphere which prevailed. The other candidates, Denis Walters, the Conservative, and Christopher Pym, a last minute nomination as Independent, were likeable characters to work with. Walters is now in the House of Commons and one of his Party's experts on the Middle East and Arab countries. He had been hoping, against the background of recent events in Blyth and the reaction to Robens' appointment and the general state of the Labour Party, to make a substantial dent in the Labour majority. Christopher Pym was typical of the kind of person we should see more often in British politics, a democrat, not by slogan, but with a deep-rooted love of democracy and principle in public life. He was an efficient and effective campaigner as well. He and his wife, who stayed at the Star and Garter Hotel while Em and I were there during the course of the campaign, were a very friendly couple indeed. My wife did a lot of travelling between Blyth and Scotland as our daughters, Edna, Rita and Kathleen were still at school.

Polling day dawned with the kind of teeming rain that only coastal Northumberland can provide, and continued to get worse during the day. We toured polling stations, hoping against hope that the turn-out of electors would reach respectable proportions. It was 54% and the figures read out by the Returning Officer were: Milne   23,438 (Labour)

                              Pym   3,223 (Independant)

                              Walters   7,366 (Conservative) Majority 16,072

In my acceptance speech, I quoted Bob Smillie, the well-loved miners' leader, who had represented the Blyth area as a member for the Morpeth Constituency from 1923 to 1929, saying 'My job is to serve, not to rule.' I tried never to depart from that principle.

Chapter Three

There was some kind press comment about the Blyth result, but the most rewarding was from my old Aberdeen school pal, Herbert Catto, Parliamentary Lobby correspondent for the *Aberdeen Press and Journal* and other Thomson newspapers. In the Aberdeen edition Herbert said 'The Blyth by-election is not regarded in political circles as giving any new pointer to any change in the political atmosphere. Mr Milne can claim to have done exceedingly well, having followed such a prominent Parliamentarian as Mr Alfred Robens.' We returned home to our girls and Em and I were greeted by them on Falkirk Station platform. We spent a relaxing weekend, walking on the nearby Ochil Hills, and came back again to make arrangements for the swearing in at the House of Commons on the following Tuesday. Messages of congratulation flowed in from all parts of the country and a number from overseas. I was a little disappointed that no official welcome was made to me by the representatives of the Labour Party in the North East, except for the Durham Miners' representative Bill Blyton, MP for Houghton-le-Spring, who had worked for me all during the election campaign. Ted Short, then Whip for the Northern Region MPs, had been abroad at this time. Late on Sunday, I received a perfunctory telephone call from the assistant regional agent of the Labour Party in Newcastle, telling me of the arrangements for the following week in the House of Commons.

With my wife and daughters, I boarded the London-bound sleeper at Edinburgh for the journey south to parliament. Since my early days in Aberdeen, I had dreamed of such a happening. For me it was a childhood ambition realised, a boyhood dream come true.

On arrival at the House of Commons, we received a very friendly welcome from the policeman at St Stephen's entrance, who assured us that London had been beflagged for our coming, but as Scots we were not entirely taken in by this; it was after all the eve of St Andrew's Day. Again I was disappointed and surprised to discover that no arrangements had been made at the Whips office for my wife and daughters to see the swearing in ceremony from the Strangers' Gallery. Short had started off by being the unfriendly, stand-offish person he continued to be. Once a headmaster, always a headmaster! A few practice steps with Bert Bowden, the opposition chief whip (later to go to the House of Lords and become Chairman of the Independent Television Authority) and then photographs on the terrace with Ted Short officially welcoming my wife, daughters and myself to the House.

The swearing-in ceremony for a by-election victor in the House of Commons is quite an occasion. This time the Prime Minister had just completed a hectic 15 minutes of Question Time, the House was crowded and in an excitable mood. As I proceeded the five paces from the bar and bowed, accompanied by Ted Short and Bill Blyton who were my sponsors, there was much banter on either side, and the Parliamentary equivalent of cheering: a chorus of hear-hears arose from the Labour benches, to be countered by the Member for Kidderminster, Sir Gerald Nabarro shouting in his throaty tone, 'Here comes the next Chairman of the Coal Board.' Then followed an affirmation of the oath read by the Clerk of the House, a few short steps to the Speaker's chair, a handshake of welcome from Sir Harry Hylton Foster, whose help and friendship I greatly appreciated in my early days in the House, and then round behind the Speaker's chair, where Hugh Gaitskell, Leader of the Opposition, waited to greet me with a few friendly words of welcome.

I was now on my own. It was my responsibility to get to grips with the House of Commons and its procedures. In some ways I was luckier than most newcomers. For some 18 months prior to the 1959 General Election, I had served on an economic committee of the Scottish Labour Party which had drawn up the policy document *Let Scotland Prosper*. As many of the committee members were MPs, the meetings were held at Westminster, so at least I had become reasonably familiar with the lay-out and geography of the place. Also, because I had seen the problems which existed in the Blyth Constituency, and the general position throughout the North East of England, my intentions were to make my maiden speech within a week of entering the House and to get down to the job of questioning Ministers about help for the many problems which abounded throughout the Blyth Constituency. I decided to speak in the Supply Debate on the Motor Industry, a subject that had been chosen by the Labour Opposition, because of the problems through which the trade was passing and its effect on our employment prospects in many parts of Britain. Criticism had been levelled at the North Eastern MPs, before my arrival in the House, at their lack of effort on this matter. In March 1960 the *Blyth News* had said this on the subject: 'Somebody up North has missed the boat. Somebody has slept. Liverpool and Glasgow appear to have had their ear to the ground.' A local councillor had stated that there was not sufficient draught in the harbour for large vessels at Blyth. At the same time Alf Robens' Agent was complaining that more shouting was needed to get jobs up North. 'We are now engaged in a very bitter fight to attract industries to the North East. The exclusion of Northumberland almost as a whole from the Local Employment Bill came as a big shock. We as a council should raise our voice in protest.' It was against such a demand and clamour for jobs that I came to Parliament, and it was a little surprising that many who had shouted in this way should be very soon hindering and hampering my Parliamentary efforts to get the jobs the area so badly required.

It was conditions like these that some months earlier had prompted Robens, while still the MP, to talk about 'No chance for Labour without unity. All must toe the line on the Party decisions.' And the Mayor at the time of the new Blyth Valley Council, added these words ten months before I arrived in the area, 'The present lack of unity in the Party was to be deplored.'

It was with these thoughts in mind that I set about preparing my maiden speech. The Scarborough Conference still hung around the House of Commons like a shroud. Party members passed each other in the corridors without speaking, and after

43

one stormy debate on defence I was told by Bessie Braddock and Sarah Barker, then the party's national agent, not to get into trouble too soon. This followed a vote on the question of reducing our armament expenditure against an effort by the Tory Government to move for increases.

The big day arrived. Fred Lee opened for the Labour Party opposition in a rather dull pedestrian speech to be followed by Reg Maudling, then President of the Board of Trade, for the Government. I was called by the Speaker immediately the Minister sat down. I reminded the House of the maiden speech of one of my illustrious predecessors, Bob Smillie, one time President of the Mineworkers Federation who had quoted Goldsmith's *Deserted Village*:

Ill fares the land to hastening ills a prey
Where wealth accumulates and men decay

and compared some of our present plight in the South East corner of Northumberland to the situation when Smillie was making his maiden speech in 1923. Coal, railways and shipping were very much in decline. I pointed out that the length of unemployment periods were also increasing, and that people had had enough talk about the affluent society which seemed to have stopped short at the borders of Northumberland. The speech was well received by the House, and my good friend Frank Bowles, the Member for Nuneaton, who I had known in my trade union lecturing days in the Midlands, commented, 'The Member for Blyth spoke most delightfully.' In the closing speeches, Douglas Jay for the Opposition and Fred Errol, Minister of State at the Board of Trade for the Government side, had this to say: Jay's remarks were, 'I must say how glad I am to congratulate my Hon. Friend Mr Milne, who made an excellent well-informed speech,' while Errol added, 'I should like to add my congratulations to those which have already been offered to Mr Milne, who has surprised and delighted us with his very early appearance as a speaker in this Chamber.' The appeal in my speech, which was made to the Government, did not fall on deaf ears, for it was Errol, as the Minister responsible for Development who opened the first Advance factory, built

44

for *Wilkinson Sword* at Cramlington in the Blyth Constituency. The closing sentences of my maiden speech read, 'By tackling the immense problems that have been presented by the challenge of a new age, the Government may have to turn their backs on some of their traditional policies, but turn their backs on them they must, if we are to prevent the situation to which I referred earlier, and if we are to check the unhappy accumulation of wealth and the decay of men in our industrial areas.'

The Press were also kind in their references to my maiden speech, particularly Edgar Hartley, the political Correspondent of the *Newcastle Journal* whose report next morning was headed, 'Mr Milne triumphs in Maiden Speech.' It went on,

'A chorus of "Hear Hears!" rippled through the Commons last night as a dark, slightly-built man spoke of the North-East as a centre of industrial activity, then bowed to the Speaker and resumed his seat. It was the tribute of MPs to a maiden speech by Mr Edward Milne, the Labour victor of the Blyth by-election.

It was a merited tribute too. Mr Milne showed no nervousness in his ordeal. His voice was crisp and clear and the content of his speech was a wise appeal for Government aid for the North East in general and Blyth in particular.'

The only jarring notes came from the Party chiefs at Blyth, who complained that I had been congratulated by a Tory Minister and a backbencher from the same ranks, little knowing that this is traditional in a maiden speech debate, but criticism also followed for my failure to refer to my predecessor Robens in that speech. While I am in the main prepared to follow the general conventions of parliament, this was certainly one I did not intend following. The attitude of the local party hierarchy was to follow me in all my parliamentary and constituency activities, and make it doubly difficult for me to get ahead with the giant task that lay ahead in parliament. The reasons for this attitude were not to be revealed until many years later in the disclosures of the activities of T. Dan Smith, Andrew Cunningham and the Leeds architect John Poulson.

My maiden speech successfully over, I had a settling down

period for what I considered the main objectives of my work in parliament as an MP, dealing with the many problems arising from the pit closures in the area and the need for alternative employment. The Blyth Constituency and South East Northumberland were facing a challenge equal to that of the Industrial Revolution, and in many ways the effect and impact of these changes would be greater than when the advent of coal mining in Northumberland altered the whole face and structure of Britain. To maintain contact with constituents, I arranged a number of surgeries and interview sessions at regular intervals throughout the constituency, a practice which was continued until my defeat at the General Election in October 1974. It is also necessary for a Member of Parliament to keep in close contact with national and international issues as they arise. This is made more difficult if one represents a constituency, as I did, which is brimming with problems. It was necessary to get the maximum help from councillors and other Party members, but this was seldom forthcoming, and only two or three councillors in the fourteen years during which I represented Blyth gave any help of any kind. My agent, Wilf Holliday, and other leading Party figures took the view that I should only deal with coming cases from our own ranks. Indeed at the first surgery that I held in the Labour Rooms at Blyth my agent came in to see me during the course of an interview, and said that a former secretary of one of our Labour Party Women's Sections was waiting to see me, but that I should not see her as she had caused a lot of bother in the Party, and had to be removed from office. I made it clear that anyone who called to see me would be interviewed and their problems dealt with to the best of my ability. The influence of the elder Wedgwood Benn, our MP in North Aberdeen in my younger years, was now standing me in good stead. No matter how a person had voted I was now their Member of Parliament. The question of how best to represent a constituency, and the many cross currents of Party and local tradition that went with that post, had always occupied my attention, and in the various areas in which I had lived and worked, I had always noted how the Member operated. I had never the temperament or the inclination to act purely in a Party fashion, although like every other MP of whatever persuasion, I would feel that I could quite easily accept some 90% of the Party's views and attitudes. My reading of the speeches of Edmund Burke also stood me in good stead and two of his quotes have guided me in the fourteen years I spent at Westminster. In what he called his *Thoughts on the Present Discontents*, he contrasts what an MP should be, as against what the Party would often like him to be.

'A strenuous resistance to every appearance of lawless power; a spirit of independence carried to some degree of enthusiasm; an inquisitive character to discover, and a bold one to display, every corruption and every error of government; these are the qualities which recommend a man to a seat in the House of Commons.'

'These politicians suppose . . . that you are blindly to follow the opinions of your party, when in direct opposition to your own clear ideas; a degree of servitude that no worthy man could bear the thought of submitting to; and such as, I believe, no connections (except some court factions) could ever be so senselessly tyrannical as to impose.'

An interview session at Blyth Labour rooms, some two months after my election, was to give me an insight into the manner in which the activity of leading Party figures and Council representatives was to be kept from me. It also showed me at the outset the tremendous influence being exerted on North East Council affairs by Dan Smith and those around him, and how interwoven these activities were with the machinery of the Labour Party at Regional and National level. I had arranged for a surgery at the Labour Rooms one Saturday morning as usual, and was surprised that the agent who had arranged to open the rooms at 10.30 a.m. failed to appear. I made enquiries about the keys, and finally got my interview going and had a very good session with my constituents. Judge my surprise when arriving at the Party office from London the following Friday, I was greeted by the agent in abusive fashion about what he regarded as my snooping on him the week before. I was to learn from a member of the Seaton Valley Council Labour Group, that on the week-end in question, a party of Councillors from Bedlington and Seaton Valley had visited the building firm of *Crudens* at Musselburgh by arrangement with Dan Smith, who was acting in a public relations capacity for the firm. There was nothing wrong or improper in such a visit, nor did it raise the need for such a violent attack on myself for the simple exercise of trying to gain access to the Labour Rooms, which the agent had arranged to open, but failed to turn up.

Parliament in my first two or three years provided me with a variety of interests. A back bench member has difficulty in catching the Speaker's eye in major debates, but I was reasonably lucky in my efforts. By use of question time it is also possible to cover over a period of time a wide range of subjects, and extract information and help from ministers, for no minister or his department likes to feel that they have been unhelpful to a questioning member, except on rare occasions. The system of balloting for debates also puts an MP in line for major occasions and the adjournment debate, which gives a member thirty minutes to discuss any subject he wishes with a minister at the end of each day's proceedings in the House of Commons, is a useful democratic exercise that allows an active backbencher to raise subject after subject, mainly of interest to his constituency, over a period of time. Such an opportunity came to me early in my spell in the House when in successive debates I was able to raise the question of Cramlington New Town and its industrial development, and the Port of Blyth, both matters of major importance to the future of the area. The raising of these matters in an adjournment debate led to the area being scheduled as a development district, which gave an advantage to the siting of advance factories, capable of attracting the major industrial firms of the world to South-East Northumberland. The Port of Blyth, and its deepening to meet the needs of the giant Alcan smelter, was also another outcome from a late night debate with a government minister on matters affecting the people I represented.

I was lucky in the ballot one Thursday afternoon and took the opportunity of introducing the following motion for an all day debate the following Friday. It proved to be an interesting and exhilarating experience.

'That this House, noting the increasing power of the advertising industry, its influence upon our national life and its effect on our economy, calls upon Her Majesty's Government to institute an independent inquiry to consider whether safeguards are necessary in the interests of the consumer public.'

For a back bencher to get the opportunity of a 50 minute speech in the House is an event in itself, and the post bag I received the following week was enormous, dealing particularly with complaints about advertising in and about the travel trade in Britain, a subject which was to lead me to introduce a number of Private Member's Bills on the tour operating industry, and ultimately, many years later, to Government legislation on the subject. I finished my speech with a quote on advertising by Lord Fisher of Lambeth:

'The simple word truth has lost its compelling power if it ever had it. Advertising has to enter a field where the amount of information is very small and the amount of seductive overtones and undertones so extremely large. I am not saying where and when they depart from strict honesty. I do not know. But they give the impression that honesty is not the chief purpose.'

By the time these debates were out of the way, and question time followed question time, I was completely fitted in to the routine of the House, and thoroughly enjoying the work. By the June of 1971, the Milne family had settled in the constituency, and my wife, daughters and myself were part of the Northumberland scene. It was a warm and friendly area, inhabited by some of the kindest people who ever trod this earth. As in so many areas the ordinary folk are the greatest of people, but their leaders seldom live up to the standards of the majority.

Chapter Four

Even at this early stage in Parliament, and living in the Blyth Constituency, I was aware of the growing hostility amongst the party chiefs at my activities, and what they described as my interference in local affairs and searching after publicity. The fortunate thing was that at the same time I was drawing closer to my constituents, who certainly seemed to appreciate having at last an MP whom they could approach, and who was approachable. The problems were mounting thick and fast, rising unemployment, pit closure after pit closure, the failure of the Government to designate the constituency as a development area, each one adding to the difficulties. A major clash emerged between myself, the secretary-agent and the chairman, over a contract from the Blyth Harbour Commissioners for a suction dredger, given to a firm in Scotland, when the local shipyard was seeking jobs and capable of undertaking the work. It was my first experience of the viciousness that was to be directed at me on numerous occasions in the future.

Both the constituency chairman, then Councillor Fred Smith, and the party agent, were members of the Harbour Commissioners and supported the decision to have the dredger built in Scotland. It was a unique position for me, an exiled Scot, battling with the local Northumbrians, to secure for Blyth shipyard a job they intended for Scotland. Smith, in an interview with the *Daily Express*, accused me of interference, and suggested that I was to be carpeted by the party for my actions. My reply was to circulate the full story to the party executive. The outcome was a vicious attack directed at myself by Smith and Holiday at the next executive committee meeting. I did not know Smith so well then, and when he said during the meeting, how hurt he had been at my action in getting in touch with the EC without consulting him, I apologised for having upset him in any way, but refused to retract one iota from my attitude on the dredger, or in circulating the EC with the details of the case as seen by myself. Smith told me at the end of this meeting that I was taking my work in the constituency far too seriously, and I suggested that he should place a note to this effect on the notice board at party headquarters.

This was the first of many such onslaughts by the party agent and Smith, both of whom were chairmen of their respective housing authorities. Unknown to myself at the time, they were also in touch with Dan Smith and his public relations work in the North-East for the building firm of *Crudens*, although nothing much seemed to have come of the exercise, despite at least one helicopter visit paid to Scotland by Councillor Fred Smith of Blyth. But much more was to be revealed in the months ahead. Already there were rumblings in Newcastle about the involvement of Dan Smith and Ted Short in a *Crudens* housing deal, which had been badly handled by the man who was to become known as Mr Newcastle. An enquiry had been demanded by the Housing Committee of Newcastle City Council.

Ted Short, now Leader of the House of Commons and Deputy Leader of the Labour Party, was a strong defender of the controversial *Crudens* housing contract with Newcastle Housing Committee and he intervened publicly in 1963 when a £772,000 contract for three high-rise blocks of flats was vetoed by Tory Housing Minister, Sir Keith Joseph. Up to his resignation in 1953, Short himself had been a member of the City Council and a close political ally of T. Dan Smith. Controversy first emerged on the *Crudens* issue in January 1962 at a meeting of the City Council. An enquiry was demanded of the facts surrounding the contract by Arthur Gray, the Tory leader. Negotiations had commenced in 1961, but Dan Smith had not declared his interest in the matter to the Town Clerk until July 1962. When the details of the scheme were announced after the Housing Minister's decision, the managing director of *Stanley Miller* wrote to Newcastle's Town Clerk asking for an explanation of why his firm's original scheme had not been accepted in 1961. Questions were also asked why other firms had not been allowed to re-tender, when the cost of the contract given to *Crudens* had been raised by £85,000. Short in the meantime dashed into battle, describing in the *Newcastle Journal* Joseph's decision as 'another impediment in the long series which have been placed in the way of Newcastle's housing programme by the present Government.' Earlier Short had described the contract as 'the best bargain for Newcastle,' and he continued to support the contract during the period of the local campaign for a public inquiry into the affair. The Newcastle City Council Housing Committee, in July 1963, recommended a public inquiry by nine votes to one, but by this time Smith had left the chairmanship. At this meeting Councillor Bob Brown, one of Short's strongest supporters, now Labour MP for Newcastle North and a Government Minister, moved that the period covered by the enquiry should be the previous five years and this was accepted. The move to have an inquiry was later defeated by the Labour Group on Newcastle City Council, and on July 31st, the City Council, Labour controlled, decided to reject the call for an inquiry. In April 1975, following the trial of Poulson, Dan Smith and Cunningham at Leeds Crown Court, Short issued a statement in which he said, 'I have never at any time discussed building contracts with Mr Smith or any builder or architect.'

From the time of my arrival in the House of Commons I had been amazed at the deference shown to Dan Smith by many members of the Northern Group of Labour MPs of whom Short was regional Whip at the time. To fail to attend a meeting arranged for the Newcastle City Council leader, usually with Short, Popplewell (Bob Brown's predecessor in Newcastle North), and Charlie Grey, MP for Durham buzzing around as master of ceremonies, was almost a crime in the eyes of the leadership of the MPs for the North-East of England. Ernest Popplewell, the not exactly fast-witted MP for North Newcastle (now Lord Popplewell) and Ted Short, adopted a somewhat sycophantic attitude to Dan Smith. At one of the Northern Group meetings, I raised the question of the concern felt throughout the North-East at the allegations that were being made about Smith's involvement with *Crudens*, and the manner in which the Newcastle City Council contract had been manoeuvred for that firm. I recollect a particularly fierce attack being launched on me by Popplewell following a conversation in the Members' Lobby, when he told me that Dan Smith was absolutely in the clear. I retorted that if the matter was as clear and simple as he had then indicated in his role as a Newcastle MP, would he arrange to see that a statement was made by Smith at the next Northern Group meeting and the Newcastle City Council meeting, but I was brushed off. This was not the last time I was to hear the familiar criticism from Popplewell and Labour Party members that all the talk about Dan Smith was a smear campaign in which I was assisting by the attitude I had taken.

Then 1963 saw the next big step forward, the moves that were to lead Smith, Cunningham and Poulson to Leeds Crown Court and prison. A sub-committee of the National Executive Committee of the Labour Party, headed by Alice Bacon (now Lady Bacon), then a Leeds Member of Parliament and a personal friend of Poulson, who was credited with personally pushing through the contract, awarded a £35,000 public relations deal to T. Dan Smith. Peter Ward, a journalist in Newcastle and a member of the Conservative Party who later masterminded the Labour Party schemes for Smith, who was also later to figure in a corruption trial in connection with Poulson, disputed the figure of £35,000, for Ward claims to only being able to account for around half that sum.

Among the Transport House officials connected with the public relations decision, Reg Underhill, now the Party's National Agent, was active in pushing the proposal forward. Underhill was a close confidant of Andy Cunningham during his period on the Party's National Executive committee, and he was the biggest stumbling block to those in the Party who wanted an inquiry into the North-East Labour Party and the numerous allegations of corruption which flooded into Transport House during the sixties. When Brian Bastin, a Wandsworth councillor who had been pilloried by Underhill and Transport House for demanding an investigation into Smith's activities in the London area, visited Transport House in 1970 with a further demand that action be taken, he was laughed at by Underhill who turned down flat the request by saying, 'You must not think that we at the top are children.'

This is the issue to which I earlier referred, the controversy in the Scottish Labour Party during my membership of the Executive committee over employing a public relations firm. It was difficult to understand the value of a contract of this kind for the regions concerned, as the Labour Party, despite its poor showing in the 1959 General Election, had done considerably better in those areas than in the rest of the country. The outcome of the arrangement, set up by the Bacon sub-committee, although I cannot believe it was the intention, was to give respectability and easier access to the efforts of Dan Smith and Cunningham in their contacts with the leading Labour Party figures who dominated the council chambers in many areas of Scotland and the North-East. The public relations work that was done for the Labour Party was in any case a ramshackle affair. It consisted mainly of employing journalists, already working in those districts, and getting them to collect material about the Labour Party for publication in the local press. In my own constituency, a Bedlington freelance journalist, working part-time with the *Morpeth Herald*, was recruited onto the Dan Smith team. The two main constituencies in the area enjoyed majorities of twenty-five and eighteen thousand respectively, so there was not much need to pay large sums of money to improve the Labour image there. But since South-East Northumberland was a development area the contacts made with the local council leaders by the Dan Smith firms could be used to obtain work from other public relations customers.

At the beginning of 1964, Brooman White, the Conservative member for Rutherglen, who had been my opponent in the 1959 General Election, died after a painful illness, creating a by-election in the constituency. I was asked by the Rutherglen Party members to take part in the campaign, and to speak at the eve of poll in support for the Labour candidate Gregor Mackenzie. There was some opposition to this from Will Marshall, Labour's Regional Officer in Scotland. On arrival at the Labour Party Headquarters for the campaign, the first person I met was Peter Ward, a reporter from the *Evening Chronicle* in Newcastle. I was surprised to see him in Scotland, and he told me that he was handling the publicity work in the Rutherglen by-election arising from the Dan Smith public relations contract with the Labour Party. He had left the *Evening Chronicle* and would be, as he put it, masterminding the Labour Party publicity in the North-East and in Scotland in the run-up to the General Election, which had to take place later that year. It was obvious that Peter Ward knew little about Rutherglen, whatever he may have known about the Labour Party, for he had been a member of the Conservative Party in Newcastle when I had met him previously. But I was getting accustomed to the strange antics of the Labour leadership in the North-East particularly in regard to Ted Short, Dan Smith and Alderman Andrew Cunningham of Chester-le-Street, which latter as Regional Chairman of the Labour Party, a member of the Party's National Executive, the Union boss of the General and Municipal Workers' Northern Area, was rapidly forging to the front as a dominating figure in the events which were to occupy the centre of the local government and political scene for more than a decade. I found it immensely surprising to see Peter Ward, one time Conservative, leading a Labour crusade with the blessing of as motley a crew of politicians as ever graced—or disgraced—the scene around them. As the learned judge was to say at a later date in summing up the trial of Ward and ex-Labour Lord Mayor of Newcastle, Roy Hadwin: 'I have the worry that there are bigger people who should be serving terms of imprisonment. You are the tiny men.'

The October General Election of 1964 lay ahead. With the Profumo scandal in recent memory, and the emergence of Sir Alex Douglas-Home from the Tory leadership struggle, in succession to Macmillan, Labour hopes were high. At one stage an opinion poll gave Labour a lead of about 120–130 seats. It was therefore not surprising that the Labour Party approached the coming campaign with eagerness and expectation. But despite the much boosted assistance from the Dan Smith machine, Labour became the Government by a margin of only three seats in October 1964, and although it is fair to say that Labour gains in the North-East and in Scotland helped considerably, other parts of the country fared equally well. Alex Douglas-Home got little credit and certainly no bouquets for losing an election, but his feat in almost bringing off the impossible is worth remembering. From its utter collapse after Profumo and the loss of Macmillan, the Tories had come within a hair's breadth of continuing their thirteen-year rule. But history seldom records or remembers those who come second.

The 1964 campaign in Blyth was a harmonious one, and co-operation from Wilf Holliday as agent was at its best when Councillor Smith struck again. I had prepared a report of the election for the Blyth Labour Party Management Committee, paying tribute to all who had worked in the election but pointing out that we could not rest on our laurels, that the party membership instead of staying at just over 1,000, could at least be raised to around the five thousand mark with some effort. Before the meeting Smith leaked it to the local press man Jim Harland, and joined by Holliday, attacked me for rocking the boat. Obviously, the Chairman and Secretary were sensitive to possible criticism that they were not doing as much as they could. It was clear that the report could only have reached Harland from the party office for only two copies of the report had been done at this stage and they contained alterations not present in the handout to party members. In my fourteen years at Blyth, and in my previous jobs in other parts of the country, I had nearly always had a top class relationship with the Press, but I was obliged to call a meeting with the editors of the *Evening Chronicle*, the *Newcastle Journal* and the *Sunday Sun* before the 1964 General Election, to discuss leaks which had been given to the Press from meetings of the Blyth Labour Party EC after a decision had been taken to issue a statement, in situations where it was not possible for my viewpoint to be put. The editors were most helpful and co-operative and they agreed that no reports would be published concerning the Blyth Party and myself without an approach to me for a statement on my own viewpoint. This was very satisfactory, for not only did it help myself and the party, but the Press as well. It transpired that two or three officials of the Blyth Labour Party were in contact with two leading sub-editors on the papers in question and also with a local reporter, and that Councillor Smith had at one time been doing some sort of freelance reporting himself for the *Journal*.

56

The first meeting of the Parliamentary Labour Party held in Church House immediately after the 1964 Election was a joyous, buoyant affair, and optimism was in the air. A new era was emerging: our election pledges would be honoured, and, said Harold Wilson, he was in the process of choosing a talented team of Ministers comparable to any in the past. I sat listening to the speakers and to the announcements of the first appointments: Bert Bowden, Labour Chief Whip prior to the Election was to become Leader of the House and Lord President of the Council, with Ted Short as Chief Whip charged with the responsibility of maintaining Labour's majority of three in the Division Lobbies of the House. The former headmaster of Princess Louise Road School in Blyth had come a long way. After the war, he had formed a partnership with Dan Smith on Newcastle City Council, and together they had been involved in political activities that had dominated two decades of North-East politics. I wondered that night in Church House whether Hugh Gaitskell and Nye Bevan would be walking and talking in the Elysian fields, with Nye recalling the remark he had made about Short in the fifties, when one of his friends warned him during one of the party's fratricidal disputes, that Ted Short would stab him in the back. Nye's reply was that Short would never stab anybody in the back, he would hand the dagger to somebody else to do the job.

Next came the Cabinet appointments, then the junior ministers and the Wilson posts were filled. Some of my trade union colleagues and many of my constituents asked if I had been disappointed at not receiving an appointment. Of course I was disappointed, but I had never really expected a post from Harold Wilson—after all the Prime Minister had a wealth of talent at his disposal. It was natural to feel left out however, for there is no politician worth his salt who does not aspire to speak from the Government Front Bench. But I was surprised when I received a summons from the Chief Whip to his office in 12 Downing Street where he offered me a job as one of the Government Whips. I thanked him for the offer but said that being in the Whips' office was one job I felt I could not do. I jocularly added that if he had wanted me to be Prime Minister, I would have taken a stab at it, but I was not suited by temperament to be a Whip. He pointed out that the job was soon to carry an extra £1,000 per year in salary, and he was more than surprised to be told that this made no difference to my decision. Although it is said that every man has his price, there are fortunately exceptions in Parliament and I did not intend to allow anything to interfere with my right to speak out, as would have happened if I had become a Whip, nor to cut down on time given to my constituents.

Then followed an approach from Tam Dalyell, one of my Scottish colleagues and one of the most effective and hard-working back benchers in the Commons, to sound me out on becoming Parliamentary Private Secretary to Dick Crossman. I decided no with some reluctance, for working with Dick Crossman at Housing and Local Government would have been an interesting and exciting adventure, but not with Bob Mellish in the same Ministry. I had decided that my back bench parliamentary and constituency activities would be enough to keep me more than fully occupied in Parliament, when Frank Soskice asked me to come to the Home Office with him as his PPS. This I agreed to do, and I continued happily at the Home Office until Sir Frank Soskice was succeeded at the Department by Roy Jenkins. Frank Soskice was one of nature's gentlemen and a much more formidable figure at the Home Office than one would think from the credit he was given. Together with Dundonian Sir Charles Duthie, the last of the great Civil Service heads of department, he formed a powerful partnership, one of the most successful of the Wilson appointments.

I accepted the post for a number of reasons, but mainly because of the help given to me by Frank when faced with a libel writ from Ernest Marples, when he was Minister of Transport in the previous Government. I had asked a question in the House from the Prime Minister, seeking information on the business appointments held by his Cabinet Ministers prior to taking office, especially Sir Keith Joseph, head of *Bovis Holdings* and Marples of *Marples Ridgeway*. The day following my question in the House, I was asked by a *Newcastle Journal* reporter in a telephone conversation, if it related to the statement of Marples on the Channel tunnel and its effect on the company owned by the Transport Minister. I said that it did not, but obviously it was something that needed looking into. Marples sued the *Journal* and myself and subsequently I had to pay £500 damages. Frank Soskice was keen on fighting the issue through to the courts, a decision which I am certain would have displeased Marples and the Tory Party with the 1964 General Election looming ahead and the impact of the Profumo affair still disturbing Conservative voters. But Ted Short and the other Party chiefs decided otherwise. Short from the Whips' office did a good job in a whip round of my Parliamentary colleagues including USDAW MPs. USDAW also made a contribution, as did Bobbie Clough, the then editor of the *Newcastle Journal*, who handed over £250 towards the legal expenses. So the financial strain on my family and myself was reduced to the minimum. Ted, in malicious fashion some years later, in defence of his money collection for Dan Smith's defence in the Wandsworth Council corruption and conspiracy trial, tried to indicate a similarity between the Marples action against myself and the Dan Smith-Sporle affair, with which I shall deal later.

After leaving office, Marples sold the *Marples Ridgeway* firm in 1965 for £454,847 in cash to the *Bath Portland* Group, and a further agreed sum of £123,750 which was payable over approximately three years. On the basis of contracts in hand at the time of sale, the profits of the new *Marples Ridgeway*, now a subsidiary of the *Bath Portland* Group was estimated to be at an annual rate of not less than £100,000. Ridgeway became managing director of the new subsidiary and all present co-directors joined the new Board. Poulson and Marples were linked in a highly successful design for flyovers. Sir Keith (*Bovis*) Joseph returned to become vice-chairman of the *Bovis* Board, which was another Leeds parliamentary link with Poulson, who was the consultant architect for the Bradford based *Arndale Property Trust* whose major building enterprises were undertaken by *Bovis Holdings*, the family firm of Sir Keith Joseph. I was to become involved in a major row concerning the contract for a town centre at Blyth, arranged for *Arndale*, but later turned down as the result of an enquiry ordered by Tony Greenwood, who had succeeded Dick Crossman as Minister for Housing and Local Government.

59

During 1965, I was approached by the secretary of the Blyth Chamber of Trade and a number of residents in the central area of Blyth about the reports of the council's discussions on the building of a town centre development at Blyth. The matter had been very hush-hush, and in keeping with the attitude of the Council, particularly of the Housing Committee of which Councillor Fred Smith, later Alderman, was Chairman, as well as being Chairman of the Blyth Constituency Labour Party; no press were allowed to attend committee or Council meetings. But matters came to a head when I made arrangements to hold meetings with the Chamber of Trade and those local people who felt they were likely to be affected by the proposed town centre redevelopment scheme. On the Friday arranged for the meetings, I was holding my usual surgery and interview sesson for constituents, when I was told by a number of councillors that I had no right to be discussing town centre plans, as this was a Council matter and had nothing to do with the Member of Parliament. This was an attitude that I had encountered on a number of occasions and which I had always ignored, very much against my will, because my constituency work just did not allow me the time to get embroiled in matters that would interfere with it. I was also told that Smith was not too pleased with my activities, and that he resented the statement I had made that day, that following the Friday meetings with constituents, I would be raising the question of town centre redevelopment with the Minister, Tony Greenwood, when I returned to Westminster the following Monday. I met the Chamber of Trade and was greatly disturbed to hear, not only of their concern at the way in which the council were handling the town centre plans, but also of the secrecy surrounding the whole deal, secrecy which was excessive even by Blyth standards.

I returned to London on Monday and sought a meeting with Tony Greenwood, who very helpfully arranged for me to meet the three officials in his department who were handling the Blyth Town Centre project. In discussions some things emerged quite clearly. As traders and residents had claimed, and despite the secrecy they appeared to have been well briefed on the matter, the officials of the ministry held the view that the scheme was too grandiose for a town the size of Blyth. They saw no need for a public inquiry into the matter and believed that the council should be more forthcoming in the information they were providing about their development plans. I returned home to Blyth at the week-end and met the constituents affected by the developments, and I also discovered at my meeting with the Chamber of Trade that they were concerned at the national level with the manner in which town centre plans were being pushed through. I agreed to meet the officials of the National Chamber of Trade and their legal adviser to discuss matters at Blyth and elsewhere. The Chamber of Trade had considered setting up their own organisation to deal with the problems of town centre development on a national footing. The firm involved at Blyth was *Arndale*. In the early sixties, according to Muir Hunter QC, acting for Poulson's creditors, Poulson, Smith and the giant construction firm *Bovis* formed a consortium for the purpose of obtaining contracts to redevelop town centres. A letter confirming this arrangement, from Poulson to Harry Vincent, then *Bovis* chairman, was read at the bankruptcy hearings which said, 'Smith will introduce the towns to you. He will have done 99% of the necessary spadework. He will be paid $1\frac{1}{2}\%$ of the contract and he can cover his expenses out of this $1\frac{1}{2}\%$. I doubt whether he needs such a large organisation, but that is up to him.'

On 18th June, 1962 Vincent replied: 'We would be most grateful if you could inaugurate such a system. It is understood that you [Poulson] would be architect, with Smith as the consultant.'

I reported fully to my constituents at subsequent meetings held in Blyth following my return from the House of Commons, concerning the town centre scheme against the background of my discussions with Tony Greenwood's officials at the Ministry of Housing, and the Local Government Department indicated that a full scale public inquiry would be held.

Alderman Fred Smith, chairman of the committee responsible for the Town Centre Redevelopment project and of the Blyth Constituency Labour Party, reacted by moving in committee at the Council that I be reported to the Minister for leaking information. It is not without significance that Smith failed to secure nomination for a further term of office as chairman of the Blyth Labour Party at its Annual Meeting in May 1966 and was succeeded by George Adams, who was later to become a leading figure in the Seaton Valley Council, in the period prior to reorganisation. On 28th April, 1966, the Minister of Housing and Local Government, Tony Greenwood, announced the findings of the Town Centre Development Inquiry. It was in effect what had been argued by the townspeople and myself, and contrary to the council's decision, namely that the scheme was unsuited to Blyth, too large and grandiose for the area's requirements, and a smaller scheme was more suited to the needs of the district. The Minister also promised his full support and cooperation in any further scheme the Council proposed, and his officials would give help where needed. This offer was never taken up with the Ministry concerned and *Arndale Bovisgate (Blyth) Ltd* of Bradford faded, or seemed to fade, from the Blyth scene. Poulson did however secure the job of architect for the new Blyth Swimming Baths which were under discussion around this time. On Friday 4th January, 1974, the following news item appeared in the *Whitley Bay Guardian and Gazette:*

POULSON TELLS HOW HE MET DAN SMITH
The former international architect John Poulson told Leeds Crown Court this week how he met Mr T. Dan Smith, who was working at the time on a town centre development scheme at Blyth. He continued to see him because when Mr Smith was introducing *Bovis*, with whom he had an agreement, he could introduce Poulson too. Mr Smith was nationally known in town centre development for which there was a vogue at the time. He admired Mr Smith, who as far as he knew had done nothing improper on his behalf.

Another outcome of the Blyth Town Centre redevelopment plans came to light during police investigations in the North East in 1973, when Mr Edwin W. Carter, Town Clerk of Blyth, wrote on 20th June, 1973 to the Attorney General, Sir Peter Rawlinson in the following terms.

Dear Sir,

One Member of Parliament has recently raised in the House of Commons allegations of non-cooperation with and obstruction by Local Authorities in the North-East of police officers carrying out investigations in connection with the Poulson case. The local Member of Parliament—Mr Edward Milne MP—has also expressed similar concern and asked for Parliamentary and Public Inquiries into this matter, and, in the *Journal* newspaper on 19th June, stated that he could name five Local Authorities who have been obstructive. . . . I would like to place on record the fact that the Borough of Blyth is not to be numbered amongst any Local Authorities who have allegedly failed to cooperate with or have obstructed the police officers working on this investigation and, on the contrary, have been at pains to give the fullest cooperation in the production and copying of files and documents. *Further, I think it should also be placed on record that I myself was seriously perturbed regarding the firm of J. G. L. Poulson as long ago as 1966* when I asked the then Ministry of Housing and Local Government whether an inquiry should be made into the leakage of information from that Department. I enclose copies of the correspondence in question. I have sent a copy of this letter to Mr Milne and to the Prime Minister.

Yours faithfully,
Edwin W. Carter, Town Clerk (L/1/4.0.1)

The italics are my own.

This confirmed the general position of many in the area who wondered what was really going on in Blyth and the North-East. Dan Smith and his minions were appearing everywhere, backed up by the Party chiefs at Transport House, throughout the North-East and in the House of Commons. Towards the end of 1965, I approached Ernie Fernyhough who was then Parliamentary Private Secretary to the Prime Minister for an interview with Wilson. I spent over half an hour with the PM and expressed my concern about matters in the Blyth Constituency and about the way any enquiry or examination of local affairs would erupt into some sort of party quarrel. I told of the increasing pressure being directed at me by party officials in the constituency, who in the main were also councillors in their local authorities. As is the experience of most people who have a talk with Wilson, I had to do more listening than anything else, but he did appear to be concerned and promised to send an officer from Transport House to look into matters and let him have a report. This promise, like so many from the same quarter ever since, was never kept. The Labour leader seemed to show no interest in uncovering issues of the kind we raised, rather than investigating and examining as he ought to have been doing. Along with Ted Short, Bob Mellish and John Silkin, he shares a heavy responsibility for the way things developed in the sixties, and for the appointments he so liberally bestowed on Smith and Cunningham and those around them.

The 1964–1966 Labour Government was a successful one. Despite a wafer-thin majority in the House, its legislative programme went ahead rapidly. The Government and the country were moving together towards better things. Looking back on that period it can be seen as the best for Labour of any administration and at least the equal of the great Attlee period of 1945–51. But the future lay ahead. Economic squalls loomed on the horizon and a General Election was to come sooner than anyone expected. In the closing weeks of the 1964 Parliament, I tried under the Ten Minute Rule to introduce a Private Member's Bill, seeking to register clients of public relations companies who were engaged in political activities. This arose, as one would have guessed, from the attitude I took to the appointment of Dan Smith and firms carrying out work for the Labour Party. It was also made necessary by the growing number of councillors, who appeared to be working on the fringes of the public relations firms, and who in many cases were influencing council decisions in a much stronger way than their Council membership alone justified. To me these activities were a threat to democracy and used mainly to prevent local issues being fully aired in public. The electors, even that relatively small number who vote in council elections, deserve to be told the unvarnished truth about council decisions, especially where they involve public expenditure. The gloss and publicity razamataz with which public relations firms dress up and often misrepresent council activities, deceive the public and add to its growing cynicism where politics and politicians are concerned, as well as to its frustration at so seldom being able to find out what is really going on and how its rate money is being spent. The real tragedy to me of the growth of this sort of exercise was that public relations were more concerned with concealing matters than revealing them. The Bill, Public Relations Companies (Registration of Political Clients) as it was legally termed, sought to provide for the registration of those clients of public relations companies who are engaged in political activities. In the course of introducing the Bill to Parliament I stated, 'Public Relations has suddenly come into the open as the business that has failed to do for itself what it effectively does for others: either through incompetence or because of other hidden reasons. The performance and technique of public relations have given it a mystique without increasing public confidence in its value or its necessity.' In my attempt at legislation in this field I had the support of the Institute of Public Relations, whose President said at the Association's Annual Conference, that the Bill would at 'one blow sweep away the element of secrecy from pressure group activities.' Needless to say the Bill did not increase my popularity with my colleagues in the Northern Group nor with the Chief Whip, Ted Short. No definite moves were made when I introduced the Bill, but a number of Northern Members took the trouble to tell me that they doubted the wisdom of such a Parliamentary move. If the Bill had been likely to get off the ground, I feel certain it would have had a much more hostile reception from the source mentioned. Rather surprisingly Dame Irene Ward, my next door Parliamentary neighbour at Tynemouth, opposed the motion supporting the Bill, but did not press the matter to a vote. The attitude of some of my colleagues did not disturb me, for I had encountered similar opposition when introducing legislation to register travel agents and tour operators to protect consumers, and discovered that a few of my parliamentary colleagues were actually working for travel firms in an advisory capacity. This question of public relations work by MPs was to emerge in subsequent parliaments. Fortunately, the press often acts as watch-dog and brings into the open matters which many MPs would prefer to have undiscussed. On this occasion *The*

Times, in an editorial the next day, had this to say on the matter.

NOT SO PUBLIC RELATIONS

When Mr Edward Milne sought leave yesterday to introduce a Bill to provide for the registration of clients of public relations firms engaged in political activities he was, in a parliamentary sense, engaged in an academic exercise. Nevertheless he was touching upon a subject which troubles the public mind. More and more the practice has spread of political bodies, and particularly foreign Governments, employing public relations firms to represent their interests. The methods employed by such firms, and particularly their relations with Parliament and its members have on occasions seemed repugnant. (*Times* 22/7/1964.)

Moving towards the 1966 General Election, changes were taking place in the constituency which seemed to be for the better. Holliday had retired, and after a struggle to retain him as a part time agent by some members of the EC had been defeated, a local party member, Ron Hepple, was appointed to the post. Ron had been a full time agent in Derbyshire, then moved to Jarrow with Ernie Fernyhough, and because of ill health wanted to come back to Blyth, where he was still living in order to cut out most of his travelling. Both he and his wife approached me before the selections to press the case for appointment, and because of the circumstances I supported Ron Hepple for the job. This was strenuously opposed by Fred Smith and others, but Ron Hepple nevertheless got the job as secretary and agent to the Blyth Constituency. At the 1966 Annual Meeting, George Adams of *Seaton Delaval* became Chairman of the Constituency Party in succession to Fred Smith, who had failed to secure nomination. Adams had a good background, was registrar at the Northern Counties College and became a prominent local councillor. He is at present leader of the Labour majority group on Seaton Valley Council having been responsible for a great deal of the re-organisation work on the Seaton Valley Urban District Council, prior to its merging with Blyth Burgh Council on the setting up of the new

66

authorities in April 1974. Both of Adams' parents had been Mayors of Berwick-on-Tweed, and life-long members of the Labour and Co-operative movements.

The 1966 General Election campaign went well. Wilson had judged the timing to a nicety. Following a very successful by-election at Kingston-upon-Hull, the Prime Minister moved quickly, dissolved parliament and secured a most convincing verdict from the electorate. In the campaign most of us took the view that this election would herald something like the long term of Labour rule in Britain, which our Scandinavian counterparts had enjoyed for so long. But it was a different parliament and indeed a different nation that emerged from the 1966 General Election. It has often been said, but never more applicably than at this time, that things in Britain would never be quite the same again. I was myself out of parliament for a few months in 1966. Returning from addressing a Union week-end school in Bridlington, I collapsed in London and was taken to Westminster Hospital, where a stomach operation kept me for some five to six weeks, and the subsequent convalescence delayed my return to parliamentary and constituency activity until after the Summer Recess, when I returned to Westminster in October.

In 1968, Ron Hepple died and there was difficulty in finding a successor. One of the local councillors, Peter Mortakis, con-tacted me and was interested in the job. At that time he was employed as an insurance agent, but seemed dissatisfied with the job and was seeking new outlets. Mortakis had been a good party official and generally taken much the same line as myself on political and constituency matters. The only doubt in my mind was that Mortakis had not overly distinguished himself in any of his previous jobs. However there was only one other applicant, and the Executive Council gave the job to Mortakis with a minority voting against. He settled into the job very well, but the office side of his activities was generally in a tangle. One of the conditions of his employment was that he gave up his seat on the local council, which he did immediately on appointment.

With Adams and Mortakis in the key positions in the con-stituency party, matters moved as smoothly as they had ever done in Blyth, but not for long. During 1968, many complaints

67

were reaching me about council activities and other related matters following the rejection of the town centre development project, and the involvement of local councillors with a Birtley builder called McCullough. At a later stage in the talks about corruption in Blyth, Dan Smith said that he thought McCullough would be the man behind any broad corruption in Blyth. The Birtley builder was a close associate of Andrew Cunningham and Alderman Fred Smith, chairman of Blyth Housing Committee. The national press and the media were paying close attention to the Blyth scene, and one of the lobby correspondents had provided me with the information on which they were working. They were interested in the two houses being built in the nearby Whitley Bay Council area by McCullough for Smith, and the flash new car being driven by Smith, which they claimed was provided and maintained by McCullough. After I had discussed the matter privately with officials at the Ministry of Housing and Local Government, I raised questions in the House about the secrecy surrounding council decisions, both in committee and at full council meetings. About this time, George Adams told me that he had been invited to a dinner at the Red House in Newcastle by Dan Smith and asked if I thought it advisable for him to go. I replied that the decision must be his, but that I personally would not touch it with a barge-pole, but that I was likely to receive an invitation from that quarter anyway. I also showed Adams the documents and information I had received from the journalists and reporters doing their investigatory work in the area. Adams went to the dinner and told me afterwards that Smith had gathered a wide range of people around him, and that at the dinner there had been people from all walks of life.

Immediately after this I received a report from one of our young ward secretaries at Cramlington, David Browning, son of Tom Browning the secretary of Blyth Trades Council, that Councillor Jim Collier of the village Seaton Delaval had been attacking me at party meetings. On receiving this information, I immediately asked for a meeting with Collier, Adams and Mortakis. I was amazed at the attitude taken by Adams at this interview. He backed Collier to the hilt, and attacked me so viciously that Mortakis feared he would resign the chairmanship of the constituency. Indeed not long afterwards, and before the 1970 General Election, Adams moved house out of the Seaton Valley Council area to Whitley Bay, and in consequence resigned both from the Council and the chairmanship of the constituency party. I was sorry to see this happen, and at the Annual Meeting paid tribute to Adams and his work, while my wife made a presentation to him on behalf of the Constituency Party. Apart from our clash at the meeting with Councillor Collier to deal with my complaints about his conduct, relationships between Adams and myself had been cordial and friendly, and any departure from that had been occasioned only by Collier's actions in Nelson Village, Cramlington and other areas of the Seaton Valley Council District.

Friction had been brewing in Blyth over the secrecy of the local council ever since the clash on town centre development, and matters were brought to a head in a speech made by Tony Greenwood at the Labour Party Local Government Conference at Harrogate on 15th February, 1969, when he said that in his view two things were essential if local authorities were to convince the public that they were keeping pace with changing ideas. The second was that 'far more of them must throw off the murky cloak of silence. The public have a right to know what councils are doing in their name, and why they are doing it. Every councillor should search his conscience on the way his council operates the Public Bodies (Admission To Meetings) ACT. . . . Councils should see that the Press are informed about what is happening. If journalists are kept in ignorance, and if decisions are taken behind closed doors which should be taken in public, councils have only themselves to blame if they have a hostile Press and an apathetic public.'

In his book, which took its title from the Greenwood speech, *The Murky Cloak*, Roger Burke wrote the following:

'On 17th September, 1969, the Prime Minister, the Rt. Hon. Harold Wilson, OBE, MP, addressed the Annual Conference of the Association of Municipal Corporations at Scarborough, and in the course of his address he dwelt on the need for accountability by local authorities to the communities they serve. He recalled Anthony Greenwood's speech to the

Labour Party Local Government Conference earlier in the year. Among his audience were Alderman Fred Smith, the leader of Blyth Borough Council, and Councillor William Woolfrey, chairman of the Council's establishments committee. Whether they squirmed in their seats only they or perhaps the Town Clerk, Edwin Carter, who accompanied them, can tell. Certainly they should have felt uncomfortable although from all events this seems unlikely. Indeed, within a few days the two members were present at a council committee meeting which recommended that a copy of the Prime Minister's speech should be circulated to every council member. Which is all very strange because at that time Alderman Smith and his colleagues were involved in a mighty tussle to exclude the local Press from their committee meetings—in defiance of Mr Wilson's advice. (*The Murky Cloak*, page 34-35.)

I tabled a further question to Tony Greenwood on the subject and stated that people who enter public life and undertake public activities should conduct them in public. Speaking some days later to the Blyth Labour Women's Federation, I accused the Council leadership at Blyth of ineffectiveness and indecision. In this demand for an open approach to council matters I was supported by my agent, Peter Mortakis who said that Blyth should take a lesson from nearby Bedlington Council which was also in the Blyth Constituency area, and whose relationships with the press were excellent, while they should acknowledge the role that newspapers have to play in political and local Government affairs. He added that he doubted the sincerity of Councillor Raymond McClure, a Liberal councillor, who had also raised the matter in Blyth Council. The question of my interference in local government affairs was raised at a number of party meetings but never when I was present. Councillor Donohue of Blyth Council did attack me prior to one meeting, when I asked him how he was getting on. He replied, 'None the better for anything that you have been doing lately.' Donohue was one of the first honorary members of McCullough's night club in Whitley Bay, *The Sands Club*. The councillor also endeavoured to get a vote of censure on myself moved at a subsequent meeting.

While all this was happening, the case of the MP for Sunderland South, Gordon Bagier, and his public relations work, erupted onto the pages of the national press. In October 1968, the *Sunday Times* had been involved in a legal battle, which had gone to the High Court, to secure the right to publish a report compiled by *Maurice Fraser and Associates* on behalf of the Greek Government, in which it was stated that Fraser claimed he had recruited a British MP to work secretly on their behalf. Bagier had denied his involvement with Maurice Fraser, but he changed his mind under pressure from the Government Chief Whip, John Silkin, after a controversial showing of the programme *This Week*. Strong pressure, not for the first or last time in matters of this kind, was exercised by the Independent Television Authority for the programme to be banned. In this they were unsuccessful because the reporter handling the programme, John Morgan, managed to make it clear that definite evidence was available linking a particular MP to the firm of *Maurice Fraser and Associates*. When he made his statement, following discussions with the Chief Whip, Bagier denied doing anything for the Greek Government in the course of his work for the Fraser organisation. At the same time as this denial, the Chief Executive for International Relations of *Maurice Fraser Associates*, Howard Preece, was claiming that the firm did not have any public relations work apart from the Greek account, which was netting the firm something like a quarter of a million dollars for 1968 alone (253,000 drachmas). All this emerged during one hectic week-end. Many of us wondered why the Chief Whip and Wilson did not issue a warning to the party about involvements of the kind that were engaged in by Bagier and others. The press and radio and television interviews given by Bagier, following his admission to being on the Fraser payroll was handled by a local reporter Sid Foxcroft. Official Labour circles gave the impression of wanting to hush up the matter as quickly as possible. The Prime Minister made the usual fluffy statements he reserves for matters of this kind. Vague talk, about the rights and wrongs of Members of Parliament having outside interests, managed to warn off any MPs on the Labour side who may have felt inclined to raise awkward questions in or out of the House of Commons.

I was particularly incensed, and had a clash with Syd Foxcroft over the point, when Bagier said, on television, that what he had done was being also done by others, and as he put it, everybody in the House was doing the same. At the meeting of the Northern Group of Labour MPs the following Wednesday, I challenged the Bagier statement, but there was an immediate closing of ranks, headed by Jim Tinn, the Member for Cleveland who launched into praise for Bagier's work as secreof the Northern Group at their meeting. Next business was promptly moved, and the Bagier indiscretion was forgotten. I found it a particularly unpleasant affair and of course cut right across party policy regarding our relationships with the Greek Colonels' junta. What happened was that at Easter 1968, Bagier had led a parliamentary delegation to Greece which included Ted Garrett, the Member for Wallsend, and the Liberal MP for Inverness, Russell Johnston. Fraser's move into the international public relations business seemed to have been of recent growth, for he obtained the contract to handle British and European public relations for the Greek regime early in 1968. His most important work was done amongst British MPs, and even his own staff were unaware of the relationships with Bagier till he phoned one day, asking for Fraser who was unavailable because he was in Athens. He then spoke to Howard Preece, and said he would be glad if arrangements could be made for his cheque for the month to be paid into a different account. (*Sunday Times*, 'Insight' 9/3/69) Bagier ran into further trouble more recently, because of a visit paid by him to the South African Government, accompanied by MPs Hugh McCartney and Albert Roberts. It is not surprising that one veteran miners' MP, Dick Kelly remarked that some members whom he described in derogatory pit language, spent more time in the embassies of reactionary foreign governments than they did in the House of Commons. Maybe the reason the three MPs who made the South African visit were saved from the wrath of the party, was because Bob Mellish's memory had so failed him that he could not recollect whether he had given them permission to go or not.

Ted Short was given the responsibility some time ago of

drawing up the procedure for a declaration of the interests of Members of Parliament, but he has been no quicker in moving on that matter than he has on giving the House of Commons an explanation of his own outside interests. When one looks back and reflects on the activities of people who are returned to the House of Commons to serve the interests of the country and their constituents, and who move off in totally other directions, leaving the people they were supposed to serve to fend for themselves, it should not really occasion surprise. For if Labour Party headquarters at Transport House, with a National Executive Committee always containing a fair sprinkling of MPs and at times a Cabinet Minister, can give the lead in employing Dan Smith, and aiding his work in setting up an army of paid lieutenants in the Town Halls of the North-East and other parts of the country, can others be blamed for doing likewise in the public relations field, whether contrary to the Party's declared policy or not?

I thought at the end of 1969 that things could not become more hectic, feeling that my battles in the constituency and in parliament were bound to bring me allies, and we would move into calmer waters. Ten years of opposition on issues, which on the surface appeared consistent with the declared policies and principles of the Labour Movement, should be enough for one member's decade in the House of Commons. But it was not to be.

Chapter Five

I had been brought up in the traditions of the pioneers of our Movement and had sat at the feet of some of its great figures. Jimmie Maxton was my boyhood political hero, and having worked with him from the late 1930s until he died, I could not fail to bring into public life some of the standards he set and the philosophy of living of which he was so much the embodiment. Bob Smillie, who was MP for the South-East Northumberland area from 1923–29, expressed it in his own simple terms, when he said that the duty of a Member of Parliament was to serve not to rule. Possibly the greatest lessons we have to learn from past leaders in the light of the present-day widescale corruption, is from Herbert Morrison, whose organisational and propaganda work in bringing the Labour Party to power, first in the City of London, and then at the 1945 General Election is given too little credit by those who never knew him. Wilson himself has said that this movement of ours is nothing if it is not a crusade, although over the years we have become accustomed to the Labour leader saying one thing and meaning another. Words are meant to mean what I mean them to mean, seems to be his slogan. Morrison once remarked that 'the only thing for which I would preserve capital punishment would be jobbery, bribery and corruption in the public services, or robbery from public funds.' On a visit to America, he was so shocked at the methods of the American city bosses, that he proclaimed that he would 'sooner clear out of public life than run the spoils system,' adding the remark, 'I should not make a good American politician.'

Morrison built the London Labour Party into the most powerful local political party in the country. The weak machine he took over as London secretary in 1915, had by 1934 shown an example to the rest of Britain, and held control of most of the London boroughs and the London County Council. In 1920 he was Mayor of Hackney. His knowledge of local government was unsurpassed and laid down simple rules. It has often been argued, in the words of Acton's oft repeated dictum, that power corrupts but absolute power corrupts absolutely. If anyone proved otherwise it was Morrison. He disproved the theory that one party rule must lead to corruption, or that only one party is capable of it. He mounted an offensive against graft in London, when he entered public life and local government jobbery and corruption was an established fact. He preached the lesson that Labour must not be tainted with the charge of corruption. All the evils, which we have seen to-day revealed in the North-East, were rampant in the London that Morrison was to transform into the best example of local government administration in modern times. The net result of the actions of the corrupters and the corrupted, as the examination of local government made by Morrison and his colleagues then proved, and as is known by many of us now, is that local government is brought into disrepute and burdens the ratepayers with increased charges, which hit hardest at the poorest sections of the community, and damage, sometimes beyond repair, the proper provision of services in the areas that local representatives were elected to represent. From party headquarters Morrison issued document after document showing examples of corruption that was brought to his notice. He was prepared to expose the slightest irregularity, kept a close eye on the work of all committees and ruthlessly dealt with nepotism and jobbery. He repeatedly cautioned his fellow councillors not only to be above corruption, but to be seen to be above it, and gave then examples of how this could be done in all aspects of counc: work and activity. In the nineteen-thirties, Morrison drew up code of conduct which even to-day could well be copied wit advantage by Labour groups, and others who serve on loc: authorities throughout the country. Its concluding points wer 'The Labour Movement, generally, has earned honourab respect for the rectitude of its public work; that tradition shou be scrupulously maintained.' If improper practices or influenc were discovered, the local Labour Party Executive would in no case defend them: indeed it would not feel able to refrain from joining in exposure and public condemnation.' In an excellent review of *Portrait of a Politician*, written together with Bernard Donoghue by G. W. Jones, Senior Lecturer in Political Science at the London School of Economics, and reviewed by himself, he had this to say of Herbert Morrison.

'His period of influence coincided with the emergence of the Labour Party in British local government, and his ideas helped shape how Labour behaved, not just in London, but over the whole country . . . To Morrison, the only reward for a member was a sense of public service . . . Morrison's views on corruption were based on his theory of the public interest. The public interest was, to Morrison, something of substance, quite apart from the clash of personal and group interests. Representatives of the public, elected by the public, were charged with a responsibility, a public trust, to seek and to champion the public interest. The ever present danger was that they might be diverted from this duty by personal or sectional interests.

Morrison's insistence on strict personal rectitude in govern-ment seems to have become unfashionable. It was too moralistic for the permissive society. His quest for an ob-jective public interest also seems inappropriate in a political system, which now emphasises pluralistic bargaining be-tween groups as the way to uncover the public interest. However if Morrison's precepts had been followed, if indeed the Labour Party's Local Government Handbook had included a forceful passage on the dangers of corruption and how to avoid them, then it is possible that our present discontents might not have arisen.'

Following the Bagier episode, there was thinly veiled hos-tility to myself on the Northern Group. The disappearance of Will Owen, formerly MP for Morpeth, from the political scene, following an Old Bailey trial arising from his associations with the Czech Embassy, where revelations were made about his contact with a travel agency operating from Czechoslovakian sources in London, and of payments made to him by officials from the Embassy of that country, although he was found not guilty, heightened the tensions between the Northern Group and myself. Will Owen, like Stonehouse and others, was a sponsored member of the Co-operative Party in the House of Commons. It was obvious from issues emerging almost in quick succession inside and outside the House of Commons, that anyone with an investigatory mind was to become highly unpopular with the powers that be. In any case, at this stage I still believed in the power of parliament and that there was a desire by officials at the top level in the party at Transport House, to get to grips with the issues. After all, the Labour Party's interest in remaining the government of the day, was surely enough reason for rooting out any wrongdoing, whether it came from the actions of those in Local Government or Parliament. But as day followed day in the closing months of 1969, and into the years that followed, I realised how mistaken I had been, because what had happened to the Labour Party, and those who dominated it, was beyond understanding.

There were rumblings in the North-East about a likely scandal involving Dan Smith and the Wandsworth Council, with talk about feelers being put out to raise money for the Poulson organisation, although at this time it was not realised that the issue was the likelihood of bankruptcy, rather than the raising of more capital for the organisation. Further ripples began to appear after the collapse of a block of flats in East London where five people had lost their lives: Ronan Point. The revelations which came to light, arising from the list of suggestions that were sent to all local authorities for strengthening similar blocks, to avoid the progressive collapse which had occurred at Ronan Point, brought to light a number of issues that linked together Wandsworth, Dan Smith, Cunningham and the Felling Urban District Council Housing Committee contract for the building of flats at Crowhall Lane and Nursery Lane. At the time of the placing of the contract, Cunningham was chairman of the Felling UDC Housing Committee, which reported to the Council on 30th May, 1963, 'Your Committee were advised that their Chairman, together with the Chairman and Vice-Chairman of the Planning and

77

Development Committee, the Clerk and the Surveyor, after consideration of the appointment of consultant architects in connection with the erection of multi-storey flats, had interviewed the firm of John G. L. Poulson L/F RIBA of Pontefract, and it decided to appoint Mr Poulson as Consultant Architect.' In fact it was stated at the time that Cunningham's committee had only interviewed Poulson for the job. This procedure was repeated the following year, when Felling UDC on 31st December, 1964, received a report from an all-Labour Sub-Committee of the Housing Committee, 'that they had seen films on the various industrialised building systems of four building contractors, and have inspected the development of various sites in accordance with such systems, and they recommend that the proposed development at Nursery Lane and Crowhall Lane should be carried out by *Crudens* and *Taylor Woodrow (Anglian) Ltd.*, and the Council's Consultants should be informed accordingly and be asked to advise as to which sites should be developed by each of the respective companies.' So the familiar pattern was followed once again where the architect, Poulson, was chosen, all competition having been eliminated by council decision, and the contractors selected without the job being put to tender. And of course Poulson, as the Council's consultant, decided how the job should be allocated between the firms concerned. Not only were the jobs arranged without tender, but neither builder put in an estimate of the costs, which were later agreed with the Ministry of Housing and Local Government, as £72,000,000 each for *Crudens* and *Taylor Woodrow*, with consultants fees to Poulson of £320,000. Some months later, protest was made at a meeting of the Council about the deal, when Councillor Horace Freeman said, 'And what brought about this decision? None of that was disclosed. And not a single item of information about methods or materials has been put to the ears or eyes of this Council. For this Council will obtain tender for a few dozen lavatory seats, door handles etc. . . . but when it comes to industrialised building work, £72,000,000 worth of it, we do not bother about pattern or price, construction or competition.'

Immediately following the Ronan Point disaster, Poulson wrote to Felling Council and indicated that in his view the

Ronan Point disaster could not be repeated, as in dealing with the industrialised flats at Nursery Lane and Crowhall Lane, he had in mind the likelihood of inherent instability and appropriate action had been taken to prevent it in the Felling flats. John Donkin, the then Clerk of the Council, was not so sure and he wrote to Poulson, indicating a claim of £1,000,000 in connection with the strengthening costs of the flats. This has been denied by the present clerk of Felling, Mr Thomas Myrddin-Baker, who claims that Felling took counsel's advice and decided to take no action, while Felling's only claim against Poulson was for £9,700 for expenses incurred by an extension of the contract. However Bernard Conlan MP, claimed in the House of Commons in 1970, that the rent loss for Nursery Lane alone had amounted to £110,000, a figure he described as both substantial and crippling. When Felling Council finally decided to strengthen, they were given a 50% grant by the Ministry towards the cost of structural repairs, loss of rent and tenants' moving expenses. This grant was later raised to 75% but local estimates of the cost to Felling ratepayers caused by the strengthening work was around £500,000 and central government grants would have added another burden in the region of £1,000,000.

Another significant point that emerged in discussions with local Durham councillors, as revealed by John Donkin, was that he had written to all affected local authorities after the Ronan Point disaster, to ask them if they would take combined action against the contractors and consultants of industrialised buildings. Donkin claims that the only response of any value that he got in reply, was from the Town Clerk of Wandsworth, Barry Payton, who was sacked not long afterwards under circumstances that were exceptionally dubious. The Wandsworth Clerk had discovered, following the Ronan Point disaster, that the structural engineer employed in the area had been paid £147,259 for work at Doddington Road, where eleven huge blocks of flats were under construction, and that until 1968 he was consulting engineer to nearly all of the district's main construction schemes. As Wandsworth contained more high rise blocks than any other local authority, the Town Clerk sought the opinion of two legal experts, and was advised that there was a *prima facie* case for damages in negligence against the consulting engineer. Barry Payton advised the Council that the consulting engineer should be sued for negligence. The Wandsworth Town Clerk had formidable support for the suggested action. He had previously convened a meeting of local authorities, with problems similar to that of Wandsworth, to discuss the question of legal action for reclaiming the costs of strengthening and improving the Ronan Point style flats. He received almost complete support for his proposals to take action against the consulting engineers concerned. Indeed a number of authorities indicated to him that they had already been given sanction to offer help with the legal costs involved. But as Barry Payton and the rest of us were to discover, the casualties in the fight against corruption came from the ranks of those who were opposing the disease and not from the corrupt or the corrupted. Events then moved rapidly, both in Wandsworth and elsewhere. The Town Clerk, in a recommendation to a Housing Committee meeting arranged for 22nd May, 1969, advised suing the consulting engineer for negligence. Twenty-four hours before the meeting, 34 Tory Councillors summoned a special council meeting, and a vote of no confidence was passed on Barry Payton. He immediately resigned, and almost before he had left the building, copies of his report were collected up, and the leader of the Tories on Wandsworth Council was trying to prove that the QCs consulted by Barry Payton had recommended differently from what had been reported to them.

Other problems were of course moving in fast on Wandsworth and *Mr Newcastle*, because the chairman of its Housing committee, Councillor Sporle, had been engaged by Dan Smith to work for one of his firms at a salary of £1,000 per year. The Wandsworth Town Clerk had been dismissed for trying to save the Council money on losses incurred in industrialised building, while the Councillor who became chairman of its Housing Committee in 1965, when the Council was Labour controlled, was actually being paid a commission on every unit of industrialised building sold, buildings of a type which proved so costly to local authorities throughout Britain—and to ratepayers and taxpayers throughout the land—following the

80

Ronan Point disaster. At the Wandsworth trial, from March to July 1971, Sporle received a six-year prison sentence, reduced to four on appeal, for accepting bribes from Smith, whilst Smith, on trial separately, went scot free and was so elated by the decision that he told reporters he was returning to take up public life in Newcastle. At one time it seemed as if this was likely, because Smith had powerful friends. George Brown had appointed him Chairman of the Northern Economic Planning Council in 1965 and Dame Evelyn Sharpe, later Baroness, gave character evidence in support of Smith at the Wandsworth trial, as Lord George-Brown was to do later for Cunningham in the Leeds Crown trial in 1974. At that time she said of Dan Smith, 'He is one of those people who are in local government for what he can put into it and not for what he could get out of it. In his approach to all his public work he had total integrity. I think he is an imaginative idealist.'

The Wandsworth case is interesting in that it reveals how difficult it was for anyone to get to grips with the complex problems surrounding the activities of Smith and Cunningham in their connections with Poulson. Almost every facet of public life in Britain was drawn into the net. Anyone, as the case of Barry Payton has shown, who dared to demand action or investigation, was ruthlessly dealt with. People in high places moved in swiftly to protect the wrongdoers, and above all to prevent further disclosures. Dan Smith had access to the top echelons of the Labour Party, and had employed Michael Ward in his local authority work. Ward and Smith served on the Labour Party's advisory committee on local government, of which Ward acted as secretary.

Labour leaders like Short, Mellish, Underhill, Hayward, and the Northern Regional officer Ron Evers, have declaimed about the harm done to Labour by the demands for examination and enquiry that I had been asking for into the allegations of corruption that were being voiced from many parts of Britain, but particularly the North-East of England. The Wandsworth trial should have revealed to them all how intertwined the political parties were in this sort of exercise, and of the mass of evidence that was at their disposal if they had really got down to the business of examining the problem by getting into touch

81

with those local councillors who had become seriously disturbed about the situation that had developed in their areas. But again, as with the Town Clerk of Wandsworth, it was not the corrupt or the corrupted who were cast aside. In fact as far back as 1962–63, Brian Bastin, a Wandsworth Councillor, courageously endeavoured to get something done about corruption in his area, but was studiously ignored and pilloried for his efforts.

In some of his more hysterical moments, Reg Underhill, the National Agent of the Labour Party, has told my constituents at Blyth, my trade union colleagues in USDAW and Labour Parties throughout the country, that Eddie Milne has never asked for an inquiry into corruption or raised the matter at Labour Party level. This is of course demonstrably not true, but we shall deal with that matter at a later stage of the story. Even if Eddie Milne, Barry Payton or Brian Bastin had not existed, surely the information emerging from the evidence given at Wandsworth leading to the imprisonment of a Labour leader on the Council, should have led to some action by Transport House or the National Executive of the Labour Party. But then Andrew Cunningham was a member of the National Executive at that time, and hardly likely to give or offer to give evidence on the subject or encourage an enquiry, while Dan Smith was back in circulation after his acquittal, with the praises of many party members ringing in his ears, and Ted Short running round with the collecting can to raise money to pay for his legal costs. In fact Labour's Deputy Leader was so coy about his fund raising activities, that when Peter Hain recounted the story, he threatened legal action and the Liberals even issued an apology to Short for slandering him in this way. The Rt. Hon. Member for Newcastle Central afterwards sent me a letter, saying that he only did the money-collecting for Smith's legal costs as he had previously done for me when I had faced expenses following a libel writ served on me by Ernest Marples, one time Conservative Minister of Transport.

As Poulson was later to relate at his trial, with Smith and Cunningham, at Leeds Crown Court, he was flabbergasted the first time he met the powerful Durham alderman. Poulson already had much experience of buying men and women, but never had he met anyone so eager to be bought as Cunningham.

But I would now like to travel back from Wandsworth and Ronan Point, back from the complexities of Labour and Tory involvement in the arts of corrupt local government practice, to the harsh realities of the impact of all this on the Blyth constituency and the North-East.

In Blyth, Jack Rowlands, an official of the Constructional Engineering Union had been appointed chairman of the Blyth Constituency Labour Party in succession to George Adams. I had met Rowlands on a number of occasions in connection with the fight to save the Blyth Shipyard from closure, and in the long drawn out battle to bring the Alcan smelter to the Northumberland coast. He was a lackadaisical, but quite likeable character, and one of his first actions as secretary, was to bring Mortakis and Alderman Fred Smith back into contact with each other by arranging a handshaking session at Smith's home one Saturday morning. The effect of this was to secure for Fred Smith a seat on Northumberland County Council in a by-election in October 1970. Smith and Rowlands were two of the Party chairmen I was accused of failing to get on with at Blyth, and it is interesting to record Rowland's comments when he relinquished office after only a short spell in November 1971. In his letter of resignation to the secretary-agent he said:

Dear Peter,

After long and careful thought, I have decided to relinquish the Chairmanship of the Division. I do this very reluctantly, although it has not been a happy spell as Chairman of the Division, I have enjoyed mixing with the people I have come to like and respect, but I feel that next year which is the last year of my Office as a Trade Union Official is going to be most difficult for a number of reasons.

One of the reasons of course will be the Industrial Relations Bill, which is going to take up a lot of time, and secondly, I will be training a new official, it is for these reasons and these reasons alone that I tender my resignation. I have sent a copy of this letter to Mr E. Milne, MP.

Yours sincerely,
J. Rowlands.

His letter to me read as follows:

Dear Mr Milne,

Herewith find enclosed a copy of a letter which I have sent to-day to the Secretary/Agent Mr Peter Mortakis which is self explanatory.

Can I thank you at this stage for the promptness I have always received to any request I have made of you and wish you and your new association with *Tribune* to be a long and happy one.

If at any time you feel I can help you in any capacity as a Trade Union official, then please do not hesitate to ask.

Yours sincerely,
J. Rowlands.

The early months of 1970 were hectic ones. I could sense the rising concern in the Whips' Office at the increasing evidence coming in of untoward happenings in the North-East, while newspaper articles were getting more courageous in their writings and naming names in their references to local government activities. It was all the more disturbing, when it was reported to me that an employee of the Party's Regional Office in Newcastle had overheard a conversation on the telephone between Ron Evers, the Labour Party's Northern Regional Secretary, and Andrew Cunningham, in which the Durham Alderman told Evers to get through to Blyth and get rid of that 'bugger Milne'. I have never been able to get confirmation of this, but things certainly began to happen in Blyth and as I knew from long experience that if Andy cracked the whip Evers lost no time in obeying his instructions. This was easily noticeable, for Noddy, as Labour's secretary is known in the North-East, is by no means reputed to be a swift-moving character.

From that point Peter Mortakis began to be awkward. Meeting dates were mixed up, and I was more often than not expected to be in two places at one time. In the April of that year I had promised to Seghill Labour Women's Organisation that I would travel north for their birthday celebration. This involved two successive nights on the sleeper between London and Newcastle and the following night to travel from London home to the North-East for the week-end. It was a task I did not mind doing, but as I had received no written confirmation, I asked Mortakis to check on the engagement for me to be assured that everything had been arranged. I travelled home on the Tuesday night and after breakfast on the following morning, 'phoned Mortakis only to be told that the Seghill function was due to be held the following week. This may appear a small matter in itself but when I show later how the Seghill Party, and particularly the Women's Section, manoeuvred two councillors out of office and were the first and only section of the Blyth Party to seek to oust me from the Blyth Constituency, it can be seen that the spirit of the Cunningham instructions if not the letter was already being put into operation.

To attempt to get the events of this period into their proper perspective is difficult enough, but to try to clear the way before moving fully into the 1970s, it is necessary to pinpoint the manifold activities of Dan Smith, who at one and the same time, appeared to be an active Labour councillor keen on improving the lot of the people he represented, particularly in the housing field and the amenities surrounding their day-to-day existence. He was also in the pay of the Labour Party, and given the task of improving Labour's image in Scotland and the North-East. He was also in the pay of a leading architect, Poulson, eager to build up a monopoly empire in his own particular field and to employ anybody with influence to attain that ambition. There were plenty of officials and councillors around willing to be bought, and more important, many in high places who were willing and able to foster these activities whilst themselves remaining in the background, but being helpful in any cover-up operations that were required. Smith also had on his list builders who were keen to get into the lucrative field of council house building and other contracts associated with it. The most important thing was first to get a foothold in the local authorities. When figures are given to show that only a small number of local councillors and officials fall foul of the law, their numbers have to be measured against the enormous influence wielded by these people, and particularly in the one-party control areas where two or three ruthless and unscrupulous councillors or aldermen can not only decide the policy of a council, but prevent the others from knowing what is going on. Those who pry or enquire too much about the council business and the control these people have over the local political parties, as in the case of the North-East, over the National Party organisation and many of the major Unions as well, are isolated and victimized. Another feature of the North-East scene is that Dan Smith and Cunningham, linked together in so many of the Poulson and associated ventures, were not always running in double harness over the whole field where they were both operating in corrupt and conspiratorial fashion.

Cunningham was to emerge as the main promoter of the night club owner and building contractor Sid McCullough, who was to play a prominent part in the North-East after the Poulson and Dan Smith empires started to run into difficulties. At the Labour Party Conferences of 1971 and 1972, many unions expressed concern about the continuing membership of this Durham Alderman and trade union boss on the National Executive Committee. Direct action against him by a number of unions in 1972 was prevented by the information being put around by the General and Municipal Workers' Union that if the nomination of Cunningham was defeated or withdrawn the union would lose the seat on the NEC. Bearing in mind that a deal amongst the big unions generally secures the appointment of the trade union section of the NEC, it is not surprising that Cunningham escaped for a further spell. But it makes a nonsense of the utterances of Underhill, Hayward and others that there was no concern in the Labour Movement over the Poulson affair and those associated with him. In May 1973, just following the Chester-le-Street by-election, Labour's General Secretary, Ron Hayward, wrote to the *New Statesman* in scathing terms about the role of that journal in its handling of the Poulson affair and its examination of Labour's involvement in it. Hayward has not done anything since to remedy the damage done to Labour's image by his ill-advised intervention. So Cunningham remained a member of Labour's NEC until October 1973, a few months after his arrest on charges of corruption and conspiracy, and is indeed a signatory to the

86

NEC report of that year, which was dealt with by the 1973 Labour Party Annual Conference some four days before Dan Smith and Mrs Freda Cunningham were charged in Newcastle along with Poulson for similar offences.

Back in 1966 Smith had to prepare a budget for Poulson, to justify his (Smith's) spending of £20,000 per year in pursuit of the Leeds architect's interests. Many councillors and aldermen graced that list and some admitted receiving money in the form of salaries or consultancy fees. Later Cunningham was to say that he had never been personally employed by the T. Dan Smith organisation, but made no denial of the holidays enjoyed in a number of places at Poulson's expense, moneys which were subsequently repaid when the bankruptcy hearings brought them to light. In fact many others are said to have departed the Smith camp when investigations were conducted about Poulson, following examination of the details provided of the monies shown in the Poulson budget.

It is interesting to recall that Dan Smith in that same year, 1966, was appointed a member of the Royal Commission on Local Government in England, chaired by the then Rt. Hon. Lord Redcliffe Maud. The Royal Warrant for the setting up of the Commission expressed great trust in the knowledge and ability of those appointed to serve, including J. E. Bolton, Sir James Hill, Arthur H. Marshall, Victor Feather, Secretary of the TUC, Dame Evelyn Adelaide Sharp, later Baroness Sharp of Hornsey, and Redcliffe Maude (Chairman). When one considers the tremendous support and prestige that was showered on Smith at this time by the hierarchy of the Labour Party, including Wilson and Short, one wonders how far his influence in the deliberations of the Royal Commission might have led to decisions about local government reorganisation, which to-day make it difficult to examine the actions of the authorities which went out of existence in 1974. In fact the reorganisation of local government was given as the reason for not conducting an enquiry into North-East Councils and Labour Parties by Reg Underhill and other Labour Party Leaders, despite the fact that the party structure remains basically the same at constituency level. Much the same problem and difficulty was touched upon by Dick Crossman in a *Times* article of 20th June, 1973, when he said, 'The other day a police officer dealing with the Poulson affair asked to see me. All he wanted to know was whether, when I was Minister of Housing, I ever received a letter, a draft of which had been found in the Poulson files. After some inquiry, I discovered that all the files of my private office had been lost in the re-organisation which created the new Department of the Environment. My private secretary was pretty certain he had not seen the letter.' The letter in question was, I believe, the one claimed by Poulson to have mentioned the likelihood of his inclusion in the Honours List in some way or another. Whilst on the subject of Dick Crossman's article, it is useful to note some other observations of his on the reluctance of the heads of both Tory and Labour Governments to set up a Tribunal of Inquiry under the Act of 1921. Dick had this to say, 'Why were the police investigating something so trivial and remote from the main charge?' He was told, 'Well, there are 18 of us full-time on the inquiry and it is likely to last for four years . . .' Crossman went on: 'What the police officer said, has since been confirmed officially. We now know there will be no legal action for a year. This must embarrass the Government, which turned down a demand for a tribunal of inquiry on the ground that, if held, it would prevent prosecutions. For the forseeable future, we are going to get neither a tribunal nor a prosecution, but only an interminable and of course, unpunishable, police investigation.' In the next paragraph, he says, 'A judicial inquiry was first urged a year ago. I was against it because I remembered the Linskey tribunal where a luckless junior minister left the court acquitted on all charges but with his political career in ruins. Now I am inclined to think that a tribunal is a lesser evil—provided only that it is instructed to investigate the code of ethics under which elected representatives and officials at present operate and to make recommendations.' This viewpoint is one that has been pressed upon Governments both by myself and others, and in the recent Stonehouse case it would have saved the recent Leader of the House of Commons, Edward Short, some embarrassment and cleared him of the accusations of dilatoriness in dealing yet again with some misdemeanour by those in the public life of the nation. Crossman had this to say

88

of the standards prevailing in public life in the same article: 'The striking feature of the Poulson bankruptcy inquiry was not the criminal activity it revealed but the flagrancy with which undesirable conduct was tolerated and even given official approval.' Strong words from one who occupied, in the Wilson Government of 1964–66, a seat at the centre of these happenings as Minister of Housing and Local Government. The former Housing Minister went on to say 'There was the case, for example, of Sir Bernard Kenyon, the Clerk to the West Riding. For the three years before his retirement he was permitted by a formal minute of the council to manage a number of Mr Poulson's companies, although Mr Poulson had at least 30 contracts with the council.' It is not surprising that further on in his article Crossman made the comment, 'Again, there is no question of legal corruption, but only of a change in standards. What would have been surprising conduct ten years ago is normal practice to-day.'

But it is not only a case of standards, when one examines the empire that Cunningham was able to build up in the North-East. Although denying employment by Smith, he was shown on the budget prepared for Poulson as receiving an annual fee of £1,000. As Chairman of the Northumbrian River Authority, and of the police authority in County Durham, he pushed the joint project in 1967 for the building of the River headquarters, together with the new Durham Law Courts. At the end of the day the River Authority were refused permission by the Government to build the headquarters as they were considered 'too lavish and expensive', terms which keep cropping up wherever the joint activities of Poulson and his minions have been preparing the way for yet another deal. But the friends of the Leeds architect looked after him well. Although he lost the project, Poulson pocketed the fees for doing the design work, £37,000 in all.

In mid-1969, Mr Poulson was informed by his partners that he was insolvent to the tune of £100,000. In June that year evidence has been given that the Cunningham family flew off to Estoril on holiday, at a cost to Poulson of £256. Some of this was paid back after the bankruptcy hearings. What is more significant in the timing of all these matters, is that one of the decisions taken by Cunningham on his return from holiday was in his role as chairman of the Durham Police Authority to appoint an architect to complete the work on a new police headquarters for Sunderland. Not surprisingly the worthy alderman chose J. G. L. Poulson and the firm netted another £30,000 in fees from the citizenry of the North-East. A familiar technique is to be observed in this Cunningham decision, for by the time it came up for ratification by the police authority, Poulson was already at work on the police station. It was an appointment that puzzled many Durham officials, especially in the light of the furore over the River Authority building, for they had expected someone with more experience of police station work to be given the job. But no protests were made. Durham council officials did not cross the Cunningham path, and the only casualty was democracy, and of course the people of Durham county, Labour controlled from the dawn of political democracy in Britain. When one closely examines the attitudes and actions of the Labour Leadership and the Party's National Executive in their dealings with the affairs of Blyth and other areas one wonders whether the practices of the Cunninghams, and the others around him, stemmed from what had been learned by him on the Party's Executive, or if it is the other way round. For it must not be forgotten that despite all the disquiet about his multifarious activities, Cunningham was still able to emerge from the Chester-le-Street Labour Party meeting, following the death of Norman Pentland, the NUM Member of Parliament for the Division, to announce the selection of Giles Radice, the research officer of the General and Municipal Workers' Union, as the Labour by-election candidate and to boast to Pressmen: 'The Cunningham organisation still works.' Despite the turmoil at the time about the circumstances surrounding, not only the Chester-le-Street selection, but the knowledge that the Labour Party headquarters and the House of Commons, particularly Bob Mellish and his whips' office, were at panic stations about the mounting disclosures in the Poulson affair, the Durham alderman was still chairman of the Northern Regional Council of the Labour Party, although he did not take the chair at its Annual Meeting in May 1973, and had only managed to hold his seat on the Executive Committee of the Chester-le-Street Divisional Labour Party.

But for a period the main storm centre was the Blyth Constituency. Matters between Mortakis and myself, as stated, had deteriorated in the early months of 1970, but in the context of past happenings in the area it was not so surprising. Fred Smith was beginning to feel his way back into local circles following his rapprochement with the party agent, but he was foiled in his attempt to secure nomination for the county council vacancy at Bebside. The local elections went well. The Waterloo Ward had been captured for Labour in a County Council election in 1967 for the first time by Angus Galloway, a one time Shopworkers' Union official in Scotland who was now working in Blyth, whom I had met when I first came to the constituency. Angus was my political confidant. We worked together very closely, and little or nothing was done in terms of making political decisions without Angus and I talking matters over. We travelled around the constituency on many of our engagements and before or after parliamentary sessions we were able to compare notes on constituency and national problems on a regular basis. The seat was held again by Labour in 1970 and County Councillor Galloway returned to County Hall.

From around April 1970, I was to become increasingly disturbed at the reports reaching me from party members and constituents about a campaign of character assassination that was being conducted against me by the Blyth Constituency secretary-agent, Mr Peter Mortakis. On 11th May, I left for Bulgaria with an Inter-Parliamentary Union delegation. An all-party group of the House of Commons, it included Dame Irene Ward, Member for Tynemouth, and Ernest Thornton, a Labour Lancashire Member of the House who led the delegation. When we left for Sofia the idea of an early General Election could not have been further away. The Government had nearly twelve months to run, and the opinion polls, on which Wilson had relied heavily in the 1966 General Election, were certainly not running our way. The delegation had not been long in Bulgaria when matters began to move fast. Talk of election was in the air and the opinion polls suddenly predicted victory for Labour. For myself I could not understand the reason for the turnabout. I had always kept my ear pretty close to the ground in my own constituency, and if anything, there had been a shift away from Government support in the late months of 1969 and into 1970. While this may not have mattered in areas like the North-East a similar viewpoint throughout the country could spell trouble for Labour's hopes. Three days before we left for home, the Prime Minister dissolved Parliament, and the General Election Campaign was on. Two Labour Members with me on the delegation decided to travel back immediately, Bert Oram, a London Co-operative MP, and Denis Hobden, a Post Office Workers' Union MP, who held a seat in Brighton with a two figure majority. Both were enthusiastic, both felt the election date was right, and that Wilson was on his way to winning his third General Election inside six years. I was not so optimistic, although the opinion polls kept moving upwards to contrast with my outlook. Right until the Sunday prior to polling, matters were good. Returns from the constituencies confirmed the predictions of the pollsters, when suddenly the shift came. A feeling of unease, heightened some said by England's loss of the World Cup, spread throughout the country on election night and by the count in the first twenty constituencies, Heath was obviously on his way to Downing Street, and the Wilsons were looking for a place to store their furniture. Such are the ways of politics. Only history will be able to record what prompted the Prime Minister to call the election when he did. Certainly there were pressures all around, but staying on for some more months seemed the best course to take.

Chapter Six

In Blyth the General Election campaign had gone reasonably well, although the agent was in a touchy mood throughout. At Regional level the campaign had been a shambles and the visit of Wilson on a walk-around talk to the people was a disaster. The seats lost in the region did not reflect this but the failure of the Prime Minister to speak for Jeremy Bray in Middlesborough was blamed for the loss of that vital North-East seat. After the election my wife and I went to visit our daughter and family in Edinburgh, and then late on the Saturday night received a telephone call from a Trade Union colleague, Councillor Nicol Hughes of Cramlington, who had been visited that night by the Labour agent, Peter Mortakis, and was so alarmed by his conversation with the party official, that he suggested we take immediate action at union level to counteract his activities. It was, to me, the usual character assassination stuff we had to live with, almost since we arrived in the area. But in addition to the usual defamatory remarks, the agent had stated his intention of working 'to get rid of the MP'.

Having checked up on the facts of the matter and talked with a number of my local labour party colleagues I wrote to the Constituency chairman, Jack Rowlands, and asked for a meeting with the Party's Executive Council to deal with the matter. This meeting was made the more necessary because at this time the Blyth Labour Party were considering the question of a joint agency arrangement with the neighbouring Morpeth Constituency. It was an idea that had at one time appealed to me, but following the election of George Grant, the NUM sponsored member in the Constituency, I had advised against the proposal as likely to be unworkable.

At the executive meeting on 13 November, the matters raised by myself included relationships with the agent, the complete difficulty in making contact with him and a number of other organisational matters. The reply of the agent was astonishing. It confirmed the reports that had been reaching me from the time of the Councillor Hughes telephone call to me in Edinburgh. He stated that he questioned my motives and my sincerity, and that during the election campaign my conduct had been belligerent, hysterical, emotional and near neurotic. He added that I had approached him with a suggestion to fiddle the election expenses, and said that I had kept him out of the office on the day of the count. Owing to the lateness of the hour it was not possible to continue the meeting, and a further EC was arranged for 4th December. During the brief comments made by EC members during this meeting, there was a complaint, never previously mentioned, by Mrs Hilda Gray, the Party's Secretary at Bedlington, that my wife and myself had been rude to her during the election. Following the 13th November meeting, my wife wrote to the EC members and the chairman and pointed out that she had never been rude to anyone in the constituency, had 'phoned Hilda Gray after hearing about the statement made at the meeting, and was told that it was nothing that my wife or myself had said or done at the election that had upset her but a letter from my wife which said 'As far as I am aware I've always been on friendly terms with the women of our constituency and I object strongly to my name being brought in to the muck-raking session that is going on. I trust this will be rectified in the minutes of the EC meeting held on 13th November.' This letter had the wording altered to read 'to the Hilda and Eddie muck-raking session' and was circulated by Mortakis to members of the Party's Executive Committee, to the Press and to officials at Transport House. At the next meeting on 4th December I questioned the party chairman, Jack Rowlands, about the letter and the details and authorisation of its circulation to party members and others. After heated exchanges and denials, he admitted altering the letter and arranging with the secretary-agent for its distribution, in the presence of Mr David Hughes, Assistant Regional Officer of the Labour Party, Councillor Mrs W. Yellowlee JP and the two vice-chairmen of the Blyth Party, Mr J. Goodfellow, a former Seaton Valley Councillor, and Councillor J. Haig of Bedlington, a NUM representative on the executive council. After admitting the alteration, Rowlands shouted across the room to me 'and there's nothing you can bloody well do about it anyway'. After that meeting, approaches were made to me by a number of EC members and other party members in the constituency to have the matters dealt with at a meeting chaired by someone other than Rowlands. This proposal was put to David Hughes from Regional Office who afterwards said that Evers, his boss at the Newcastle office, had turned down the idea. The scene moved to the ordinary quarterly meeting of the Blyth Constituency Labour Party held on Friday 11th December, 1970. Despite a report having been forwarded to the Party's National Agent, now General Secretary, Ron Hayward, about the nature of the two previous meetings and the attendance at the management committee meeting of David Hughes, no special item was placed on the agenda. It was not till 9.15 p.m. that my Parliamentary Report was reached, an item that had been included at each previous meeting anyway, on which I was very brief. Although Hughes was present as Regional Office representative, (and in the light of my reports to Transport House as the National Executive Committee representative too) he was not introduced to the meeting, the reason for his attendance was not stated, and he was not at any time asked to address the meeting, nor did he speak during the whole of the proceedings.

After I had briefly reported on the happenings of the two previous meetings of the Executive Council, I told the meeting, that 30 minutes to deal with an issue of this kind was inadequate and asked for support in approaching the NEC for a full inquiry. The chairman immediately put the question to the meeting, when it was carried with no dissent, but no discussion was allowed, despite the fact that the chairman was closing the meeting twenty minutes before the thirty minute extension was up.

Immediately following the meeting, I issued a statement to the press that Mortakis no longer had any authority to act on my behalf, and all arrangements with my constituents would be done from my home in the constituency. Prior to this meeting,

I had discussed, at the House of Commons with Underhill from Transport House, and Herbert Pridmore, USDAW's Administrative Officer (acting for Alf Allen, General Secretary of the Union) the disturbing state of affairs at Blyth and both promised that action would be taken. I had also discussed the case with Ron Hayward in the House on 14th December, and had given him all the documentary evidence and was assured that everything would be done to deal with the situation. As I was to discover on this and subsequent occasions, nothing was ever done except to fully back the agent and the small coterie of EC members who, as it was now apparent, assisted by Regional Office officials, were out to 'get rid of Milne'. I was informed by Underhill by letter that the enquiry was to be held on Monday 15th March, 1971, with Joe Gormley in the chair, accompanied by NEC members Tom Bradley and J. Diamond of the Iron and Steel Federation (BISAKTA). Bradley subsequently withdrew and Underhill and Hayward accompanied the two NEC members at the hearing. In a previous letter Underhill promised, 'but I can assure you that you will be consulted regarding the date and other details for the enquiry should the National Executive Committee accede to the Constituency Party's request (letter dated 31st December, 1970)'. There was no consultation with me prior to the enquiry. On the day of the enquiry, 15th March, the NEC team spent the day in Blyth interviewing the Blyth Party's Executive Council members, but did not meet me at all despite requests from me to do so. Only the EC were present at the evening session and although other members of the Labour Party, including Larry McManus, Ken Roach and Angus Galloway had indicated a wish to be present this was not granted. Evers and Hughes from Regional Office were present, but did not speak. One small concession given was that my wife was allowed to be present. This brought protests from a number of members of the Blyth EC, but they were overruled by Gormley. The proceedings were a farce: no real progress being made or any attempt to deal with the issues involved. The only matter of consequence to emerge was Rowlands' rather shamefaced admission that he had forged the alteration in the letter which

96

my wife had sent to him and the other EC members, but declared that '*he was only doodling*'. There is no doubt that he had been advised to take an apologetic attitude because of the likelihood of legal action.

On Gormley's advice, the parties concerned shook hands on the matter, but I remained sceptical of Gormley's ability to conduct such a meeting. He said the hearing was best forgotten and we should try to work together in the future. Two weeks later I attended the Annual Meeting of the Blyth Constituency Labour Party, and was very well received at what I considered an exceptionally good meeting, spoiled only by the secretary-agent's manoeuvres to get himself back onto Blyth Council, which he had had to leave on his appointment as agent under his employment agreement with the Labour Party. He did this by handing a letter to the chairman midway through the meeting. The agent had, of course, without seeking permission, allowed himself to be placed on the municipal candidates' panel some weeks before.

In a letter of 28th April, 1971, Hayward gave the findings of the NEC arising from the enquiry, which said that they were pleased to learn that the dispute had been amicably settled and that it had been agreed to bury past differences. He indicated that the Regional Organiser, Ron Evers, had been instructed to supervise the affairs of the Blyth Constituency and to report at the end of six months. This was extended for a further six months, and in the light of happenings the following year was a decision of real significance. Evers, as with so many of the assignments given him, did absolutely nothing on the matter, except to advise Mortakis to seek a job elsewhere, saying that vacancies existed for agency posts at Darlington and Sunderland. Mortakis's replied that he was going to remain in Blyth until he got rid of the MP, and Evers did nothing about that threat either, except perhaps to assist in the exercise. His subsequent actions gave ample evidence of such activity.

Acting on Transport House instructions, Evers called a meeting of the officers and myself for Friday 7th May, but did not consult me about the date. I was unavailable because of constituency engagements, but arranged for a meeting with him on Thursday 3rd June. Despite this, he went ahead with

97

the meeting on 7th May, and then refused to divulge to me what had been discussed when we met for the later meeting. This was an acrimonious affair with Mortakis in belligerent mood. He was hostile and obstructive and nothing of value emerged from the meeting. At the Northumberland Miners' gathering on Saturday 12th June, a number of party members protested about his rude attitude towards my wife and myself and the comments he had been making to officials attending the gathering. I warned Alf Allen, USDAW's secretary, about the continuing hostility and in my letter to him said, 'The attitude of the agent could well lead to an intolerable situation, and prompts the question as to how much longer Union finance can be used to employ an "agent" whose main activity now seems directed at undermining the position of an USDAW sponsored MP.' There was no response or assistance from Allen.

In July 1971, Dan Smith was acquitted of the Wandsworth charges, in a trial that had a number of unusual features about it. Sporle, who earlier that year had been sentenced for receiving bribes from Dan Smith, did not appear at the Smith trial and so, as it turned out, the person receiving the bribes was punished, T. Dan Smith being luckier with the jury than Sporle. Labour leaders moved in to protect Smith and demands for enquiries into the Wandsworth affair were brushed aside. Brian Walden MP, later to declare his interests as a consultant acting for some of Britain's bookmakers and other bodies, wrote a fulsome article in the *New Statesman*, then edited by Dick Crossman, in which he praised Smith and suggested that he had not received sufficient recognition for his undoubted talents, which if he had been operating in America, would have made him the confidant of Presidents. Brian Walden, who represents the All Saints Division of Birmingham in the British House of Commons, may not have fully realised the irony of his viewpoint until nemesis caught up with President Nixon. It certainly confirmed the comparison I have often made, that in the Poulson case we in Britain had an issue of Watergate proportions on our hands.

John Silkin had disappeared into the Ministry of Housing from the Whips' Office to be replaced by Bob Mellish, whose main claim to fame at this time was to collar anybody who would listen to his denials that he had ever met Dan Smith, although in the mid-sixties they had both served on the Labour Party's Local and Regional Government Advisory Committee. Reports of the financial difficulties of the Poulson empire kept creeping into discussions in Parliament and in the press. There was certainly considerable apprehension around. I tried, on a number of occasions, to raise questions, but found them invariably ruled out of order on the grounds that no ministerial responsibility existed for such issues. And under existing Parliamentary procedures, we increasingly found that the Clerk at the Table Office was right, so many matters of vital importance to democracy and honest local government administration in Britain went unanswered. There was, for instance, the matter of the money collected to stave off the financial difficulties of the Yorkshire architect and his satellites. John Silkin was credited by the *Sunday Times* (30th June 1974) with close association in this activity with Eric Miller of *Peachey Properties* who in conjunction with others raised a sum of about £250,000 which was paid into the Poulson Bankruptcy Court to pay off creditors and prevent public revelations. This was only one of many ploys that were instituted around this time by the many people in direct or indirect contact with the Smith, Cunningham, Poulson bandwagon. Silkin and *Peachey Properties* had similar interests, and both helped Poulson. Land at Pontygwindy in South Wales had been purchased by Eric Miller, chairman of the *Peachey* organisation from the Silkin family for around £250,000 for the purposes of building the *Carrefour Hypermarket*. Everything in this transaction seems to have been conducted on the strictest legal basis, but on the question of standards in public life, and concern for helping others, I can't help wondering why I did not get any help myself from John Silkin on the numerous occasions from 1969 onwards when I sought his advice and assistance when faced with Labour hostility and extinction as MP for the Blyth Constituency. Instead I later received a sharply worded letter from his brother Sam, the Attorney General, following a letter I had written to *The Times* in January 1975, in which I inferred that following a speech by the chief Law Officer of the Crown (in which he had said that in relation to the Poulson affair we

99

should temper justice with mercy not 'just go grinding on'), that it appeared there existed some sort of cover-up operation which constituted an element of Watergate in British public life. The Attorney General wrote to me, as follows on 5th March 1975, 'I need hardly say that I am most concerned about the totally groundless allegation . . . I am concerned to ensure that any such allegation, for which there are no grounds whatsoever, will not be repeated.' Silkin's successor, Bob Mellish, was in the Cunningham mould: blustering, bullying, maybe a little less than big Andy, but bullying nevertheless, with limited ministerial capacity, lucky to have been around the Labour Party when qualifications of that kind were needed. Mellish had been at the key ministeries when the drive for Open System Building was given its heyday, and he opposed efforts by the joint London boroughs to develop a consortium of direct labour housing authorities, which gave Poulson and his associates all the room in the world to operate. The re-organisation, which led to Mellish's two main ministries disappearing with the creation of the Department of the Environment, rules out any hope of shedding some light on what went on in the 1964–70 administrations for, as already shown in the Dick Crossman article about his own private papers, a lot of information that would now be valuable is no longer to hand, and disappeared in the re-organisation. But there is no doubt, that as both the bankruptcy hearings and the Leeds Crown Court trials showed, Poulson's most lucrative contracts came from the Ministry of Public Building and Works.

On the night of the 28th October, 1971, following the House of Commons vote on the Common Market, I travelled by sleeper to Leeds to attend the opening ceremony of a block of offices built jointly for USDAW and the General and Municipal Workers' Union, which housed their Northern Regional Offices. There had been some controversy about the Union buildings in Liverpool and Leeds, and the USDAW national officials and head office staffs were rather touchy on the subject. Some of the opposition to the deal came from members of the Union's Executive Council who felt that USDAW was being drawn too close to the General and Municipal Workers' Union, but it also stemmed from the discussion in the Labour and trade union movement about the activities of Andrew Cunningham. At the meetings of the USDAW delegations in the 1970s, a small minority resisted support for Andrew Cunningham to the Trade Union section of the Labour Party National Executive Committee. Our objections were always hotly opposed mainly by Alf Allen, now Lord Allen, General Secretary, and Walter Padley, the Union's sponsored MP in the South Wales Ogmore seat, a past member of Labour's NEC. This was understandable for a long standing arrangement existed in the trade union movement to vote together, and both Padley and Allen needed that sort of support both for the Trade Union Congress General Council and the Labour Party National Executive Committee. There was comment about a Poulson connection in the union's office building activities, because the Leeds office had been named Concord House, as had the headquarters of the union occupied by Cunningham in Newcastle. In the Leeds Crown Court conspiracy and corruption trial of Smith, Cunningham and Poulson, one of the charges against the Alderman was receiving bribes from Poulson in return for influencing projects his way, through a number of bodies that included the General and Municipal Workers' Union. In fact the architect of the union's offices at Leeds and Liverpool was Mr W. G. Burrows of the Ellis/Williams Partnership whose offices are in Liverpool. This of course was clearly shown in the union's magazine and the leaflet giving details of the buildings in question.

May 1972 brought the end of the Evers overseeing of the Blyth Constituency, not that much had been done in that period by the Party's Regional Officer. Then out of the blue on the 2nd May 1972 came a letter from the secretary of the Blyth Party, Peter Mortakis. It asked me to give the party details of my engagements for the next six months, so that they could arrange a meeting with me. By decision of an Executive Committee meeting of 4th December, 1970, I had not been invited to an EC meeting since that date, although I had attended meetings of that body up till then, from my arrival in the Blyth Constituency in 1960. I replied to the letter, stating that I felt the request to be both stupid and offensive, stupid because a six months' list of engagements was continually subject to change, alteration and addition, and offensive because it implied that I was difficult to contact when exactly the opposite was the case. I had lived in the Blyth Constituency since 1961, and whilst I was in London my wife was in close and constant touch with events and happenings in the area. In fact my wife did more constituency work than the agent and some councillors put together.

At the same time as this was happening, a hastily-convened meeting of the Seaton Valley Local Labour Party was called, and the Seghill Women's Section moved that the Parliamentary Panel be re-opened, which is the Labour Party way of getting rid of an MP. This was agreed, although no reasons were given for the move, nor was I invited to put any viewpoint on the decision, or before it. The secretary of the Women's Section had previously been elected to the Northumberland County Council by the simple expedient of calling the selection conference for her appointment when the sitting candidate, County Councillor Jack Clough, the chairman of Bates Colliery NUM was at work. Regional office failed to take any action. It seldom did on actions of this kind.

I was asked to attend the EC meeting on 2nd June. It was an acrimonious wordy affair but the outcome was the calling of a special meeting of the management committee of the Blyth Constituency Labour Party to accept a motion that the party seek a new candidate at the next election. Despite the fact that Evers the Regional Officer was present, the proper formalities had apparently not been observed, and so we had to suffer the same thing again but this time with a difference. Whatever the reason for the Party Chiefs at Transport House ordering the meeting to be held again, it has to be pointed out that Evers must have had a hand in the matter, for he was present on 2nd June and saw nothing amiss that night, or at least he didn't say so.

The vital difference, was that on Friday 15th December, Councillor Collier, the chairman of Blyth CLP, and Agent Mortakis, were called for a briefing to Transport House in London. Again, as in the case of the 1971 inquiry, no contact was made with me by Transport House. 16th June repeated the process of the 2nd June meeting. By 13 votes to 5 it was agreed to recommend to the Management Committee on

30th June that the Parliamentary Panel be re-opened. 30th June was North-East Tammany Hall at its worst. Evers was in charge. I asked, prior to the meeting, that party members be allowed to attend as visitors, because the issue of getting rid of Milne had aroused tremendous interest, and resentment against the party leaders in the area. The request was refused.

Earlier in the afternoon, I had numerous 'phone calls and callers at my home. The Party Treasurer, Jack Fulthorpe of Seaton Valley, had visited a number of NUM delegates to inform them that they could not attend the meeting that evening. Despite the tremendous interest aroused by the action of the EC in seeking to sack me, only 76 of the 98 accredited delegates were allowed to attend the meeting. Some were refused admission on technical grounds, some did not come at all because of the actions of Fulthorpe, and others were notified that they would not be allowed admission.

Prior to the meeting, I had asked Evers to have a roll call of the delegates and the organisations they represented, but this was also refused. The meeting started 25 minutes late. It is useful to note, that despite the fact that 13 members of the EC had voted at the previous meeting for my removal, the case against me, including the chairman's remarks at the start of the meeting, occupied only nine minutes. The vote, at what is now locally referred to as 'the hanging party' was 40–36 in my favour. Following the declaration of the result, a vote of no confidence in the Party's Executive Committee was moved by a number of delegates, but was firmly ruled out of order by Chairman Collier, strongly—if that word be can used in connection with Evers—supported by the Labour Party's Northern Regional Officer. The delegates were successful in tabling a motion for a future meeting, which was not held until 22nd September. The most curious outcome of all the bizarre happenings in this saga of getting rid of the MP, was the behaviour of USDAW's General Secretary Alf Allen. On the Wednesday prior to the management committee meeting, I received a telegram from Union Headquarters in Manchester, saying that Allen was at Dilke House, the union's London office, was meeting Mortakis that afternoon, and could I come along. It has been a noticeable feature of the long drawn out struggle at Blyth, that Allen has leant over backwards to lend support to the efforts of the secretary-agent. I replied to Allen that to meet Mortakis at that stage was to court disaster at constituency level. He, Allen, knew the whole history of the struggles at Blyth, and if I went back to the Friday meeting and had reported any talks with Mortakis at that time, my whole credibility would be destroyed and Allen as a seasoned negotiator should know this. In fact I am certain he did, and that is why he acted in the way he did.

22nd September found me in Sweden with a Parliamentary delegation, but the meeting to consider the vote of no confidence in the agent and the EC went ahead. Delegates were again treated as they had been at the June meeting, and this time two delegates from an USDAW branch were refused admission on the grounds that Walter Sawyer, the local organiser and Mortakis, had closed the branch down. This matter was reported to the USDAW Head Office, but no action was taken.

Some surprise was expressed by delegates at the manner in which this meeting had been rigged—and for anything of that kind to raise comment was quite remarkable in the Mortakis era. Rigging had become the order of the day. But it transpired that the Blyth Labour Party Agent, with or without the blessing of the Regional Officer, had hired a doorman to keep order and to see that certain people were kept from the meeting. It was what the local press were later to describe as the case of the 15-stone doorman. Wilkes, the doorman in question, 'phoned me at my home when I returned from Sweden, because he had not realised the type of task he had undertaken following an approach made to him by Mortakis. He told me amongst many other things of how a local taxi proprietor, who if a member of the party had only been so for a week or two and was certainly not a delegate to the Management Committee, had turned up with some four or five delegates' credentials in his possession. Somebody was making sure that this vote was not lost. And the Regional Officer did nothing about it, nor did Transport House or USDAW Central Office, when the matter was reported to them by Angus Galloway after 22nd September 1972. Wilkes also wrote Wilson, but Wilson had other matters on his mind at that time and failed to respond. He was possibly watching the Blyth scene with not a little anxiety, for the Poulson bankruptcy reports were getting increasingly worrying. Concern was also being felt at Local Party level. At a County Council by-election in 1970, Mortakis had complained that support for the party was dropping, and that party workers had failed or refused to turn out to support Alderman Fred Smith, Labour leader of Blyth Council. One veteran party member remarked at the time, that it was not possible to work in the election, because you could not get near the committee rooms at all, because of builders' men working for Smith (McCullough).

Following the meeting on 30th June, at which we narrowly escaped the holding of a new selection conference at Blyth, I was surprised to note that the official paper of the Labour Party, *Labour Weekly*, carried no comment or report on the proceedings, although it had, previous to the Management Committee meeting, talked about demands for my resignation at Blyth. I wrote to the Editor, Donald Ross, and received an astonishing reply. 'The information about Blyth in our 23rd June issue was received from an outside correspondent and appeared to be confirmed by other press reports. *However, I was later informed by the National Agents' Department that such demands were entirely unconstitutional and was advised to let the matter drop.*' I wrote to Hayward on the matter, pointing out that Ron Evers had been present at all the Blyth meetings, and that Collier and Mortakis had been briefed at Transport House prior to the decisions being taken at Blyth, that there had been plenty of opportunity to be given information about the Blyth Party and myself, if indeed the action taken for my removal had been out of order. At this time the Party was in turmoil, following the Common Market vote in the House of Commons and Dick Taverne's challenge at Lincoln. He, and Edward Lyons at Bradford West, were facing party meetings to explain their attitude in the Division lobbies. I pointed out in my letter to Hayward on 14th September the difference between the procedural arrangements in these constituencies and the manner in which affairs had been handled at Blyth by the Regional Officer and other Party Officials. Hayward passed the buck to Underhill, the party's hatchet man, on occasions such as these.

It has to be remembered in all these proceedings that Cunningham still dominated the scene at Transport House and in the Regional Office at Newcastle.

In a lengthy letter, the Party's National Agent, who was later to handle the 1974 inquiry at Blyth, and supervise the General Election campaign of the February of that year, made the following points. 'Although the Editor of *Labour Weekly* has complete editorial freedom, Ron did point out that it would not be helpful to all concerned to continue to deal with the Blyth matter in the way it had been covered in the paper. I am surprised that you should link this with the visit that the Chairman and Secretary-Agent made to me on the 15th June . . . and I should be very upset if any motive other than the one I have given were read into the visit by the two officers.' Underhill went on to say, 'I can assure you that in both the cases of Blyth and Bradford West, the procedures followed as far as they went in the respective cases, were fully in accord with the Party Constitution and the procedure laid down by Conference. We are very scrupulous in this Department in ensuring that no-one puts a foot wrong in matters of this kind,' Underhill continued, and said 'It is unfortunate that people hear garbled versions of what took place at various meetings and such matters are then the subject of inaccurate discussion between Members of Parliament.' In my reply to Underhill I had stated: 'Your paragraph about garbled versions becoming the subject of inaccurate discussions between Members of Parliament has also been noted. It is obvious that Members of Parliament are not the only ones guilty of garbled versions or inaccurate discussions.' It was curious, that in the long letter to me about procedure in the cases of Bradford West and Blyth, Underhill made no mention of the position of Dick Taverne at Lincoln as I had linked both Bradford West and Lincoln constituencies in my letter to Hayward.

The line I took in beating off the efforts to remove me at Blyth, was best expressed in a quotation I used from one of my predecessors in the Blyth Constituency, Thomas Burt MP. Burt was the first trade union candidate to become a Member of Parliament. At the time he was a full time official with the Northumberland Miners, later to become the Northumberland

Area of the National Union of Mineworkers. In 1872 faced with a situation similar to my own, just 100 years later, he issued a manifesto to the union membership which stated: 'So far as I am concerned, I tell you honestly that, while I desire to be of service to you to the utmost extent, I do not care, nor have I ever cared, an iota for the situation. If you wish me to continue in it, I can only do so on certain conditions, most of which I have already understood to be implied, if not distinctly expressed, in the very relationship that exists between us. Who are my masters? This is to me a vital question. Long ago I made up my mind never to have for my master a tyrant. I object just as strongly to a number of tyrants. It is often said that working men are the greatest tyrants on the face of the earth. To this I do not subscribe. It is too general, it is too sweeping. But I can say from bitter experience that there are in the ranks of working men some of the greatest tyrants it has ever been my ill fortune to meet with. Are such men my masters? I do not myself regard them as such, and I will never do so. It has been said at some places that I have had the situation long enough. Perhaps I have. If I have had it until I have lost the confidence of the men, I have indeed had it too long. I ask, and must have, the same personal rights as you yourselves possess. I came to you as a free man, and can only continue with you as such. I choose my own company. I shall correspond with whom I like. I claim to have, or that I ought to have, some little time to call my own, and this leisure I dispose of in my own way. (Manifesto issued to Northumberland Association. Cowpen Quay. Blyth. 3rd April 1872. Quoted from 'Thomas Burt—*A Great Labour Leader*' pages 116–117.)

But more eventful happenings were on the way for us in the North-East. It was sparked off by the tragic death of Norman Pentland, the well-liked Member for Chester-le-Street in County Durham, in January 1973 during the Parliamentary recess. This resulted in the calling of a by-election for the 1st March. Other events were moving apace. Dick Taverne, having been removed as Labour Member for Lincoln following his vote with the Heath Government on the Common Market, resigned his seat and the Lincoln poll was fixed for the same day as the Durham decision. In addition the Labour seat at

Dundee, held by George Thomson, who had been appointed by Ted Heath to become a Commissioner for Regional Affairs at the EEC Headquarters in Brussels, had also become vacant and the third of the by-elections to be held. All this was against the background of further revelations involving leading figures in the North-East with the Poulson affair.

Matters had moved quickly, following the announcement of the Chester-le-Street vacancy. The selection conference at Durham had focussed attention on the way in which, due to pit closures and other matters including the introduction of new industries to the area, the General and Municipal Workers were beginning to dominate the political as well as the industrial scene. Tom Urwin MP a former Minister for the North-East, with a full complement of Northern Regional MPs, was moved into the constituency. There was an air of anxiety about; electors were asking about the involvement in the Poulson bankruptcy case of leading local councillors and public figures. For a seat with a majority of nearly 20,000, the ground work preparation seemed over reacting, it was more like the run-up campaign to defend a marginal.

Then came the *New Statesman* of 23rd February, 1973, and the questions being asked locally could no longer be brushed aside by Regional Officer Evers and the other Labour apologists. In a trenchant article entitled, 'Find the Source of Power' by Richard West, he took his readers back to a visit paid by him to County Durham some ten years earlier, and told of an interview with Dan Smith (from *The New Statesman*, 8th February, 1963) in which the then Labour leader gave the reasons for his receiving the Public Relations Contract from Labour Party Headquarters. It was 'to get the Labour Party a better image in Scotland and Northern England.' 'I know the Labour Movement inside out, and why they picked me is really because of that.'

'Why,' asked West in the *New Statesman*, 'should a constituency which as been Labour since 1906 and has enjoyed a majority since the war of at least 20,000, be facing a fighting challenge from the Liberal Party, which has not contested the seat since the twenties.'

As one local miner put it, the answer was 'It is not about

Liberal versus Labour but about dissension within the Labour Party.' Andrew Cunningham lived in the contested constituency, as did his son John, the Member of Parliament for Whitehaven since 1970, both in houses built by Sid McCullough, who was being freely mentioned in the North-East, following the 1972 attempts to unseat us at Blyth, as my likely successor in the constituency.

I was interviewed by a Lobby Correspondent and others, because of the *New Statesman* article, and asked why I had not gone to work in Chester-le-Street along with almost every other Northern MP. I stated that 'the article by Richard West adds considerably to the requests many of us have been making for a complete examination of the party's organisation in the Northern Region, and the published allegations increase the need for an official investigation by the Party's National Headquarters at Transport House.' I added that I had been concerned for some time about certain activities within the North-East Labour Parties and in reply to a question as to whether the article should have been published at that time, said, 'The *New Statesman* has a responsibility to its readers and to the Labour Movement.'

In view of the consternation caused by my intervention, and the story being put about that I had quit the Chester-le-Street campaign, I issued a press statement the following morning. Two main points which needed clearing up were, firstly that I had never asked for a probe into the Chester-le-Street Party: that was a job for the party members in that constituency. What I had asked for was a complete examination of the party's organisation in the Northern Region. This I had been asking for in Blyth for over three years. Secondly, I did not quit the by-election fight. I was never invited to take part. A circular was sent to all Northern MPs asking them to help in the Chester-le-Street by-election. I chose to help in Lincoln, since the Labour candidate was a personal friend and a Union colleague of long standing. If Roy Jenkins and others can campaign in Chester-le-Street and not go to Lincoln, surely I can also make up my own mind on the matter. How I allocate my time is for me to decide. Neither the Tyne Wear Party or the Parliamentary Labour Party could send me to a by-election area. I had had experience of fighting a by-election in Blyth in 1960, defending a majority similar to that of Chester-le-Street. It does not need a mass of MPs to defend a 20,000 majority if the local party is in good fettle. The *New Statesman* article also raised new issues which needed answering. Is it too much in a free society, to ask that these answers should be given by those responsible for the by-election campaign?

Labour's majority at Chester-le-Street dropped to 7,000. Mellish did his usual rampage around the tea room in the House of Commons when things aren't going his way, describing me in passing as a 'nutter' in the normal gracious manner the Labour Chief Whip has. The following Wednesday came the hanging party, namely the weekly meeting of the Northern Group of Labour MPs. Prior to the meeting John Horam, who shares with Bernard Conlan the distinction of representing Gateshead in the House of Commons, approached me and in rather shamefaced fashion told me, that as John Cunningham would not be at the meeting, he was going to raise the question of my conduct at Chester-le-Street. At the meeting the matter was actually raised by Tom Urwin who claimed that my actions had resulted in the drop in the Labour vote. Up till the Saturday, when the Journal report of my remarks had brought the *New Statesman* article into prominence, everything had been going well in the campaign. I told the meeting that if this was indeed the case, then it was time they gave me some responsibility for organisation in the North-East, because if I could sway some 14,000 voters, then somebody at Regional Office was wasting their efforts. The meeting was an acrimonious affair, but no-one was prepared to propose any drastic action. Towards the end, John Cunningham turned up and adopted a more-in-sorrow-than-in-anger sort of attitude. John Cunningham of course had powerful friends on the National Executive of the Party, including Jim Callaghan, whose Parliamentary Private Secretary he became after entering parliament at the 1970 General Election. Both Cunningham and Callaghan were directors of the Sir Julian Hodge banking group, involved with the support of Andy Cunningham in trying to persuade the Labour Movement to a motor insurance scheme for the purpose of helping party funds, and of course the Hodge organisation.

This scheme was defeated heavily at the Party Conference after a lot of useful spadework by the CIS Agents' Branch of USDAW. Ted Short issued a statement attacking the *New Statesman* as a 'squalid Liberal rag,' and George Grant the Morpeth MP, after mumbling a few words at the Northern Group meeting, returned to his constituency to persuade his Morpeth Labour Party to send a motion of censure to Transport House about my attitude. This, and a motion from the Birtley Labour Party at Chester-le-Street, was the only adverse action taken against me. But Underhill was not to leave matters in that way. He was smarting under the failure of the Blyth Party to reach a decision about me remaining the official Labour candidate at the next election. I was summoned to appear at Transport House to explain my actions at Chester-le-Street to Underhill and John Chalmers, who was later to appear in Blyth at another enquiry held by the National Executive on the eve of the February General Election in 1974. It came as no surprise to me to be told by John Chalmers, when I telephoned him the day before the meeting, that he had not received any of the documents with which I had provided Underhill to state my case. In fact, a next door neighbour of ours delivered these papers to John on his way to work next day. It was a rather subdued Underhill, whom we met at Transport House. What was I supposed to have done wrong? Wasn't there concern in the North-East? Underhill has written to countless Labour Party members and organisations saying that Eddie Milne has never complained to Transport House about those connected with Poulson in the North-East. What did he think was the basis of my complaint about the position in Chester-le-Street and the North-East, didn't he take the trouble to read and inwardly digest the article in the *New Statesman*. After all, as one of the Labour Party officials who was closest to the decision which gave the Public Relations contract to Dan Smith, he had a special interest in these matters. And then, a prominent member of the Party's National Executive Andrew Cunningham was just a few weeks away from arrest on conspiracy and corruption charges involving Dan Smith and Poulson. It must have been a sorely disturbed and disappointed National Agent of the Labour Party who on the instructions of the National Executive wrote me on 25th July, 1973, 'I am instructed to convey to you the conclusion, that although it was unnecessary for you to have made any reference to the Chester-le-Street By-Election, as those remarks could be misunderstood, nevertheless ³ the committee was generally satisfied with the statement you made at the interview, and decided that the matter should now be closed.' Signed H. R. Underhill, National Agent.

And so the matter seemed to end. The next move did not rest with Underhill, but with his minions at Blyth. The Selection conferences to choose the Labour candidates for the District Council Elections to the new authorities arising from the re-organisation of local government were taking place. One of my most active supporters, Councillor Larry McManus, was due to attend the selection conference for the Seaton Valley Ward. Larry came bottom of the poll in the list of prospective candidates. The *Whitley Bay Guardian*, in an editorial at the end of the week, had this to say.

THE IDES OF MARCH

Does it not seem strange that Councillor Larry McManus, one of Seaton Valley's most respected councillors, and chairman of the local Labour party group, should come bottom of a poll for candidates for the new authority elections?

Perhaps it is not so strange when one remembers that Councillor McManus was one of Mr. Edward Milne's staunchest supporters in his fight against efforts to have him deposed as MP for Blyth.

Mr. Peter Mortakis 'scales' the heights of profundity by saying that when there are more candidates than seats someone is bound to be disappointed.

The whole business has more than a faint whiff of the Ides of March about it.

(*Whitley Bay Guardian*, Friday, 30th March, 1973)

Larry McManus himself explained the whole position in a letter to the *Whitley Bay Guardian* the following week:

Some readers may have misinterpreted my motives in re-signing from the Seaton Valley Labour Party and deciding to stand as an Independent candidate in the new district council elections in June . . . It may look as though I was bitter because I was defeated in a democratic election. This is not true. I have been active in public life long enough to accept a fair defeat. However I am sure that the votes were carefully weighed against me at the meeting to select district council candidates.

A bus load of voters arrived from Seghill. They made up more than half the members there. Elsewhere this important meeting had not been well advertised and only 47 members turned up.

You drew attention to the connection between this vote and the campaign last year to depose the Blyth MP, Mr Edward Milne. The first group to vote against retaining Mr. Milne as Blyth's Labour candidate at the next General Election was the Labour Women's Section at Seghill. They are normally a social rather than a political body. I firmly opposed them then.

Perhaps this makes it less surprising that so many members of the women's section turned up at a meeting many other party members did not know about. Whether or not members were told how to vote would be difficult to prove, but many of those voted against me, and the fact is that I, as an active Labour Group chairman received 22 fewer votes than one elderly councillor who, at this very meeting, admitted never having spoken in Council once during five years service.

(*Whitley Bay Guardian*, 6th April, 1973)

I decided to follow up with a letter of thanks to Larry for the contribution he had made to the Labour movement in the Blyth constituency. Councillor McManus had a life-time of activity in the Trade Union and Labour Party. Larry was at the election conference which selected Alf Robens for the 1945 General Election, a coal face worker and an active member of the National Union of Mineworkers. Apart from the support he had given me since coming to the Blyth Constituency in

1960 to become its Member of Parliament, he incurred the wrath of Councillor Collier, also a Seaton Valley Councillor, and chairman of the Council. Larry had been instrumental in getting five NUM delegates admitted to the June 1972 meeting and their credentials upheld as valid, after Peter Mortakis and Jack Fulthorpe, Secretary of Seaton Valley Labour Party and Collier, had ruled them out of order. In such a meeting, where we only got through by four votes, Larry's action was vital. Later in the year he was to make the following statement on the local position.

After the Poulson and Cunningham business, Eddie Milne is dead right to ask for an inquiry. It seems to me that in Chester-le-Street, Cunningham just used his influence for his own ends. The Liberal revival shouldn't have a chance here, and it wouldn't if the Labour Party was properly run. Because it isn't Socialist, I had to resign; mates of mine at the colliery are stopping their dues to the party and saying, 'It's corrupt, they're all tarred with the same brush.'

My letter to the *Whitley Bay Guardian* sparked off another attempt by the local party to have the Parliamentary panel at Blyth re-opened. It read:

I should like to take this opportunity of expressing my thanks to Councillor Larry McManus for the support and assistance he has given to me in my Parliamentary work in the Blyth Constituency over the past twelve to thirteen years.

His attendance at meetings and surgeries has been of immense value to me, as well as to the many people in the Seaton Valley area who had benefited from his guidance and advice.

It was disturbing to learn of the proceedings at the meeting which led to Councillor McManus deciding to contest the district election on 7th June as an Independent Candidate. These proceedings may form the basis of the enquiry so many Labour Party members have asked for during the past three years.

As Larry McManus wrote in your columns, he remains a Socialist. I look forward to the day when it is possible for him to return to a Labour Party that has recovered its basic principles of democratic Socialism in a free society.

Sgnd. Edward Milne.

(*Whitley Bay Guardian*, Friday, 13th April, 1973)

The outcome in the June elections was the re-election of Larry McManus in the Seaton Delaval Ward, unseating one of the councillors preferred to him at the selection conference. Former Alderman of Blyth Council and leader of the Labour Group, Fred Smith, was defeated in the Waterloo Ward of the New Blyth Valley Council and Secretary-Agent Mortakis was bottom of the poll in the Croft Ward, in which he resided. Previously he had been bottom of the list of candidates selected by the Ward Labour Party.

In the June of that year I received a letter from Prime Minister Heath, notifying me of his decision not to set up a Royal Commission or a Tribunal of Inquiry into the Poulson affair. In his reasons for the decision, he concentrated on the Tribunal of Inquiry difficulties in regard to future prosecutions, but no reference to the setting up of a Royal Commission was mentioned. And for the time being that seemed where the matter must rest. But event was piling up on event. The background affairs leading to the arrest of Andrew Cunningham and the termination of the public hearings of the Poulson bankruptcy proceedings were very much the subject of talk inside and outside of Parliament. For the first time, a section of the Labour Party in the North-East joined in my calls for an inquiry into what had been going on. A behind-closed-doors meeting, lasting over two hours, of the Chester-le-Street Constituency Labour Party, called for a police investigation into allegations of irregularities in land and building deals levelled against two councillors in a recent BBC *Nationwide* programme. The three top officials of the party sought a meeting with the Chief Constable and the new MP for the area, Giles Radice, who said he backed his constituency Labour Party's decision and commented, 'We want no witch-hunt or wild allegations. Justice must not only be done but must be seen to be done and the proper agents for justice are the police and the courts.'

The following week-end I was besieged with callers and telephone calls at home after returning from the House of Commons. Numerous interviews had been arranged throughout the North-East for appointments to the new local authorities which were due to take over, arising from the re-organisation of Local Government in April 1974 and following the council elections just held. What was disturbing a great number of officials was that police investigations were going on throughout Durham and other parts of the Northern Region, and whilst these investigations were being conducted by Scotland Yard and outside police officers, they nevertheless did not feel that confidentiality would be assured on any evidence they might give. What troubled them most was that Andrew Cunningham was still chairman of the Durham police authority and a member of many of the committees making the appointments the council officials were interested in. As many of these officials and those they represented came from Newcastle and County Durham, I suggested that they consult and seek the help of their own Members of Parliament. The answer I invariably received was, 'Mr. Milne, you must be joking.'

In view of the concern expressed to me and the information they had provided me with, I made arrangements to meet the Attorney General on my return to London with the Solicitor General, Sir Michael Havers, in his room at the House of Commons, prior to the vote at 10 p.m. I passed on the information I had received from the Town Hall officials and expressed their viewpoint. The upshot of the meeting was that the Attorney General issued a statement by agreement with myself, and I was quoted as saying, "I am satisfied that no one who can speak in these enquiries has anything to fear. I was invited to ask anyone who may have information to send it to the Attorney General of the High Court of Justice in London." I had stressed that two main fears were uppermost in the minds of local authority people, first that any information they might have would reach the local police and secondly, that if it did, it could affect their prospects of promotion. At that time many outside people felt that this was an exaggeration, but they did not know of, or have to live and work in the Durham of 'Godfather' Cunningham.

But July 1973 still had a long way to run. Two effects from the visit to the Attorney General were in some way predictable. A number of local authority people contacted me to thank me for my intervention on their behalf and a lot of evidence found its way to the Royal Courts of Justice that may not have reached the police authorities. The Chief Constable of Durham was not too pleased about the matter, and in a statement to the press, wanted to know why I had not got in touch with him on the issues I had raised with the Chief Law Officer of the Crown. I told him that I did not get in touch with my own Chief Constable in Northumberland on matters of this kind. Any constituency or parliamentary issues raised with me were always first brought to the attention of the Minister responsible for dealing with it. If the Attorney General had felt that consultation with the Chief Constable of Durham was needed he would have said so.

In the midst of all this I was engaged with the Table Office in an attempt to get some information from various Ministers about the Poulson involvement with Government Ministries, particularly with the Scottish Office, the Ministry of Public Building and Works and the Ministry of Housing and Local Government. The conviction of Poulson and Pottinger, the Scottish Civil Servant, had sparked off a number of questions that needed answering. For beginning to emerge clearer every day now was evidence that the principal actors in the Poulson saga could not have operated so successfully without friends and assistance in high places, who if they did not indeed actively help or benefit from what was going on, certainly aided and abetted by doing nothing to stop it. For as Nye Bevan once said in another context, that is applicable to this one: 'It is not enough to plead that because you cannot prevent a crime, you are justified in becoming an accessory to it.' The questions I wanted answering fell into a number of different categories, but they concerned the timing of the auditor's report and its contents on the work done by the Poulson companies varying from the Ministry of Public Building and Works (with Mellish as Minister) to the Secretary of State for the Environment.

In my view there was too much fuss being made at official level of the difficulties surrounding the setting up of the new departments, and the elimination of the old. It was in my recollections, as mentioned in an earlier chapter, that Dick Crossman had encountered the same difficulty when talking to a police officer about a letter from Poulson in his former department. We also wanted to know why the report, having been to Cabinet level, should not have been released to Parliament. One press report referred to the auditors' complaint about Poulson's cavalier attitude and his failure generally to explain in adequate fashion a variety of expenditures on sums of up to at least £25,000. I was also interested in getting a reply from the Minister as to what further steps he intended taking to inquire more deeply into the matters concerned. It was also my intention, if I could get a suitable wording from the Clerks at the Table Office, to ask if any steps had been taken by any government department to recover the sums of money about which Poulson was reported as giving unsatisfactory evidence. To me, one of the most important questions of all, was why the Poulson-related companies were allowed to continue on the Register of Government Contracts. It was obvious that someone at the departments concerned had slipped up in letting Poulson and his associates loose in the first place, but it was certainly criminal to allow the evil work to continue. I considered the press comment on Poulson's cavalier attitude to be justified, for he was aware of the influence he was able to exercise on the areas of power in governmental circles.

It may interest my readers to know how the power of backbenchers to raise matters of urgent and important public business can be curbed and restricted. Following my efforts with the Table Office and a visit to the Chief Clerk of the Table (and let me hasten to add I am not complaining about their decisions for I have always found the Table Office staff most helpful, often finding strategems to circumvent an obstructive ministry or department), I raised a point of order with the Speaker. The following exchange in the House was the result.

Mr Milne (*Blyth*, *Lab*) on a point of order, asked for the guidance and protection of backbenchers seeking to raise questions on the subject of the Poulson inquiries and related matters. The first of the two matters he wished to raise was the transference of a tribunal of inquiry question from the Prime Minister to the Home Secretary.

The Speaker That is not a matter for the Chair.

Mr Milne said he understood that one of the Speaker's roles was the protection of backbenchers in the execution of their duties. In view of the ruling, he would seek to raise the matter in other quarters. The second point was the use of the sub-judice ruling by the Table Office. He asked a question and added the words 'in view of recent happenings in the local government field.'

The Speaker said there was here an important ruling, which had been repeatedly stated by his predecessors. If an MP was dissatisfied with a decision of the Table, he should first consult the Speaker privately before raising it in the House. Mr. Milne had not come to him about the matter. (Labour interruptions.)

Mr Milne I discussed this matter this morning both with your office and with the Chief Clerk of the Table Office. I am now asking for your ruling in the House.

The Speaker I do not want to shut Mr Milne up, but it has been established by my predecessors that a private representation to the Speaker is the proper course first. The matter has not been referred to me. If it is referred to me privately I will consider it. If I rule against Mr. Milne, he is entitled to raise it in the House. It is a matter of saving the time of the House.

Mr Milne My constituents sent me to this House of Commons and while I try to observe the responsibilities of this House and to carry out its procedures, my duty is to raise matters in this Chamber and not necessarily with the Speaker privately. (Labour cheers)

Mr Speaker My predecessors have repeatedly ruled that a matter of this sort should not be raised in the House until it has been raised first with the Speaker. The purpose is to safeguard the time of the House. (Conservative cheers)

Mr Milne It is not necessary for Speakers in their duties as Speakers of this House, to follow the bad precedents of their predecessors. (Renewed Labour cheers)

The Speaker said later: It may be that I may not take the same view as my advisers. If I do not, it is not necessary for Mr. Milne to raise it. If I agree with the advice, he can still come to the House afterwards. As Mr. Milne had persisted, he would consider the point. (*The Times* Parliamentary Report)

These exchanges give an insight into the difficulties facing backbench MPs in matters of this kind. Doubly difficult was the fact that the House was only a matter of eight or ten days from the Summer recess, and for questions to be reached it is necessary to table them at least two weeks before, so effectively the matter was closed until the House re-assembled in October.

The next move was to raise the issue once more at Parliamentary Labour Party level. The comment of some of my colleagues had encouraged me in the exchanges with the Speaker in the House, and so I notified the Chairman of the Parliamentary Labour Party, Douglas Houghton, that I would be raising the matter on Thursday, 12th July. At the party meeting there was no support for my further appeal for an examination to be made of the public relations contract which the party had concluded with Dan Smith and which was now being revealed as inextricably bound up with developments and evidence in the Poulson case. The matter was referred to the Shadow Cabinet.

But Short and Mellish were not inactive. It was now obvious that a concerted effort was being made to crush our protests. Cunningham's arrest lay just ahead. On my way to the Chamber after the Parliamentary Party Meeting, Percy Clark, the Labour Party Director of Information, stopped me in the Members' Lobby. It was unusual to see Percy in the Lobby although he had Press Gallery facilities to be there. He was very agitated and began to tell me that I was wrong in thinking that Dan Smith had a contract to do public relations work for the Labour Party. I suggested that we go to the tea-room where the matter could be talked over. When Percy repeated his story about the public relations charge I had made at the Parliamentary Labour Party meeting at which he had been present, I said to him, 'I cannot understand why you are trying to convince me of this now. There is no use Percy Clark or Eddie Milne trying to kid each other. You know that Peter Ward was handling this matter for Dan Smith. One has only to look at the Party's Annual Report from 1963 onwards to know that the contract was made and existed for a number of years. From my experience on the Labour Party Scottish Executive, I know when the discussions on this matter started, both at Scottish and National level.' Percy did not pursue the job of trying to convince me about the Smith contract with the Labour Party and left for a meeting at Transport House. It looked as if a cover-up operation was on the way, for Percy Clark was too experienced a press man to try to convince me off his own bat about Dan Smith's public relations work for the Labour Party. At the Poulson bankruptcy hearings in September 1972, the QC appearing for the creditors remarked that he felt there wouldn't be an alderman or councillor in the North-East corner of England that Mr. Poulson didn't know. Amongst other contracts listed by Muir Hunter QC, were the wife of a Chief Justice, borough architects, hospital administrators and hosts of others including politicians. One name included was A. D. Allan, deputy general manager of Peterlee Development Corporation, who was to be the object of the Labour Party Director of Information's denials. Allan's connection with Smith was a two-fold one. From 1961–67 Dan Smith acted in a public relations capacity for *Peterlee Development Corporation* and from 1968–71 he was chairman of the *Peterlee and Aycliffe Development Corporations*. In the *Northern Echo* of Saturday 14th July, 1973, Ken Allan, now described as a Newton Aycliffe chief official, was defended by Dr. Hughes MP for Durham City against allegations made concerning his work for the Labour Party by Mr Percy Clark. Dr Hughes accused the Labour Party's Director of Information of 'character assassination,' saying that he intended to go immediately to Transport House when he returned to London on the following Monday and that 'he would be looking for answers.' The statement from Percy Clark which roused the ire of Mark Hughes, was that none of the £35,000 paid to the Dan Smith organisation was for work done by Allan. The Labour Party Director of Information said, 'We had a list of journalists, members of the National Union of Journalists, who alone were permitted to work for us. Mr Allan was never on the list.'

Clark continued, 'I personally overlooked the scheme from Transport House. We received regular reports on all the work done for us in the field. We received no reports of anything done for us by Mr Allan.'

Dr Hughes claimed that he had in his possession copies of documents relating to work carried out by Mr Allan, and also the copy of a letter sent to Mr Allan by the then general secretary of the Labour Party, Mr Len Williams, in January 1963 concerning a draft contract for the work. It did appear as if certain people were a little coy about the Labour Party Public Relations work done by Dan Smith, for in addition to the other evidence mentioned by Hughes, there was also a letter sent to Clark by Ken Allan showing how more than £3,000 had been spent. Hughes was on the war-path, but whether he did anything tangible was never revealed. Like many others at that time, the issue he raised was conveniently forgotten. Although the Durham Member was to add:

'In the atmosphere of smear, this sort of carelessness gets very near to the point of criminal negligence in allowing the good name of a person to be put at risk by the uttering of false information.' In fairness to Percy Clark, it may have been that the Chairman of the Party's sub-committee, headed successively by Alice Bacon and Andrew Cunningham, kept many matters of this kind to themselves. Strange things were possible in the Transport House of that period. That much I learned, when on a delegation from Parliament to study the effects of EEC entry on the Commonwealth Sugar Agreement, I stayed for a few hours at the residence of the Governor of Mauritius, Sir Len Williams, former General Secretary of the Labour Party, appointed to the Mauritius post by Harold Wilson, and like myself a former lecturer with the National Council of Labour Colleges.

On leaving the Chamber after raising the points of order with the Speaker about Parliamentary questions on the Poulson affair, I met Geoffrey Rhodes, the Newcastle East Member, who told me of an attack made on myself by the Northern Group at a meeting which had been arranged to discuss the newly issued Hardman Report with Kenneth Baker, Minister for the Civil Service. I had told the chairman, Ted Garrett, that I would not be at the meeting as I had to be in the House for question time. When I questioned Jack Dormand, the Northern Group secretary about this, later in the day, and complained about secret meetings, I was approached by him, by Bob Brown, another Newcastle member, and Dr John Cunningham the Member for Whitehaven, and in a reference made in hostile fashion by Dormand (MP for Easington, Co. Durham), I was told it was high time 'I was shut up.' At the next meeting of the Northern Group I asked for the minutes to be read concerning the attack on myself and was told none were available.

This was made all the more surprising, because at the Parliamentary Labour Party next day, I was again the subject of attack from Ted Garrett, based on the Northern Group's supposed decision the day before. Again this was a meeting at which I was not present. I had previously approached Douglas Houghton to inform him that I would not be at the Parliamentary Labour Party meeting on Thursday evening, as I was flying north for an important constituency engagement. Despite this the meeting still dealt with the report on my previous week's request for an inquiry into aspects of the party administration at Regional and Transport House level.

Douglas Houghton reported to the meeting that the Shadow Cabinet had turned down the requests and demands made by me at the meeting the week previous, because it was a matter for the National Executive of the Party. This, of course, the National Executive countered by claiming that it was none of their responsibility. Following Houghton's statement, I was bitterly attacked by Garrett, Labour MP for Wallsend and chairman of the Northern Group of Labour MPs, who accused me of causing serious embarrassment to my colleagues in the North-East. According to press reports there were murmurs of 'Hear Hear' from other members of Labour's Parliamentary Party, when Garrett went on to say about me, 'He is a Don Quixote, dashing around tilting at every windmill in sight.' No suspicion rested on any members of the Northern Group regarding the speculation and gossip that was coming from various quarters, Garrett went on to say, in criticising my activities and method of getting publicity. A *Journal* headline the following day reported a Northern Group comment that they were 'fed up with Milne.' What was surprising to many, both inside and outside the Labour Party, was that Labour's spleen and displeasure should be reserved for myself in a week in which the Party's Regional Chairman, and longstanding member of the Labour Party National Executive Committee, Alderman Andrew Cunningham of County Durham, was arrested on charges of corruption with Poulson. To many this was a measure of Labour's shame, a betrayal of the principle of Socialism.

But the ten eventful days of July were not yet over and the greatest surprises were still in store for us. On Friday, 20th July, the *New Statesman*'s London Diary carried the following item connected with the arrest of Andrew Cunningham.

All credit to Edward Milne, the Labour MP for Blyth, who wants an investigation into the party in the North-East. I take a personal interest in this, having fallen foul of the North-East Labour Party during the Chester-le-Street by-election. I wrote an article in the NS describing the influence in the area of the local GMWU boss Alderman Andrew Cunningham. Although what I wrote at the time was well known in Chester-le-Street and also a cause of concern to the Labour Party, the article was portrayed as devilish Liberal propaganda. At least six Labour MPs— including Bob Mellish, Shirley Williams, Roy Hattersley and Michael Foot—wrote in to the editor of the NS to complain. Of the North-East MPs, only Milne spoke out on the issue. He refused to take part in the Chester-le-Street by-election and was publicly pilloried for his pains. I hope his colleagues now have the grace to apologise.

As always, or so it seems, the last word rested with the Rt. Hon. Harold Wilson. My wife and I had travelled to see our daughter and son-in-law in Manchester on the day the NS article appeared. Around 5 p.m. the telephone rang. Peter Hetherington of the *Guardian* was on the line. Had I started to write Harold's speeches for him? enquired the *Guardian* reporter and then proceeded with a quote or two. I was amazed, feeling at first that someone had been playing a trick, for Wilson had already concurred with Heath in agreeing that no action should be taken on the Poulson matters and the the prosecutions should be allowed to run their course. But Harold had descended on County Durham in preparation for the Durham Miners' Gala the following day. And in the centre of the great heartland of the Labour Movement in the North-East, he was due that evening to open a new Civil Hall at Shildon. Other functions of this kind performed by Wilson included the opening of the Garden Farm Hotel nearby, built and owned by Sid McCullough, the builder friend of Alderman Cunningham, who had been given the planning permission for the site after two refusals in other directions had been made, circumstances that had become almost normal in the County Durham of the Cunningham ʻera.

As Peter Hetherington had indicated there was nothing in the Wilson Shildon speech that could be disagreed with, it was a classic assessment of the way in which inquiry and investigation should be made into the evil of corruption. It sounded convincing not so much because, in June, when I had received a rejection of my demands for either a Tribunal of Inquiry or the setting up of a Royal Commission from Prime Minister Heath, there was no support from Wilson, in spite of the sentiments expressed in the Shildon speech. The speech was a typical Wilson performance, brilliant analysis but false as hell.

Let us have a look at the speech itself and reflect on how many of the sentiments expressed that July night at Shildon have been put into operation, or indeed were intended to produce any action. It is true we got the Royal Commission set up by Wilson in April 1974, but only after sentence had been passed on Smith, Cunningham and Poulson. Now to Shildon—and to what I can only call hypocrisy. Wilson said:

> It is right that we in Britain should address ourselves to the anxieties being expressed here about the quality and standards of democracy in Britain, national and local.
>
> The price of retaining confidence in British democracy is constant vigilance against any abuse, any individual dishonesty or weakness on the part of those who have been elected to position of trust, vigilance which must be applied

without fear or favour, or political considerations. If only a very small minority give way to the temptations which beset them for personal gain or other unworthy motive, then the whole of public life is sullied.

The price we face is that fewer and fewer people will concern themselves with local or national issues, with the workings of local or national democracy.

The price, too, is that for every case of corruption which comes to light, a hundred other devoted public servants find it that much harder to do their job. *Men and women of all parties who have given their whole lives to community service find their efforts greeted by cynicism. The dedication which inspires them no longer appears to their constituents to be the crusade which was proclaimed.*

That is why we must root out, without mercy or any personal or party considerations, any who by their actions debase the standards our democracy requires. For in so doing, they betray the people who elected them and endanger the system by which they and indeed all others are elected. *The first requirement is that Parliament must give a lead.*

After ruling out the setting up of a Standing Commission on corruption he went on to say:

But I do believe there is an urgent need for an inquiry into the wider issues that are now plaguing the minds of public and of local and national elected representatives.

Apart from any changes that can be made in law and practice, the first safeguard must be a free and independent press enabled by all legal means to turn over the stones of our public and business life to see what may be concealed beneath them.

In order to be able to do this, there should be no inhibition of the kind created by the issue of writs which the plaintiff never intends to proceed with. Equally the press should not be inhibited by the existence of court proceedings which for whatever reason have dragged out so long as to be virtually moribund, and which through the sheer passage of time may relate to a world or to a state of affairs which has changed almost out of recognition.

Heady words, but meaningless in the light of the Shadow Cabinet and Transport House attitude towards myself. It is certainly true, as we were to discover later, that following the strongly worded summing up of Justice Waller, in sentencing Smith, Cunningham and Poulson at Leeds Crown Court the following April, Wilson who had become Prime Minister in the meantime, set up a Royal Commission under Lord Salmon. On the other hand to my regret I do not think he did anything on the National Executive or Parliamentary level to stop the action being taken by those closest to him to terminate my parliamentary activities.

To underline his belief in the need for a Royal Commission, he concluded his Shildon speech by saying that he had examined all the alternative ways of dealing with the problems that corruption created:

On the whole, however, I would favour a Royal Commission. But whichever it is to be, I believe it should be appointed and got to work as a matter of urgency.

Chapter Seven

A curious sideline from Wilson's Shildon Speech was provided at the Whips' Office on my return to London on the following Monday morning. Usually copies of the Leader's week-end speeches are around in profusion. Not on this occasion. I had to ask Harry Mitchell, Assistant Secretary of the Parliamentary Labour Party, to get me a copy from Transport House. Some weeks later I discovered that a copy had not been provided for the special file in the Research Department of the House of Commons Library reserved for the speeches of Cabinet Ministers, members of the Shadow Cabinet and even the Leader of the Opposition.

Wilson's Shildon speech could have been the launching pad for a new initiative to get officialdom to realise the harm that corruption was doing to the Labour Movement. I had a large number of letters on the subject, and I knew that many people had been in touch with Transport House and the Regional Office on the matter. Chester-le-Street and its consequences were still live issues in the North-East Labour movement. But steps were taken by Transport House and other parts of the Labour top level areas to tone down the demand. Then came the arrest of Andrew Cunningham. At least there was substance in the rumours after all. Many people still cannot understand why Cunningham, jointly charged with Mrs Cunningham, Dan Smith and Poulson, should have been arrested prior to the others. Dan Smith and Freda Cunningham were not arrested until the beginning of October, the Friday that marked the end of the Labour Party Conference. One theory that had some credence was that it was to allay the suspicion, fast growing, that a cover up operation was being conducted on the matter, and to back Wilson's Shildon speech. In fact one gets the feeling from all the actions of the Labour Leader that he tried very hard to keep ahead of the events in this case, and that on the Friday of his Shildon speech, he was already talking with the Cunningham arrest in mind. Another factor was that the arrest of the Durham Labour leader could prevent further talk on the case at that stage in the North-East.

As we moved nearer to the Labour Party Conference of that year, matters became more difficult in the constituency and I decided to approach the National Executive Council of USDAW. I met the National President, Alf Allen, General Secretary, and the two North-East representatives of the Council at the House of Commons, but it was an abortive meeting. The only point of substance that emerged, was that I made perfectly clear to my Union colleagues that I would rather go out of public life than ever work with Mortakis again. Following this I had a meeting with Allen at the Union headquarters in Manchester. He was in a hostile mood, saying that he had many reports about my actions in the constituency, but refused to give details. He said that many matters brought to his attention were of a private nature and could not be divulged. I was, of course, not unmindful that Alderman Fred Smith of Blyth had been for a number of years a member of the National Co-operative Wages Board and had heard from a number of USDAW officials of stories emanating from Smith. What was particularly disturbing, as I pointed out to Allen, was that at no time had I been given an opportunity of answering any of the attacks made on me in this way. Allen's only concession was to suggest a further meeting with Mortakis present. I argued strongly against this, but decided in consideration for Allen, a mistaken gesture as I afterwards discovered, to attend it. It was, as I had expected, abortive. Matters were made worse in a clash I had with the Union General Secretary, prior to meeting Mortakis and Pridmore, the union's administrative officer. Before travelling to Manchester for the second meeting, I asked Allen to let me have the USDAW file on Blyth, in order to see what Allen had been talking about in the stories passed on to him about myself and the Blyth constituency. I was angered to discover, on arriving at Central Office from the sleeper, that only

129

two short letters had been laid out for my examination. When I met Allen, Mortakis and Pridmore, the General Secretary said that I must have misunderstood his remarks at the previous meetings just before the 1973 Labour Conference as there were no letters about myself, nor a private file. This attitude was in keeping with the obstructionist attitude that the union secretary had always adopted when approached to take action on my behalf.

This was clearly demonstrated, when following the abortive meeting with the Blyth agent, Allen arranged for a meeting with him and Councillor Collier, the Blyth Constituency Labour Party Chairman, during the Labour Party Conference in Blackpool, a meeting which Collier travelled to Blackpool to attend. No discussion took place with myself on the meeting, and indeed if the Union President, Mr J. Hughes, had not let the information slip in conversation with me, I might not have known. I pointed out to Hughes that this sort of arrangement was most irregular and that if they were to have a meeting with the Blyth Constituency representatives, then the delegate from Blyth to the Party Conference, Tommy Climson of the NUM, should also be invited, or at least Allen and Hughes should have a talk with him and seek his viewpoint on the Blyth constituency matters. But this was never done. And adding to my suspicion of the reasons for Allen and Mortakis working so closely together, was the information, contained in a fringe document circulated on the Thursday of Conference, in which it stated that amongst Cunningham's nefarious antics in the North-East, was trying his hand unsuccessfully to oust Eddie Milne at Blyth.

Travelling home from the Labour Party Conference, delegates were to hear of the arrest of Mrs Freda Cunningham and Dan Smith. This gave added weight to the demands made at the conference for an enquiry, which of course had never reached the conference agenda, but which might have done so if the events of the two months prior to the conference had been known to delegates prior to the agenda being drawn up. The question being asked of myself and others at Conference was why the Shadow Cabinet were so reluctant to sanction an internternal party inquiry. Positive action at this time would have averted the embarrassments of 1974, and maybe of the years beyond. But somewhere at the top the veil had to be drawn over the events of the 1960s. The persons arrested were too much in close contact with the top Labour leaders to allow such a thing to happen. Immediately following conference, I wrote to Allen asking to meet the union's full executive to discuss my position as a member of the union's main Parliamentary Panel. But Allen was determined that I was not to get a hearing on this matter, that although a meeting was arranged for Sunday, 11th November, he arranged for three representatives of the Blyth Party Executive to be present, along with one other to represent both viewpoints on the local party.

After arriving for the meeting at Union Headquarters on 11th November, I was approached by Mr Pridmore, Chief Administrative Officer of USDAW, and asked if I would meet the EC along with the Blyth representatives. I told the Union's Administrative Officer that my complete case had been presented to all members of the executive, that I had asked to meet them, and no-one else, and would prefer the meeting to go on as arranged. I then met the EC and left, only to be followed into the EC meeting by the representatives of the Blyth Labour Party, Councillor Collier, Mortakis, Councillor Bosworth and the person who was supposed to represent my viewpoint on the Blyth EC, Ned Murray, a delegate from the Colliery Mechanics, who, not long after this meeting, was placed on the list of council candidates by the Labour Party.

I was very pleased by the response of the EC members during my interview. All of them had known me during the long period I had been in the union. The only jarring notes were struck by David McGibbon, one of the Scottish representatives on the EC, who asked me if the facts I had stated in the document were true. I told McGibbon that if he had known me for around forty years and needed to ask that question, there was nothing I could say more to convince him whether it was true or not. In the course of exchanges with Allen, he referred to my maladjusted mind. This was in keeping with the campaign being conducted at this time to label me as an eccentric, if not worse, with Mellish and the other MPs in the Whips' Office participating. Garrett, the Wallsend MP, had in his constituency and at the Parliamentary Labour Party described me as a Don Quixote, tilting at every windmill in sight. Although Hughes, the union president did not ask Allen to withdraw his remark about me, at a later stage in my interview when I talked about not wishing to walk in the gutter with the General Secretary, he asked me to withdraw my remark. The outcome of my meeting with the USDAW Executive was an approach by them to Transport House for a full scale inquiry into the Blyth Constituency Labour Party.

In the meantime, the party at Blyth had also moved by calling a special meeting to censure me for writing to the press in connection with the exclusion of Larry McManus from the list of Labour candidates. But Allen was obviously not going to let matters rest just by allowing my request for an inquiry to be backed by the union's EC and forwarded to the Labour Party National Executive for consideration. In a press handout from the union's Public Relations officer, the meeting was correctly reported, but in an interview with the *Guardian*, Allen talked about the union widening its split with Milne. Indeed the Manchester and London editions reported differently on the matter, and only London carried the split headline. I raised the matter with the Speaker and pointed out to Allen in a telegram that his statements were misleading. He had also, in a union press statement, said that the meeting had not dealt with my claims about the involvement of leading councillors with Poulson. This had never been mentioned by me although Allen, like so many others, had always fought shy of giving any assistance to myself in the efforts we were making to have a complete investigation into the affairs of the Northern Regional Labour Party and the local authority representatives in the North-East. Allen's statement on this matter also differed from the official press handout of the meeting provided by the union's PRO.

Writing in the *New Statesman* of 23rd November, 1973, Christopher Hitchens summed up the matter:

The situation then is one in which Eddie Milne is in trouble with his local party and to a lesser extent his union USDAW. But he has managed to get the latter to support an inquiry into the former. He is considered a nuisance by Transport House and by the North-East group of Labour MPs which is chiefly distinguished by its large number of massively elected mediocrities. In the last five-year period that he calculated, Andrew Roth found that they were always over-represented on parliamentary free trips and such-like facilities. They have not forgiven Milne for his refusal to canvass at Chester-le-Street, and they are unlikely to be pleased with him for releasing to me the text of a letter from Edward Short which admits having tried to help raise money to pay for T. Dan Smith's defence at the Wandsworth corruption trial.

Eddie Milne has taken on all these forces. He will stand as an Independent if unseated. Whatever happens now the rule of 'omerta' has been broken.

Around this time there was intense speculation in the North-East at the activities of certain local authorities and their relationships with the Co-operative Movement. These officials of the Co-operative Movement felt, and rightly, that if their position in regard to the wider Labour movement gave them no special preference as far as Labour councils were concerned, at least they were entitled to equal consideration with the property developers and their trading rivals. At a seminar arranged by the Co-operative Party in conjunction with the Northern Group of Labour MPs on 26th September, 1973, the following report was given by the Estates and Property Controller of the North-Eastern Co-operative Society. The Co-op had made application for a Superstore and District Shopping Centre in Doxford Park, Sunderland.

This was a £750,000 project and had been presented with much effort and expense to the appropriate committee of Sunderland Corporation. The short list of applicants was reduced to four, and the Society was led to believe that their scheme and presentation of it was as good as any other. Judge their surprise to find that their financial bid of £50,009 per annum was put to one side for a bid from another company amounting to only £7,500 per annum. As the Property Controller of the Society reported to the meeting, they were still trying to find out from the Sunderland Corporation the reasoning that lay behind their decision, and why the details of their intentions in the area, as well as the actual financial bid, were never really put before the full Council which finally ratified the committee's decision to place the project with another developer. The Co-op referred the matter to the District Valuer, and decided that if no satisfaction was gained from this move, to approach the Department of the Environment on the matter. I tried to get the officials of the Northern Group of Labour MPs to discuss the matter, but was overtaken by the events at Blyth in 1974 which led to me losing the Party Whip and being unable to attend further Group meetings. A similar report was given in relation to the Town Hall Site in Central Sunderland with the comment: 'The attitude of the Corporation does seem peculiar and I think the best word I can use for it is un-commercial.'

Naturally the report which took my attention most was that of Blyth. This I give in full:

The attitude of the local authority here is also beyond explanation. In contravention of their own Town Centre schemes they agreed an option to sell four acres of land to a private business concern (*Allied Suppliers*) for them to erect a supermarket with a private car park. This will have the effect of taking away literally all car parking from the centre of the town and allow one retailer to have 200 car parking spaces all to himself.

We are the biggest retailer in Blyth and were not even given the opportunity to offer more money for the site which we certainly would have done. Again we have an un-commercial illogical approach. (*sic*) However, we have made a technical objection the result of which is that after a long struggle, which has taken about two years, we may well get another site adjoining the one offered by the local authority to this private firm. However this will cost us money in that we are having to deal through a property developer, because contact with the local authority is simply a waste of time. (26th September 1973)

The attitude of Blyth Council towards the Co-operative Movement is the more difficult to understand when one realises that at least two of its leading figures, Alderman Gilbert

Barker, chairman of the committee which appointed J. G. L. Poulson as the architect for the building of the local swimming baths and Alderman Fred Smith, who had two houses built in nearby Whitley Bay by Sid McCullough, a friend of Andrew Cunningham, and whose building contracts with Blyth Council reached massive figures, were top figures in the Co-operative Movement and gained what political prominence they possess from that association. Barker was a long time member of the Board of the Blyth Society prior to its amalgamation with the North-Eastern Co-op and Fred Smith served for a period of time as chairman of the National Wages Board of the Co-operative Movement, a post which brought him into close touch with Alfred Allen, USDAW General Secretary and other top USDAW leaders.

I must now come to Peter Ferry, who was appointed Chief Executive of the Blyth Valley Council, formed from the former Blyth Borough and Seaton Valley UDC, and later to figure in the Blyth Constituency scene as the Returning Officer in the controversial General Election of October 1974. Ferry was a somewhat drab lifeless figure. It occasioned surprise when he received the Blyth Valley appointment, for it was felt that someone with legal knowledge and experience was required. Before the Council re-organisation he served on the National Committee of the Urban District Council's Association and gave evidence for that body to a Select Committee of the House of Commons which was collecting information on the allocation of house improvement grants. In his meeting at the House of Commons, Ferry revealed that the officials of the Council and not the Councillors were responsible at Seaton Valley for the allocation of grants. Some 700 applications he revealed had been received by his Council but only five were submitted for approval to the Councillors. The officials decided the rest. This was despite the fact that there had been widespread complaint both to councillors and myself about the Council's methods of dealing with this vitally important allocation of public money. Ferry and his Council's dealing with the highly controversial allocation of grants to the *London and Tyneside Properties Ltd* of the Jesmond district of Newcastle upon Tyne, for the modernisation of 181 houses at the former pit village of New

Hartley, caused widespread public interest well outside the boundaries of South-East Northumberland and great concern to myself. The houses were built by the National Coal Board on land leased to them by Lord Hastings of Seaton Delaval Hall. Lord Hastings had decided to sell the land to the *London and Tyneside Property Company* because he could not obtain planning permission to have the area tidied up and more pleasant to live in. The residents had been pressing both the National Coal Board and Seaton Valley Council for improvements to be carried out in the village, ever since the pit closed in the early 1960s. The houses were occupied mainly by retired employees of the NCB, who were protected by the Rent Act but were under pressure from the property company to have their houses modernised. As many of the houses had recently been much improved by the occupants, many felt this was a waste of public money and there was widespread local protest. I was attacked by the councillors for attending meetings of the residents, although the local councillor had called me in because she had been overwhelmed by the strength of the protest from the local residents.

Trouble really started when the Coal Board served notice to quit on 25 service occupancy tenants whose legal right to the housing accommodation stemmed from their employment by the Board. It was further cause for alarm when the miners discovered the kind of alternative accommodation they were being offered by their employers. In fact if the Northumberland officials of the National Union of Mineworkers had done their job properly, the service tenants could have remained at New Hartley, or at least the NUM could have put up a strong legal case on their behalf to do so. But, as so often in the North-East, nobody argued with the Labour Authorities about their deals with the property companies. Matters really came to a head when it was reported that the houses had been sold by the Coal Board to the *London and Tyneside Property Company* for £480 each! The alternative housing offered the National Coal Board employees was deplorable, and again it was not the National Union of Miners who championed the cause of the New Hartley Tenants but councillor Larry McManus, who readers will recollect was removed from the Council panel of the

Seaton Valley Labour Party. Commenting on one of the alternative houses offered by the Coal Board he said, 'The house had been empty for a long time and was in a bad state. There was a piece of wood over the back door and a notice warning people not to use it. The house was in a shocking condition.' A coal board official said that he thought everything that could be done for the tenants had been done. He had not taken the trouble, as Larry McManus had done, to visit the house in question but said that if it was not in a good state of repair, it would be put right. Despite the fact that the house had been allocated, the Coal Board official said further that the tenants had ceased to be the responsibility of the Board the previous Saturday and they had tried to do what they could. In this way the folk of New Hartley were deserted by their councillors and by the Coal Board. The two councillors mainly concerned, the chairman of the council, Councillor Collier (also chairman of the Blyth Constituency Labour Party) and Councillor Jack Patterson, later to become Mayor of the new Blyth Valley Council, a past vice-chairman of the Blyth Labour Party, refused to meet the New Hartley residents, although they had both figured prominently at a promotional lunch given by the property company in the Victory Club in the heart of the village.

Mr Peter Dyke, a director of the property company, was critical of the role played by the Coal Board, when he stated that the company had warned the Coal Board that a human problem was going to arise from this, but they did not take much notice. We are concerned, he said, about the welfare of these rent-free tenants. Three offers had been made to the Board to ease the situation, continued Mr Dyke. Lord Hastings also agreed that a muddle had developed, and that it was bad luck for the people living in the houses. 'It is somebody's fault and it looks like the Coal Board's', he summed up.

It needed meeting after meeting to sort out the problems of the New Hartley people and the only councillor playing a part was Larry McManus. An excellently run local residents association was formed and they gained concession after concession from the authorities concerned, and even in the long run managed to get an interview with the local council and to persuade the local councillors to attend their meetings. This of course was achieved mainly in the run up to the local elections.

One other mystery surrounding the problems of the New Hartley folk was the price paid for the houses by the *London and Tyneside Property Company* to the National Coal Board. The figure being freely circulated was £480. I wrote to Derek Ezra, the chairman of the NCB on the matter and suggested that if Coal Board houses were to be sold, then the occupants, most of whom had given a life-time of service to the coal industry, should have first refusal, particularly if the price mentioned in the sale to the property company was in the bargain basement category, and also subject to a substantial grant for improvement purposes. Ezra wrote back to say that the figure of £480 per house was not the correct one. I replied that I would continue to give the figure concerned in all my reports, but if he would supply me with the correct figure then I would be pleased to amend my one. I am still awaiting a reply from Mr Derek Ezra and from his Land Agent Mr Dickie who was, prior to his appointment to Hobart House, London office of the NCB, responsible for the Coal Board land deals in the Northern Region. I have met Mr Dickie on a number of occasions but have never been able, even with his help, to unravel the many mysteries surrounding the sale of Coal Board property in the North-East or elsewhere.

It was rather ironical to discover, after the battles on behalf of the members of the National Union of Mineworkers in New Hartley, that a move had been made at executive level in Newcastle to carpet me for what the NUM leaders described as interference in their affairs. I met them in Newcastle on my way to London one Monday morning and went over the matter fully with them. But no action was taken by them to defend the interests of the New Hartley members. That job was done by the local people themselves. Under excellent leadership, the Residents Association performed miracles in the face of official opposition from all quarters.

Support for their stand came indirectly in the questions being asked from all over the country about the property speculation surrounding the improvement grants. There was strong pressure from local authority associations for amendments to the Housing Acts, because it was alleged that speculators were making quick and easy profits by improving old houses with the help of Government grants. The Rural District Councils Association claimed that since 1969, when the Government dispensed with the condition that grants should be repaid if properties were sold within three years after improvement, there had been an increase in the number of grants paid to 'people whose interest is purely speculative'.

The New Hartley episode and its connection with the building world sparked off new controversies in the local government field, and with the appointment of the new councils at the June elections, speculation was rife about the importance of police investigations taking place in the area. This was greatly heightened by reports of houses being built by Birtley builder Sid McCullough for people and councillors including the Cunninghams to whom he was beholden. McCullough, readers will recollect, was the builder mentioned by Dan Smith when he said, 'I think he would be the man behind any broad corruption in Blyth.' Interest was added to the matter, when reports surfaced that houses had been built for Alderman Fred Smith, Blyth's Housing chairman for many years, for Councillor Matt Allon, a brother-in-law of Andy Cunningham, and also Arthur Moss, the Blyth Burgh Surveyor. A McCullough-built house was in preparation at Seaton Delaval for the new chief executive of Blyth Valley Council, Mr Peter Ferry. It was also being freely said that cars were also being provided by Mc-Cullough. The news naturally caused panic in many quarters. Peter Ferry and Alderman Fred Smith reacted to it immediately. Following my return from the Labour Party conference, I received a note from Fred Smith who had called to see me while I was away in Blackpool. His letter said, 'I'm having the mother and father of rows with the *Sunday Times* about an article that appeared some weeks ago, part of which concerned the Blyth Labour Group.' The point in dispute between Smith and the *Sunday Times* concerned the visit of Dan Smith to the Labour Group in Blyth in either 1962 or 1963. Smith said that if the report was not corrected he would write the Press Council and could I help him on the matter. I replied that I had no information regarding the meetings of the Blyth Labour Group, and in view of the arrest of Dan Smith and other issues, any information which I had would be forwarded by me to the proper authorities, which I had in any case been doing for some time.

Ferry adopted a different course. He sent a letter to the members of the newly elected Blyth Valley Council due to assume office in April 1974.

Dear Councillor,

With this letter is a photostat copy of an Article and sub-Article which appeared on 6th October, 1973. I was shown the paper some time after its publication and immediately sought legal advice upon its innuendoes and possible defamatory content.

The Seaton Valley Urban District Council in common with many modern Local Authorities decided when the 75% Improvement Grant was introduced to streamline the processing and approval of applications for a Grant.

As a result of the Council's decision to delegate its powers in this respect to me I have formally approved applications from *London and Tyneside Properties* for the village of New Hartley.

I should like to make the following points about the sub-Article:

(i) The sub-Article is headed '£150,000 Deal'. The word deal is open to a number of interpretations, one of which at least infers dishonesty. This I refute absolutely. I have no connection whatsoever with *London and Tyneside Properties*, and there has been no deal with them.

(ii) I have not decided 'to pay £150,000 of ratepayers money to *London and Tyneside Properties*'.

   (a) The total amount involved in approved applications is £139,000.

   (b) The sum so far issued on approved completion is £83,000, and the remainder will not be paid unless and until the remaining improvements are completed and each one is individually approved by the Council's Building Inspectors.

   (c) Grant money is only provided as to 10% by the

ratepayers. The remaining 90% is contributed by the Government.

(iii) I have entered into a contract with S. McCullough Limited to have a house built by them. There is no impropriety in that. The connection of my name and others with the name of Andrew Cunningham, who is at present awaiting trial on charges of corruption, I consider completely scurrilous.

Yours sincerely,
Peter Ferry.

Only one point needs comment arising from this letter. Many of the Seaton Valley ratepayers who applied for a modernisation grant would have welcomed the time scale accorded to *London and Tyneside* in receiving the monies due to them from the payment of the grants.

The question of corruption had certainly been uppermost in the minds of those of us in the North-East, far too few unfortunately, who had been living in the shadow of the problem for so long. The argument used by many around us, was to the effect that people like Smith, Poulson and Cunningham were really doing a good job of work and if they received payment in return, it was no more than they might have gained if they had used their talents in the business and commercial field. The simple answer of course was that they did not operate in that field but in the realms of public life where the practice of democracy still was, or should be, the dominant factor. What was also forgotten were the economic and social consequences for the great mass of the ordinary people of the country who had to pay for the misdemeanours of the misguided few. It was therefore, refreshing to receive a report on this matter from the United Nations which carried a statement from the Secretary General of that organisation. It read 'Many countries face the problem of bribery and corruption, which exacts economic and social costs of serious proportions . . . Governments need to approach this difficult problem from a number of different angles . . . Administrative and legal reform is equally implied.' (UN Secretary General to the General Assembly 1973, A/8844 para 86.)

When I met the Attorney General, Sir Peter Rawlinson, he was most helpful in dealing with the problem created in Durham about police enquiries into the activities of local authorities, because of Andrew Cunningham's chairmanship of the Police Authority. Reports of harassment by the police of individuals and councillors making complaints, and the attitude of the Durham police chiefs when approached about the way in which local affairs at council level were being conducted, has caused concern for a number of years. Generally the complaints were brushed aside at police level by the remark that they were political matters and did not come within the scope of the police. In County Durham particularly and to a larger extent in Northumberland, police and political matters were equally controlled by Andrew Cunningham and those around him. His chairmanship of the Regional Council of the Labour Party and the various council and regional posts which he held and dominated throughout the counties of the North-East gave him a power base unequalled anywhere as a Councillor. For a comparison, one would have to go to the America of the 1930s, or Mayor Daley's Chicago, or the various New York administrations for anything like Durham's long years of Tammany Hall type politics.

This is why one sometimes despairs of getting officialdom to grapple with the problem of corruption. At whatever level in British public life one approaches the issue, the road blocks barring progress are formidable. Public trials have been held, convictions have been secured, people are still facing trial and further exposures of corrupt practices and actions are being revealed daily, but I believe the barriers and cover-ups remain.

The trial process can drag on for years. The Royal Commission under Lord Salmon will be of immense help, but the final decision will be with Parliament. But so far no party or its leaders have shown any real desire to get down to the roots of the matter. As things stand the one hope is that public demand for action, in the wake of the Royal Commission Report to Parliament, will stir the police, judiciary and the politicians into actions much more drastic than any they have undertaken in the past.

But the battle at Blyth still waged fiercely and interference with my Parliamentary duties continued apace. Trade Union meetings were told by Councillor Collier and others that until the local dispute was settled no engagements could be fixed with me. Following the Transport House announcement that the Blyth Inquiry, requested by USDAW, would be held on Sunday 27th January and Sunday 3rd February, chaired by John Chalmers of the Boilermakers, with Alex Kitson of the Transport and General Workers, and Underhill as the other members. The response of the Blyth Labour Party officials to this was immediate. I was due to address the Constituency Management Committee meeting to give my Parliamentary Report, which I did every quarter. Mortakis cancelled this and summoned a special meeting of the EC to consider action on the reopening of the Parliamentary panel to find a successor to Milne. Despite protests on a widespread scale, the meeting was allowed to continue and Transport House did nothing to help in the matter. I decided to hold a public meeting to acquaint my constituents and as many party members as possible about what was going on under the guise of democracy. Councillor Collier said that the need for a special meeting of the EC arose because I had demanded his resignation following efforts by him to prevent me from meeting the Transport and General Workers Union branch at the *Brentford Nylon* factory at Cramlington near Blyth where Collier and other Labour officials were employed.

Prior to the Christmas recess, I had made arrangements for an interview with Harold Wilson, but after a lot of coming and going with his private office, I was notified by Albert Murray, former MP for Gravesend, who along with others, ran Wilson's private office, that the interview had been cancelled. Whether the Labour leader had ever been notified of my request for an interview will never be known, but what was obvious was that although Albert Murray might have been the political secretary in Wilson's private office, Marcia Williams and her relatives had their say. Before the House resumed in January, I wrote to both Wilson and Callaghan, the latter as chairman of the Labour Party, and again endeavoured to get things moving. To Wilson I said, 'I was disappointed that the meeting arranged with you before the Christmas recess had to be cancelled. Now that the

Poulson/Pottinger trial is under way, I think it is becoming increasingly evident that a wide-searching examination of the implications of the Poulson affair is needed.'

In my letter to Callaghan I outlined the happenings at Blyth over the years and said, 'I was glad to learn that the NEC had decided at USDAW's request to hold an Inquiry into the situation in the Blyth Constituency . . . It would take too long to go into all the detail, but I hope that the forthcoming Inquiry will show to the public at large and the members of the party and my constituents at Blyth that democracy is still a live factor within the Labour Movement. They look to you, with your considerable influence and reputation, to play a part in clearing up once and for all a situation that should never have been allowed to arise, and once it had arisen should never have been allowed to continue.' I was to realise very soon that the loyalty that Callaghan and Wilson owed, was less to the Labour Movement than to the cronies they had around them, and that those who suffered as a result were the great mass of ordinary folk whose immense sacrifices had created the opportunities for the Wilsons and the Callaghans to achieve power and influence, built on the great Movement that others had made possible.

And so to the Sundays of the Transport House Inquiry. Over the years in various parts of the country I have been fated in one way or another to have dealt with this sort of occasion. Always, hatchet man Underhill, or someone cast in the same role seemed to dominate. The trivia of the whole thing is frustrating and boring, for one knows and feels that the outcome is predetermined. On this inquiry one factor was unknown. The two Sundays of evidence and counter-evidence was to lead to a third, an election adoption meeting at Blyth and the emergence of another Labour candidate which Underhill had worked so hard to achieve. A date with destiny lay ahead. Those around me at Blyth had always felt from the 1972 'hanging party' which we survived by four votes, that Transport House and Cunningham and his allies in the regional office and in the Blyth party, would continue to shoot at the target they had set themselves.

So no-one was surprised at the trend the Inquiry took. The most significant remark of the whole two days was made by

NEC representative Alex Kitson when he blurted out during one hectic spell, 'Watergate has nothing on this'. Underhill had invited members of the party to write to him if they wished to give evidence. Some twenty or thirty did so, but it was not till nearly 4 p.m. on the second day of the hearing that individual witnesses were reached and the number still around to give evidence was then reduced to four. Not that it mattered anyway for the issue was well on the way to being decided by that time. It was therefore no surprise, when John Chalmers changed the order of procedure and allowed Mortakis to wind up the proceedings and speak last instead of myself as arranged. It was a small matter in itself but hardly the action of the chairman of an important sub-committee of the National Executive who claimed to be impartial on the matter, and who as the General Secretary of a Union with headquarters in Newcastle, must have had some idea of what was going on in the region and what was happening in Blyth, and more importantly, why it was happening. At that time of course Andrew Cunningham had not yet been convicted, and it may be that the top levels of the Labour Party were hoping that things would turn out all right.

The attitude of Chalmers was disappointing, as was that of Kitson, both of whom had known me during the years I had been in the movement, particularly in the period in Scotland. Prior to the winding up session Chalmers adjourned the hearing, and I was invited along with Collier and Mortakis to join the inquiry team in an ante-room. There Chalmers appealed to me to go through another hand-shaking act, and everything would be all right. I pointed out that prior to approaching USDAW to seek this inquiry I had made it clear to Allen that I would rather go out of public life than work with the Mortakis set-up again. The Gormley type solution of the last inquiry simply was not on. In any case, if I had agreed to that step being taken, it would have been used against me at Blyth in any subsequent meeting and the vote to oust us would have been taken against that background. In fact, as was later revealed, moves had been made in support of the candidature of Ivor Richard, who when his Barons Court constituency disappeared, was without a seat at the next General Election, and the 1975 moves to reopen the Blyth Parliamentary Panel were designed to remedy this.

I went back to Westminster in a week in which General Election talk dominated all other matters. This culminated in the Prime Minister dissolving Parliament and calling for a General Election on 28th February. Prior to leaving for home I had talks on the situation created by Heath's announcement on the Blyth position with Jeffrey Thomas, a Welsh MP and QC and John Silkin, former Chief Whip. Both assured me that the election declaration solved my problems in the Constituency, as once an election had been set going, then re-adoption was the order of the day. I had nothing to worry about, said Silkin. I was not so sure and reminded both my colleagues that rules in Blyth differed from elsewhere, that I did not trust the impartiality of Evers and Underhill, and that as far as I was concerned the outcome was very much in doubt.

The adoption meeting was called for Sunday afternoon at 2.30 p.m. On the morning, two hours before the meeting, Allen 'phoned me from the Union Central Office where the Executive Council were in session. He urged me to accept Mortakis as my agent at the election, as the inquiry report of the Labour Party's National Executive would not be received for a number of weeks and matters were therefore still, as he described them, sub-judice. I told Allen of my talks with Silkin and Thomas and said that if the inquiry made it impossible to discuss my allegations, then my re-adoption would be automatic, and I expected his support if anything happened to the contrary. I also reminded him that I had made it clear to him and the union that under no circumstances would I work with Mortakis again, and indeed had told USDAW's officials on many occasions that it was time union money ceased to be used to subsidise an agent whose avowed aim was to get rid of an MP they had sponsored for the Blyth Constituency ever since Alf Robens had been adopted prior to the General Election of 1945, a period of close on thirty years.

The adoption meeting was like the inquiry meetings of the previous weeks—pre-ordained. I was invited to speak. Generally the adoption of the candidate is moved, seconded and adopted, prior to the candidate addressing the meeting. This was significant, but I made no protest. Evers was not in attendance, but he had sent David Hughes, his assistant. USDAW had also made arrangements for one member of the EC, Jim Coleby, to be present. Why Allen made this move will never be known, but it showed the contact with Transport House on the Blyth situation and how much consultation there had been between these two bodies. For at any time in this dispute, if the Union's General Secretary had cared to raise a finger on my behalf, the whole situation in Blyth of the last four or five years could have been drastically altered. But the Union General Secretary was on his way to the House of Lords. Prime Ministers with favours to bestow must not be crossed.

The questions I was asked at the meeting were few and routine in character. The vote was the big issue. There was no criticism of my work as member and no question as to who would be my agent if adopted. The matter already decided, the vote was a formality: 30 votes for adoption—41 against. My spell as Labour Member of Parliament was over.

I received a further telephone call after the meeting from Allen, saying that I could still attend the selection conference, which had been fixed for the following Thursday, and that the Union had agreed to nominate me again.

This was in no way an attempt to be helpful on the part of Allen, and was either intended to complete my humiliation or was possibly a gesture intended to make him appear impartial for the record. But I was not playing that Tom and Jerry game.
I told Allen that I was not prepared to sit in the gutter outside the Labour Club at Blyth, waiting for the same meeting headed by Collier and Mortakis who had turned me down only a few hours before, to reverse their decision in my favour. I also wanted to know from Allen how he could have known of a meeting arranged for Thursday, when the decision at Blyth that afternoon had to be ratified by the National Executive Committee or the Election Committee headed by Callaghan and Underhill in London the following morning. So the plot thickened, as had been suspected in all the discussions since the battle started in 1970; Allen and Underhill along with the Party's Regional Office, were very much the central figures, in the moves which finally succeeded that afternoon to get rid of Milne at Blyth. The call issued by Cunningham to Evers on that far off afternoon had been answered.

147

All Sunday evening, callers kept coming to our home. The first to arrive was my friend and comrade Angus Galloway, formerly a Union colleague in pre-war Scotland as secretary of one of the large NUDAW (later USDAW) branches in Glasgow, now a depot director in Blyth, who had been my political confidant since arriving in the Blyth Constituency in 1960. Angus had just forwarded his resignation to the Labour Party on hearing the news. Councillors Winnie Yellowley JP, Ronnie Mordue of Blyth and Malcolm McDonald, also of Blyth, and Jimmie Black of Bedlington, all expressed a similar viewpoint of resignation from the party. The main NUM officials in the constituency offered to sign my nomination papers, and the chairman of one of the local councils called with a donation saying that he was also resigning later in the week. Party veterans like Jane Allison, a former Mayor of Blyth, and Harriet Napier, a past chairman of the Women's Federation, also joined in the campaign. We talked that night of the steps to be taken, but decided to make no move until the decision of the Blyth Party that afternoon had been confirmed by Transport House; an announcement had been promised by Underhill for 12 noon next day. It came, and as expected, backed the Blyth Constituency Management Committee's decision of the previous day. Transport House had dealt with Eddie Milne in just 14 hours.

Chapter Eight

The first press comment on the dismissal came from the *Newcastle Journal*. Its *Opinion* Editorial was headed:

CAN BLYTH FIND A BETTER MP

Not much is certain in political life—but it does look like the end of the Parliamentary road for Eddie Milne. But it may well be argued that his place in the hearts of the voters in the Blyth Constituency is as secure as it has ever been. It is scarcely conceivable, no matter what the special circumstances of a particular contest, that Blyth would not back an official candidate. He will need to be as keen a believer in open government and in political sincerity to provide anything approaching a substitute for Eddie Milne.

A campaign committee was quickly formed and a meeting called for the following Friday. Between 120 and 130 turned up to help in the fight. Many Labour Party supporters, who had left the party over the years, or been turfed out, rallied around us. As Larry McManus said, on the night the nomination papers were handed in, 'Many people are beginning to enjoy their politics again.' It proved, as expected, to be a happy, friendly campaign, but the bitterness from the official party was deep-rooted. The character-assassination and the innuendoes of strange behaviour on my part continued to be circulated. But our policy was to maintain our own position and to ignore the other parties entirely. It was a four party contest and there were excellent relationships during the campaign between the Liberal and Tory workers and ourselves.

Ivor Richard was selected as the official Labour candidate, as expected. His election address set the tone for the type of campaign the party conducted. It was headed: 'I give you my promise that I will use my efforts, if elected, to represent the interests of the Blyth constituency—*interests which have been far too neglected in the past.* Most, if not all, of his speeches were centred on the same theme. As an incoming Londoner, he was of course at a great disadvantage in the area, no fault of his, but it placed him in the hands of the local Labour party as far as policy and campaigning plans were concerned. The corruption issue was quickly seized on by the Labour candidate, tradinghis knowledge and experience as a barrister and former junior minister, to show how much he knew about the North-East and what Cunningham, Smith and company had been up to. As the newspapers summed it up, 'Corruption charges blew up as the big issue in the bitter Blyth election campaign.' Ivor Richard claimed at one meeting that we had been conducting a smear campaign and hinting at corruption for several years, but that top level investigations had revealed nothing. This displayed a startling ignorance of the situation, since leading Labour Party figures were facing trial in different parts of the country. A strange lapse for a barrister, even one fighting a seat in the North-East of England. The same night that this was being argued by Richard, a newspaper columnist was talking of the strange evidence emerging from the Poulson-Pottinger trial revelations. On 17th February he said:

During the Poulson-Pottinger trial it was said that Sir Douglas Haddow, head of the Scottish Civil Service, when Pottinger's relationship with Poulson was becoming a matter of public discussion and concern, told Pottinger that it was proposed to answer a question relating to the matter in the Commons.

The answer would be that official inquiries within the Scottish office had confirmed that Pottinger had in no sense misused his official position. But that his private relationship with Poulson would be investigated through the Civil Service.

It was further said by Pottinger during the trial that Sir Douglas Haddow assured him that the worst that could happen to him would be a 'bit of a wigging,' and that the

Civil Service plan was to 'play the whole affair cool and hope no further publicity erupts.'

Did Sir Douglas Haddow really say those things to Pottinger? Was he really going to cover up for Pottinger in the fashion which Pottinger suggests? In fact was Pottinger telling the truth or was he lying? Now that the trial is over, should not Sir Douglas Haddow tell us exactly what he said to Pottinger?

But the piece de resistance was reserved for Transport House and, of course, Underhill. It took the shape of an over £300 advertisement in the local press entitled 'The Facts About Blyth Party and Eddie Milne.' It was, as I described it at the time, not so much a document of lies as a lying document. Ivor Richard said that he believed the advertisement would prove effective in losing Mr Milne votes. 'It has had a remarkable reception.' It lied in that it claimed to be a report of the inquiry of the previous two weeks to the election. In fact that report was only presented to the NEC of the Labour Party at its May meeting more than two months after the February General Election. It was signed or purported to be signed by each member of the National Executive Committee, including Padley the USDAW representative, Harold Wilson and the North-East's leading politician over a number of years, Mr Edward Short.

The advert went on to claim that I had quarrelled with five chairmen and three agents. In fact the Party seemed to have a phobia about agents, for whilst agents were being dismissed all over the country, the party reports were deploring the reduction in their numbers, and scheme after scheme was being discussed to attract party members to the agency service; Blyth itself of the Parliamentary constituencies had a full-time agent from 1948 and earlier in the former Wansbeck constituency. The two agents appointed during my term as Member of Parliament both approached and sought my help in getting them the job. As far as party chairmen were concerned, I have had considerably less trouble with those at Blyth than Transport House officials have had with Chairmen of the NEC. The only one I heavily clashed with was Alderman Smith and he came around for a time seeking to help us as he described it 'against Mor-

takis'. Alderman Smith has been mentioned earlier in connection with the Birtley builder McCullough, and it may be that which caused the friction. The NUM were brought into the advert with a letter forwarding £100 to help Richard. In previous elections the Mineworkers' contribution was usually £150. A letter from the Northern Group of Labour MPs, stated the obvious when saying, 'Mr Milne is disqualified from membership of the Parliamentary Labour Party and there are no circumstances in which he could be accepted into the Northern Group.' To make weight, a letter from USDAW was also included. It ran, 'The Union will not be giving Mr Milne any financial assistance or support. Mr Arthur Hamilton, USDAW Organiser in the Northern Region, will be appearing on the platform in support of Mr Ivor Richard. Arthur Hamilton is the brother of Willie Hamilton who has served for a number of years as MP for Fife.' So that was that.

The campaign was exhilarating. Some 300 people played a part in it and there were joyous scenes when the result was declared. It ran as follows.

Milne	22,918	(Indep. Lab)
Richard	16,778	(Lab)
John Shipley	10,214	(Lib)
B. Griffiths	8,888	(Con)

Majority 6,140.

The result was regarded as a vindication of the stand our folk at Blyth had taken, and locally it was regarded as a rebuff to Ted Short, whom I had challenged to come to Blyth and back up the attacks being made upon us in the Labour Party Advertisement. He had replied that he had 'no time to waste on Milne'.

The figures were interesting. The local party claimed that we won because of Tory votes. It is of course true, as it is of any MP, that he picks up votes irrespective of party but Evers the Party Regional Officer had predicted before the election that I would poll 1,000 votes. Many constituents vote for a member because he has helped them in some way. But at Blyth the combined Labour and Independent vote as against the joint Liberal Conservative vote showed a majority of 21,000, much as had normally been the case in the two-candidate elections which had previously been the pattern at Blyth.

And so it was back to the House of Commons. The response from top party ranks was frigid, particularly from Wilson, Short and Mellish. In the early days, those with ministerial appointments and particularly those who still hoped to have appointments, were extremely reluctant to be seen around with me or near to me. And on many occasions when chatting with former Labour colleagues in the tea-room, they would stop the conversation by saying they had to leave, generally adding 'it is not because I am with you, Eddie.'

As was to be expected my postbag after the election was of massive proportions, posing problems for my secretaries, but we did try, and I think succeeded in seeing that everybody had a reply. The letter which gave most pleasure was from a QC who had played a leading part in the Poulson prosecution, a Labour lawyer, who congratulated me on my stand.

Against the background of much moral support from members of the bar, it is interesting to note the anxiety of the Blyth Labour leaders and their chosen candidate from the ranks of the legal profession, Mr Ivor Richard QC, lately Labour candidate at Blyth in the February General Election. Returning to the North-East in March to address the annual meeting of the Seaton Valley Local Labour Party, the section of the Blyth Party which had removed Larry McManus from office a year previously, he plunged into the corruption controversy again. He told the delegates he would be approaching the Attorney General the following week because it was time that Mr Milne's 'unspecified and unproven allegations were dealt with once and for all'. He wanted an old friend of his, Sam Silkin, the Attorney General, to see Mr Milne and demand from him his 'evidence'. Richard also claimed that the corruption issue had lost Labour the seat. 'If we had had another week we would have won,' said Richard. 'Another fortnight and we would have crucified him.' I described Richard's comments as 'Playing his part in the operation cover-up.' After all Richard had been an MP for ten years and was on Labour's Front Bench when demands for an inquiry into corruption had been made. Sam Silkin would have already had the evidence I had given to his predecessor Sir Peter Rawlinson as had numerous other people. I received a letter from Ivor Richard's solicitors complaining about and threatening action about my cover-up comment, but heard no further word on the matter when I refused to withdraw my statement. But we were not to have the pleasure of Mr Richard's company in the North-East for long. He was off to pastures new. The Prime Minister had decided that he was another to be rewarded for services rendered. The unsuccessful Blyth Labour candidate was to become Her Majesty's Ambassador to the United Nations in New York with a salary believed to be around £270 per week, a figure for those like Denis Healey to remember, when he is lecturing miners and railmen about the social contract and the inflationary effect on wage rises. Richard was Parliamentary Private Secretary to Denis Healey in the last Labour Government at the Ministry of Defence and later Richard became Minister for the Army. Some day someone will write about the power of privilege, and those around Wilson who have benefited from it.

One of the first callers to see me at the House of Commons on my return after the election was Albert Roberts, Labour MP for Normanton, a sponsored member of the NUM. Despite my Poulson probing, Albert had always adopted a friendly approach to me and often engaged in conversation when we met in the corridors and around the House. He had a close interest in the Leeds office of USDAW and mentioned on occasion his visits there with the Union's Regional Officer N. B. Capindale, who was also a member of the regional hospital board. Roberts came to my desk-room to ask about the election, as did so many others. He reminded me of a statement I had made during the election, when in reply to a question about any likely return to the Labour Party on my part, I had said that under no circumstances would I return to the Party while Short was deputy leader and Mellish continued as Chief Whip. 'Why,' asked Roberts, 'had I said this?' I told Albert Roberts it was because I considered that Short and Mellish had been the two main persons blocking my efforts to get some sort of examination into the Labour Party in the North-East about the Poulson affair, and when I had reported to them about happenings in Blyth they had done nothing when both of them had the power to do so much. I also referred to what I considered the cowardly attitude of Short at the General Election when I had challenged him to come to

155

Blyth and justify the advert used to attack me, and signed by himself, along with other members of the National Executive. Roberts was quite surprised at all this, he said. 'I thought it was because you knew that Mrs Short had worked for Poulson.' I was absolutely taken aback at this, for whilst a lot of names had been bandied around at the time of Mrs Cunningham's arrest, the name of the wife of the Labour deputy leader never came into the reckoning. It was a matter which was to crop up again when the police visited the House of Commons on 21st June, 1974 to investigate the allegedly forged Swiss Bank documents distributed to MPs and attributed to Ted Short. On the occasion of his interview with me, Detective Superintendent Wood of Scotland Yard, who was accompanied by Detective Inspector Marsden, asked if I could recall the conversation with Albert Roberts. When I said that I did, he asked me to sign a statement on the matter, which I agreed to do, and this was signed in a committee room of the House of Commons. I will deal again with this later on in the story. It will also be within the recollection of many who have followed the Poulson disclosures, that in reply to a question from Muir Hunter, Poulson had said that he had paid Roberts for specific jobs undertaken on his behalf. Some of these specific jobs concerned the overseas activities of Albert Roberts in Spain, Portugal, Angola and Greece. Roberts was also connected with Maudling in the Gozo hospital in Malta, of which the Queen laid the foundation stone in November 1968. At the Wakefield bankruptcy hearings, Poulson told of how when he had tried to secure hospital work in Spain, the Spanish authorities had told him to get in touch with Roberts. Albert Roberts was elected during the period of the 1964–1970 Labour Government as chairman of the Inter-Parliamentary Union, which gave him a strategic position in regard to overseas visits and contacts with visiting Parliamentary delegations. It was always a source of concern to many of us who had trouble with our unions and constituencies, that MPs like Bagier, Roberts and others, also union sponsored MPs, had no criticism for their connections with regimes like the Spanish and Greek Governments who had so little in common with the aims and aspirations of the Labour Movement. Roberts appears to have done considerable PR work for the Spanish Government and was decorated by Franco's regime in 1967.

At the Labour Party Executive meeting in March, Renée Short complained about the advertisement used in the February General Election at Blyth. She demanded to know why her name—and the name of other members of the NEC—had been inserted in the publication without consultation or consent. The usual Transport House hand-out, said that Mrs Short was the first to object about the use of names and the matter would be raised again at a future meeting. A polite way of burying an awkward matter.

But a matter of greater importance emerged from the Party's National Executive Committee meeting in the statement from John Chalmers, chairman of the enquiry team and secretary of the Newcastle based Boilermakers, when he reported that the three man team, himself, Kitson and Underhill, had not completed their examination of evidence taken at Blyth when examining the affairs of the Blyth Labour Party at the request of USDAW, and that the next NEC meeting due to be held in April would probably discuss it.

It will be recollected that Underhill caused an advertisement to be used in the February election which stated, 'Moreover the report of the latest National Executive enquiry into the relations between him (Milne) and the Blyth CLP had until recently not been published. This enquiry was set up at the specific request of the Union of Shop, Distributive and Allied Workers who sponsored Eddie Milne. A report from the National Agent on behalf of the National Executive of the Labour Party dated 15th February has now been received and is set out below' (then followed the names of the National Executive Committee). It can be well understood why we classed Underhill's report as a lie during the General Election and another example of what I described as Transport House treachery. I had also described the adverts as a disgraceful way to conduct a campaign and one more proof of the lengths to which Underhill and other Labour leaders were prepared to go to shut Milne up. And even when the report finally emerged at NEC level in May, it was never revealed to USDAW or the Blyth Constituency Labour Party, and when John Chalmers moved at the meeting of the NEC that the Report should be made public, the answer of Ron Hayward the Party's General Secretary was that it would be unconstitutional to do so. Such is the state of democracy in the Labour Party at the moment. One thing is at least certain about the inquiry team report, and that is that if it had been an adverse one as far as I was concerned, it would have been circulated on a widespread basis.

Chapter Nine

The new Parliament was slow to move. The delay and uncertainty which hung over the almost dead-heat result had a stultifying effect. Wilson himself was strangely subdued in the days which followed Heath's final surrender of power. The Liberals who had hoped, certainly Thorpe did, that a coalition with the Tories would emerge, although none of them admitted to that hope, were in a state of not knowing where to turn. Their election failure to make a break-through had taken the fighting heart from them. The Scottish and Welsh nationalists could now muster a larger contingent on the Opposition benches than those who clung to the Liberal Party. The real challenge to the power of the two-party system which had dominated British politics for a generation was now passing into other hands. The economic facts of life were increasingly to call into question the ability of either Labour or Conservative Governments to solve the problems facing the British people.

And so far as my own position was concerned I was very much on my own. The organisation which had gathered round me in February had turned into a vital political force and with four councillors on the local authority and a membership nearing 200, none of us were in any great hurry to re-forge our Labour Party links. It was suggested to me by a number of my Parliamentary Labour colleagues that I should apply for the Labour Party whip, but the attitude of those around me and myself was that it was the Labour Party that had left us and any moves must come from them. In any case my election statement concerning Short and Mellish still stood. Whilst they occupied key positions I would not be seeking re-entry to the Labour Party.

In Parliament it was still difficult to get questions tabled on the corruption issue. The impending Smith and Cunningham trials were now the reason being put forward to check too much inquisitiveness on my part. I decided it was time to test out Wilson on the Royal Commission issue or the use of the Tribunal of Inquiry Act, and in March used the time honoured device, when all other efforts had failed, of asking him to visit Shildon, Co. Durham. As will be recollected this was the spot, in 1937, when he hoisted the anti-corruption banner in the great heartlands of the Labour Movement. The question was ultimately on the House of Commons Order Paper on Thursday 4th April. Little did any of us know when the question was first tabled, of what problems were besetting the Prime Minister at that time. The day before Wilson was due to answer my question in the House, the Millhench affair hit the headlines.

During the election Wilson, Short, Mellish and other Labour leaders had made attacks on the press for smear tactics, although when I had complained about character assassination at Blyth, and challenged Short to come to the constituency in support of the Labour candidate, Ivor Richard, and deal with the issues involved, he refused to do so by saying that he had no time to waste on Mr Milne. Now Wilson reacted predictably to the Millhench affair, defending his secretary's brother and claiming that the press were harassing Mrs Williams to an undue and intolerable extent and that the whole story was a Tory election plot. He appeared to ignore the fact that the story had been in the hands of at least the *Daily Mail* before the end of the February election and they chose not to use it until after polling day. The original land deal involved the Field family which included Marcia Williams, the Prime Minister's personal secretary.

The Millhench career was a strange one. A member of the Salvation Army, he had joined the Forces and served in Germany for three years, and for a similar period in North Africa. He decided to terminate his Army career and enter the business world by forming a firm with luxurious offices in Wolverhampton, called *Lynton Insurance Management Services*. It was from this source that the path of Millhench and the Prime Minister's office staff had crossed. It started with a property deal in Ince-in-Makerfield in February 1973 and the purchase of 29.83 acres of land at £10,000 per acre. A month previous to this, Millhench had travelled to London, where he was introduced to Mr Field, Marcia William's brother who Millhench understood worked for Harold Wilson in the House of Commons. Millhench was to have at least four other meetings with Mr Field, two of them at the House of Commons and another at Aston University in Birmingham where Mr Field introduced him to Harold Wilson. About his visits to the House of Commons, Millhench describes one of them taking place in Mr Field's private office—a grubby little place, he said. From reports circulating at the time that grubby little place seems to have been a hive of activity, for it was stated that Mr Field, introduced to officials of the former Llanelli Borough Council in South Wales as Mr Harold Wilson's private secretary, had taken part in local council planning talks before buying 40 acres of farmland in Wales. After the talks concerning this transaction, the Council were informed that the firm of Dupont intended to build a very large plant on the site. As the Chief Executive of the Llanelli District Council said at the time, there were two meetings at the Council attended by Mr Field. He did not know who Mr Field was at the first meeting, but was told just before the second that Mr Field was Mr Harold Wilson's secretary. Mr Field's name cropped up again in a statement from Warwickshire County Council who reported that they had a letter on Mr. Wilson's notepaper and signed H. A. Field concerning a re-development project undertaken by Mr Victor Harper, a business associate of Mr Anthony Field. The development, at Solihull, was separate from the land deal at Ince-in-Makerfield where Mr Harper acted as Mr Field's agent. I could not help wondering at the refusal of Harold Wilson to see me just prior to my failing to secure re-adoption at Blyth, compared to the ease with which people connected with property and land speculation (or reclamation!) at Solihull, Llanelli, or Ince-in-Makerfield, could be interviewed by or interview the person who was described as his private secretary, Mr Field.

The Prime Minister acted. He slapped a writ on the *Daily Express* and initiated libel actions. This of course had the effect of curtailing and limiting public and parliamentary comment on the matter. I thought of his words at Shildon:

'Apart from any changes that can be made in law and practice, the first safeguard must be a free and independent Press enabled by all legal means to turn over the stones of our public and business life to see what may be concealed beneath them.

In order to do this, there should be no inhibition of the kind created by the issue of writs which the plaintiff never intends to proceed with. Equally the press should not be inhibited by the existence of court proceedings which for whatever reason have dragged out so long as to be virtually moribund, and which through the sheer passage of time may relate to a world or to a state of affairs which has changed almost out of recognition.'

Now to the *Newcastle Journal* of 13th May, 1974. The headline was 'Wilson drops libel actions,' and the report went on to say,

'A Libel action brought by the Prime Minister, over two newspaper articles concerning land deals, ended in agreement in the High Court yesterday.

Mr Wilson was not in court to hear his counsel tell Mr Justice Park that he had brought the action "solely with a view to clearing his reputation." '

The lead stories objected to in the *Daily Express* of 3rd and 6th April, 1974 had been headed 'Wilson Men in Land Deal Row' and 'Wilson Met Land Dealers: Commons Office Used for Talks.' Mr Wilson took the view that the stories suggested that he had taken part in dealings involving land speculation and had obtained excessive profits. On behalf of the *Daily Express* it was said, 'they had always denied any intention of making allegations of that kind.' The report concluded, 'As the newspaper publishers had signified their willingness to join in making the statement in open court Mr Wilson was content to let the matter rest.' I shall content myself with saying that I wish Mr Wilson's loyalty and support not to say activity, was more often available to those of his colleagues who live by socialist principles.

The question of Wilson's visit to Shildon reached the floor of the House of Commons on Thursday 4th April, with all the explosion from it that was expected, but certainly not visualised when the question was first lodged at the Table Office. Wilson's reply was as expected. He wanted action, as he had said at Shildon, but land speculation was different from land reclamation. There were no profits to be made from reclamation, and those of us who thought so, did not really know what we were talking about. He was questioned by a Tory MP and retaliated in the usual fashion, 'If the honourable Member is trying to follow the smear by the Tory press, I still say that any honourable Member from Durham knows the difference between property speculation and land reclamation.' Then Willie Hamilton barged into the fray with a question to Short on next week's business. Hamilton had blown hot and cold in turns on the corruption issue. He had been prominent in the early stages of the Pottinger issue and then faded from the scene as did so many others, although it has to be said that the procedures of the House of Commons do not allow much scope to MPs who have an investigatory turn of mind. Hamilton demanded, 'In view of the allegations made in certain newspapers about land transactions, will the Leader of the House [Short] give an assurance that the Prime Minister himself will be making a statement on these matters before the recess, and if there are any associates of himself or any other member of the Government involved in these transactions that they will be removed forthwith?' Short's reply was as expected. 'The House will be aware that a statement was issued outside the House this morning which makes it abundantly clear that the whole campaign is a smear based on misrepresentation of the facts.' I was not surprised. Although Leader of the House he has never plucked up courage when his own conduct has been called in question to make a statement to the House, but he is always ready to take the lead in attacking those who seek information about the actions and activities of himself or those around him.

Wilson's statement to the House the following Monday

centred on attacking the press for publishing news. The whole story was a Tory election plot. When he said that no-one had complained to him about profits made from land reclamation I pointed out that on a number of occasions along with one or two other people in the North-East, I had pointed out to him the activities of at least one MP in this field where, arising from the pit closures in the area, vast sums were being made from the clearing of pit heaps and pit spoil, and that those with the powers of planning permission in the area weren't always acting in a correct manner in arriving at decisions.

In an interview on ITN that evening, the Editor of the *Daily Mail*, Mr David English, replied to Wilson, claiming that the story did not seem at first important against the background of the election issues involved which is why they did not publish until after the election. The *Mail* editor went on to say that they would be inhibited by the writs which had been served on the Prime Minister's behalf, but the paper would continue to publish disclosures if they threw further light on the affair. He claimed that there was no substance in the Prime Minister's charge about Mrs Williams being subjected to harassment by the press, at least by the *Mail*, to an undue and intolerable extent. His main point in the interview was confined to dealing with Mr Wilson's definitions of land speculation and land reclamation in which he said that as far as he could see, 'If you dealt in buying and selling land and you were a friend of Mr Wilson's and played golf with him then your activities were land reclamation. If on the other hand you were a normal business man doing the same thing, then according to Mr. Wilson's definition that was land speculation which was of course a socially irresponsible thing.'

No sooner had the dust on the Field speculation settled than the Blyth Constituency Labour Party acted against those who had worked for me in the February election, councillors, leaders of the NUM, and other unions and members of the Women's Sections of the Labour Party received on 14th April, 1974, the same letter as was received by my wife and myself from the secretary-agent of the Labour Party, P. Mortakis. 'The Blyth Constituency Labour Party General Management Committee by a unanimous decision have expelled you from

164

membership. I am obliged to inform you that you have the right to appeal to the National Executive of the Labour Party under Clause 13 Section 3, of the Party Constitution.' Needless to say the communication was ignored by all of us. I lacked confidence in the repeated failures of the top level Labour leaders to examine the Blyth situation, and the actions of Underhill in stifling discussion at national level on the matter together with his repeated assertions that corruption was not the point at issue, all tended to make our folk at Blyth carry on with their own party organisation which was gaining adherents as month followed month, which had been named Independent Labour Party (Blyth Constituency) in March 1974.

The correctness of this attitude was proved in an article written in the *Militant* of April 1974 by Dave Cotterill, a leading member of the Blyth Labour Party Executive Committee and right hand man for the Labour Candidate in the October election. 'It is no accident,' he wrote, 'that enormous publicity was given to Milne's personal publicity campaign. He organised meetings to drum up support for himself before he was kicked out. Every dirty trick was used to undermine Labour support.' He went on to pursue the Underhill line, that Milne should approach the police with evidence if he had any, while knowing full well from the press items he condemned, that not only had ample evidence been given to the police, but to the Home Secretary and the Attorney General.

The scene is now set for the Leeds Crown Court trial which was to conclude with the jailing of Smith and Cunningham, following a summing up by Mr Justice Waller in which he stated, '*To those of us born on Tyneside, both of you have disgraced that local government in the eyes of the community.*' Charged along with Smith and Cunningham were Poulson and Mrs Cunningham. Also on trial at the same time were retired Coal Board officials, William Sales, former chairman of the NCB's Yorkshire Division and Maurice Kelly, the Board's chief Yorkshire engineer. Mr Peter Taylor QC was trenchant in his opening statement, declaring that the three men, Poulson, Smith and Cunningham, had gripped the machinery of local government and public life in a web of corruption for almost seven years, forming as he said a 'formidable triumvirate'.

Of Dan Smith the prosecuting counsel remarked that 'Some said he was the saviour of the North, but for seven years he used power and influence corruptly to secure local contracts for Poulson for substantial reward.' Cunningham he considered the 'most powerful man in County Durham and when ordinary folk regarded him with trust, he was engaged in a web of corruption and enjoying its fruits'.

Mrs Cunningham pleaded not guilty and the case was set aside, although the plea was not accepted on the grounds that it was not in the public interest to spend time and money establishing her part in the affair. Sales pleaded not guilty, and a date was set for trial while Kelly was sentenced to 12 months imprisonment and fined £2,000. The pleas of guilty by Smith and Cunningham meant that the whole story of the corruption network has not been fully revealed, but enough was demonstrated to show the extent of their activities, and for many of us to marvel at the machinations which enabled Smith, Poulson and Cunningham to escape detection for so long, or even more important, why local councillors and leading officials of numerous authorities, along with leading Labour Party figures and North-East Parliamentary and political figures, did not join the demands being made for examination and enquiry into what was going on. The trial certainly demonstrated the charges that we had been making for some time, and at least it became obvious from the Poulson bankruptcy hearings, that in the affairs of Poulson and those associated with him Britain had an issue of Watergate proportions on its hands.

Although the guilty pleas left much undisclosed and unsaid in Leeds Crown Court, enough emerged to show the formidable nature of the corruption network. It demonstrated Smith's ring of contacts from rural councils to Westminster and Whitehall and throughout the political parties. It clearly revealed the immense powers wielded and controlled by Cunningham as boss of the General and Municipal Workers and their representative on the National Executive Committee of the Labour Party, and through that association, his ability to act as Regional Chairman of the Northern Labour Party with its headquarters in Newcastle. What was also shattering in the Leeds Court context, was to reflect that if Poulson had not gone bankrupt, or if the people who tried to save him from bankruptcy had been successful in their efforts, then the whole merry game would still be going on. And anyone seeking action would have been accused of character assassination and smear tactics.

Smith and Cunningham had powerful allies as well as many people standing in the wings, hoping that the whole thing would be forgotten and their role in it relegated to the limbo of things forgotten. Smith had been appointed to the Buchanan Committee in 1963 by the Minister of Transport, Ernest Marples, to examine Britain's major road network. As has been said earlier, the Labour Party National Executive Committee paid him £35,000 to handle its publicity machinery to 'improve Labour's image in the North-East and Scotland.' Appointed by Wilson in 1965 to the chairmanship of the Northern Economic Planning Council with a salary of £7,500, and with Cunningham as a fellow member he was able to tell a *Daily Express* journalist, 'At that time I was riding high in the Labour Party. When I called down to see Mr George Brown, then deputy leader, I wouldn't have been surprised if he had offered me a Cabinet post. In fact I think I deserved one.' From conversations repeated to me by some of his more sycophantic supporters in the Northern Group of Labour MPs, Smith, and they, believed firmly that there should, or would be a knighthood or possibly a seat in the House of Lords. One thing must be said for Dan Smith is that he had an ability quite out of the ordinary. It is a puzzle and a pity that he did not set out to use it in the interests of the working folk, in whose ranks he was brought up, instead of using them to climb to where he did. Smith introduced Cunningham to Poulson in the Dorchester Hotel in London in 1963. Poulson chose his allies shrewdly: he assessed their characters accurately, for they were the two most powerful and influential Labour Party men in the North-East, and it could be claimed in Britain, able and willing, with the tools at their disposal to open the door into dozens of council chambers throughout the country. Poulson had to buy his allies, but if they were in the market place it was easy. Mr Justice Waller, when it came to sentence, said to Smith, 'Corruption is said to spread like a disease. It is a disease which was deliberately spread by you.' He remarked of Cunningham, 'In your case you not only accepted money from Poulson, but on one occasion, at any rate, you demanded it.' It is therefore interesting to recall the remarks attributed to Smith in a *Daily Mirror* interview at the time of the trial. He told Poulson that he would have to buy Cunningham as it was the only way of getting things done in the North-East. Smith said, 'Whatever you do, don't upset Andy. He's a dangerous man when he wants to be. Even Cabinet Ministers are frightened of him.' So these men, powerful and foolhardy, fawned on by so many throughout the North-East, the men who had created an army of paid lieutenants in the town halls of the North-East, went to prison, but the problems they created lingered on.

What were the lessons to be drawn? One would have imagined a lead from the Labour Party on this matter. But there is only silence from its local and national leaders, except the following words of wisdom from regional secretary Evers, who was in charge of the Northern Party machine all through the Cunningham era, and did not believe there would be an internal party inquest: 'The courts and the police are the ones sorting out the problem. After all only two North-East Labour Party members have admitted being corrupt. But there are 12,000 councillors in the region.' Mr Evers went on to say he did not believe that the Labour Party had suffered any long-term damage.

Another factor of the case which was to cause long term concern in the area was the role of the police in the whole matter. Remember that throughout the whole period of his corrupt association with Poulson, Cunningham was also chairman, and a fairly ruthless one, of the Durham Police Authority. In a recorded television interview released after the trial, Cunningham said that no politician should be allowed to hold so many posts in the future, but the most revealing statement came from the Rev David Webster, the Vicar of Great Lumley and a member of the Chester-le-Street District Council, who claimed that he had contacted the Fraud Squad with information involving possible land deals between councillors and developers in September 1970, but no notice was taken of the matter until a *Nationwide* BBC programme in July last year. Councillor Webster attacked the police committee at Durham for ignoring his complaints. He stated that he had only been a member of the Rural Council four months before he realised there was something wrong, and on approaching the Fraud Squad got what he described as the brush off. He was told to follow the matter up through political channels, as it was not a police matter. As in County Durham, both police and political channels were controlled by Cunningham, who in May 1973 was still able to be re-elected to his post as chairman of the police authority.

As was expected, press comment on the implications of the Poulson case was directed to suggest remedies and demand action. The *Observer* had this to say in an outspoken editorial:

> But now that sentence has been passed on T. Dan Smith and Alderman Cunningham for their part in a network of graft and corruption, the Labour Party, too, is free to hold its own searching inquiry into the evidence of malpractice on the overwhelmingly Labour-dominated councils in the North-East. Mr Edward Milne, whose demands for such an investigation were brushed aside earlier and who was re-elected in February as independent Labour MP for Blyth against official Labour opposition, has been vindicated in his lonely stand. We need open political parties as well as open government. (28.4.74.)

The *Guardian* the day previously had dealt with the same issue. The point they made was that corruption and the actions of Smith and Cunningham was not just wrong in itself but stressed that 'It is an affront to the immense honest majority of councillors and others who sustain British local government without reward and without thought of it. North-East England, where Poulson was particularly active, is an area where Labour's expectation of office is almost limitless. So the Labour Party for its own sake should be the first to examine itself. Mr Edward Milne, the Independent Labour MP for Blyth has been demanding a Royal Commission. Mr Wilson demanded one when he was Leader of the Opposition. A Royal Commission may be the wrong sort of inquiry. But an inquiry of some thorough sort is vital.' (27.4.74.)

In an editorial entitled, 'Poulson and Watergate,' which took up the theme which I myself had been arguing that there was a similarity between the British and American situations, *The Times* touched on the need for a Tribunal of Inquiry under the 1921 Act, which in my view was the only way open to Wilson then, alongside the Royal Commission, to demonstrate that he was really keen on getting right down to the root of the problem of corruption in public life. Summed up thus *The Times* said, 'Unfortunately there have already been indications of an attempt at a cover-up of the Poulson case. Large sums of money have been paid to the trustee, some of them allegedly with a view to terminating that part of the bankruptcy proceedings; some of these sums were paid under promise of secrecy. There is also evidence, which *The Times* has published, that police inquiries are not receiving normal cooperation from some public officials. *The Times* has for the past year advocated a Tribunal under the 1921 Act; so far this has been refused.' They concluded, 'Indeed if there is no Tribunal that well could be a matter of regret to the innocent, *but it will almost certainly be a matter of self congratulation for the guilty.*'

Possibly the last word of press comment on the Leeds Crown Court trial should be left to the *Sunday Express*.

In their hour of public disgrace there was just one solace for Mr Dan Smith and Mr Andrew Cunningham. One man came forward to set against the catalogue of their corruption their record of genuine public service—Lord George-Brown. For him, as a public man, there was nothing to gain and much to lose by doing so. But Lord George-Brown has never lacked courage. Yet, if he could do it, why were others so silent? What of the other famous names who have rubbed shoulders for 20 years with Mr Smith and Mr Cunningham at Labour Party conferences and trade union rallies? Where, for example, was Mr Edward Short, once not only a friend but even, according to Mr Smith, a business associate? Truly, when they eventually emerge from prison there is one toast that Mr Smith and Mr Cunningham will never again pledge

170

without grimace. That of absent friends. But that is in the long distant future. In the immediate present it is entirely right that Mr Edward Short, Leader of the House of Commons and Deputy Leader of the Labour Party, should be issuing tomorrow a statement declaring exactly what his connection (if any) was with Dan Smith.

But as always there was no word from the Rt. Hon. Member for Newcastle Central. But plenty more emerged in the next few days for him to answer, and as in the past, no answer was given. Immediately following the Leeds Crown Court trial I was due to attend the USDAW Conference—as a visitor. The General Secretary, Alfred Allen, had written to tell me that as I had opposed an official Labour candidate at the February General Election, I was no longer on the Union's staff and that my superannuation arrangements covering my pension rights as an USDAW employee would be terminated forthwith. On entering Parliament, USDAW, under its Parliamentary representation rules, had stated that on leaving Parliament I would return to a job not less favourable than the one I held on entering the House of Commons in 1960. Neither job nor pension rights were now available to me, wrote the Lord Allen to be. It is a pity he had not taken the chance of a talk with his one-time Union associate Andrew Cunningham, who just a short time after being sentenced at Leeds Crown Court, had been notified by the General and Municipal Workers that he was entitled to a pension of around £60 per week. Once again we see that that the list of casualties was greater for those who opposed corruptive practices than those who operated them. At this time Cunningham and Smith were still members of the Labour Party, while my expulsion and that of those who supported me had already gone ahead at breakneck speed.

On my way to Margate for the USDAW Conference, I took part in a BBC *Money Programme* on the Leeds Crown Court trial findings. With me were Ian Mikardo, Geoffrey Rippon, Paul Smith of the Local Government Reform Organisation and the chairman of the Association of Municipal Corporations. Included in the programme were pre-recorded interviews with Smith and Cunningham. I had heard snatches of the Cunningham interview while preparations were being made for the programme, and he adopted a very light-hearted approach to the enormity of the offences he had committed. Everybody was at it and he had had a few holidays—so what? It was only little Mr Milne, who thought he was a second Jesus Christ, who was really causing all the trouble. I was disappointed at the approach of both Rippon and Mikardo to the events of the previous weeks. They simply ignored the implications of what had been revealed at Leeds Crown Court. This was disturbing because if any progress was to be made within Parliament to get to grips with the whole question of corruption and the standards of conduct in public life, then these two men had a part to play. Mikardo, as a leading member of the Tribune group who had been making noises about Cunningham and others in local government, and in his other role as a member of the Labour Party National Executive, was well aware of what had been going on over the last twenty years in the North-East of England and elsewhere. It was Mikardo who earlier, after my return to Parliament following the February election, barred a move to allow me to attend meetings of the Tribune group, all for perfectly constitutional reasons but I feel it would have been more impressive of Mr Mikardo to be pushing much more strongly than he has done for the publication of a register giving the business interests of Members of Parliament. Rippon, as a Cabinet Minister in a department which covered housing, local government, planning and development, should have had his senses tuned to the story of Poulson and the stranglehold he and others exercised in the control of Government contracts in the period of their power.

In fact Rippon seemed keener, prior to the interview, in seeking the help of the rest of us on the programme in extracting a higher fee from the BBC than was normally paid for such programmes. More in the role of a shop steward than a former Government Minister. One curious sideline emerged at the BBC that night. Many people had wondered why the trial was held in Leeds rather than Newcastle. Was it because it was easier to take Smith and Cunningham to Leeds than it was to take the seven tons of evidence, mainly collected at the Poulson bankruptcy hearing, to Newcastle?

The David Taylor interview with Dan Smith was shattering. He claimed to have paid Ted Short for services rendered to him or his companies, and quoted a figure of around £500. That was on a Friday approaching midnight. It was to take Short until the early hours of the following Tuesday morning before the Civil Servants in his department issued a statement on his behalf, and even then it was couched in the most careful terms. There was no mention as to why or when he accepted the payment stated by him to be only £250. He had agreed to it by writing to Smith affirming that it must be 'a confidential matter between the two of us'. In the interview Smith had underlined the bigness of his crime and the seriousness of the Poulson adventures and their effects on government both local and national by saying, 'I don't think this is a little sordid issue, I think there is a great deal behind it.'

But before Short's statement was made public Wilson moved in two ways, firstly by defending Short, when he later stated that he had been consulted on the statement made by his deputy, and then by announcing in the House of Commons, some twelve hours before the Deputy Leader's explanation of the Smith payment to him was issued, the setting up of a Royal Commission to look into the Standards of Conduct in Public Life.

I was in Margate for the USDAW Conference and not in the House to hear the announcement, or to question the Prime Minister on it. It is always difficult to assess reasons for Wilsonian actions. Did the Leeds trial force him at last into doing something tangible on the corruption issue? Or was it the exposure of the BBC of the payment received by Short from Smith? It is anybody's guess as to the reasons, but the suggestion that the timing of the Royal Commission announcement was to take the heat out of the Short issue does not appear wide of the mark to me. Nevertheless it was pleasing in a way to find that at least part of my long campaign to get successive Governments to move on this matter had at last been answered, and to read the *Newcastle Journal* banner headline of Tuesday 30th April, 'Milne Gets His Way. Wilson Sets up Royal Commission.'

Short's promised statement on the payment made to him

by Smith was still awaited. I was interviewed on ITN's *First Report* in Dover on the Monday, and in reply to a question as to whether I was in agreement with the clamour for Short's resignation, which was coming from some quarters, I replied that I was not at this stage, but that nothing less than a statement in the House of Commons subjected to Parliamentary questioning would satisfy me. After all Short was Leader of the House. He was to be the Chairman of the Committee set up to deal with the disclosure of Members' interests, so he had a special responsibility to the House and the Nation to give a clear and unequivocal answer to the doubts his conduct had raised.

Before leaving the USDAW Conference to return to the House of Commons, I was to hear the Union's President, Mr J. Hughes, declare that discussion on my removal from the Union's Parliamentary panel and expulsion from the Labour Party could not be discussed at the ADM because the events had taken place in 1974, and only 1973 matters could be raised by delegates. So I was prevented from attending the Conference by decisions that still had to be discussed and decided, but those who kept me outside the USDAW Conference Hall also refused to allow others to raise the matter. It will be remembered that it was Jimmy Hughes along with Alf Allen who interviewed Blyth Party officials at the 1973 Labour Party Conference but refused to meet the delegate to that Conference elected by the members of the Blyth Labour Party. Now that Alf Allen has landed in the House of Lords, maybe we should look in the next Honours list to see if any further favours have been bestowed. $74\frac{1}{4}$ hours after the BBC accusation by Smith, at 1.15 a.m. on Tuesday 30th April, Short's statement was issued from the Privy Council Office accompanied by an apology for its lateness due to his being very heavily engaged on public duties and the need to verify certain facts and correspondence. It did not mention the fact that he had addressed a public meeting on the Monday, and that possibly as a believer in open government he could have issued his statement then. He praised Smith for his work, stated that he had been offered £500, but had accepted £250 for services rendered, and considered the sum a reimbursement for a substantial amount of expenses, such as entertaining, which he (Short) had incurred on Dan Smith's behalf. He denied ever having seen Poulson, to the best of his knowledge.

Short's statement did not satisfy me. Press comment was adverse and they retaliated against Wilson's attacks on them. It was pointed out that the press, radio and television had not invented Poulson or convicted Smith and Cunningham. Nor, as one paper remarked, did the press invite Short to burn midnight oil preparing an explanation of a transaction carried out over eleven years ago. Another editorial pointed out that it was not the press who hounded and disowned Mr Edward Milne, now Independent Labour MP for Blyth, for daring to demand the fullest inquiry into the North-East corruption scandals.

Short's statement certainly made him look naive even if it did not make him look venal. And a subsequent statement from Short which had a touch of the Transport House technique about it, accused the BBC of paying T. Dan Smith £250 to 'assassinate the character of Mr Short'. Short has failed to reply to a letter from Sir Charles Curran on behalf of the BBC challenging Short to substantiate charges that the BBC urged Smith to implicate other political figures. 'I have the right to expect, I believe, that you produce your evidence or withdraw the charge,' Curran wrote. Short was given the opportunity of appearing on the BBC's *World At One* to discuss his criticisms of the Corporation's reporting of his association with Smith, but refused. Curran made the point that he was entirely satisfied that his staff ascertained the truth of what they said in the programme which rested on the exchange of letters between Short and T. Dan Smith.

I returned home to my constituency to attend a public meeting at Cramlington New Town, and issued a five point challenge to Short. Give details of his friendship and association with Smith both as a former Newcastle City Councillor and as a Member of Parliament for the City. Say when he told Wilson, or any other Labour Leader about his connection with Smith. Did Short relinquish all contacts with Smith on becoming Government Chief Whip in 1964? If he did to whom did he pass them on? The last point I made was to demand a meeting with Short to discuss the whole question of alleged corruption arising from the Leeds disclosures. There was of course no response from Short. His commitments in other directions carried more importance. I finished by stating my position that as things stood, I would not expect Short to resign, but if he did not meet Parliament on the issue with a statement subjected to Parliamentary questioning, then he (Short) would seriously have to consider whether he could justifiably remain in Parliament or indeed in public life.

At the end of that hectic week, two further matters emerged to disturb Short and the Government. Former Attorney General and President of the Board of Trade in the first post-war Labour Government, Sir Hartley, now Lord, Shaw-cross entered the corruption controversy by declaring that he had incontrovertible evidence of corruption by a figure high in public life. He wrote to *The Times* and stated that at the time he was advised to remain silent. He commented 'and so the evil-doers continue to flourish'. He cited two cases which had caused him concern some twenty years ago. Shawcross said, 'Knowledge, which came to me when I was President of the Board of Trade, caused me a good deal of anxiety in regard to a person occupying a far more exalted position than the comparatively small fry concerned in recent cases. . . . In the absence of a power of interrogation I could do nothing. . . . Shortly afterwards at the Bar, I was consulted about a matter in which there was incontrovertible evidence of corruption involving large sums on the part of an individual highly placed in public life and esteem. When I advised that there must be immediate disclosure to the police my instructions were withdrawn. And the legal privilege of secrecy prevented my disclosing the matter personally, for although I had myself thought that my duty as a Privy Councillor might override the legal privileges concerned, the authorities I consulted at the time had no doubt that I must remain silent.' This *Times* letter of a former Attorney-General made me ponder. If he could make so little progress, then my efforts as a back-bencher were not too bad after all. And to whom was he referring in making the point that the evil-doers continue to flourish?

The second matter of concern went a long way into Short

territory. The declaration of interests by Members of Parliament, delayed and hindered by those in authority in both Governments for far too long, had become an issue. The Leader of the House was due to chair a meeting of the Committee of Privileges to investigate a claim by the MP for Bassetlaw, Mr Joe Ashton, that there were six Labour MPs whose services in the House of Commons were for hire by outside organisations. Ashton had written a courageous article in, of all places, *Labour Weekly*, the Transport House official paper of the Labour Movement. In it he stated that he knew the names and the details, but would not publicly disclose them. I wonder why he could not have given them to Reg Underhill who later in the month, along with Ron Evers at the Northern Regional Conference of the Labour Party was to strongly resist a motion demanding an inquiry into the running of the Labour Party in the North East. But the matter was dropped by Ashton as by many others around this time. The fate of Eddie Milne at Blyth was sufficient warning to many.

But Ted Short did not lie down. He bounced up at the week-end in an interview with the *Daily Telegraph*. He declared that he might have been indiscreet but 'I am not going to be hounded out of public life by a foul and disgusting campaign'. Ted Short isn't too particular about people being hounded from public life, as long as it is not Ted Short. Then he jointly attacked Dan Smith and myself. His attack on me rested on linking money paid to assist in the libel writ served on me by Ernest Marples, one time Minister of Transport in a Conservative Government, and the money he had recently collected to defend Smith in the Wandsworth corruption trial of 1971. In fact Short had denied that he helped Dan Smith to raise the Wandsworth money, and secured an apology from the Liberal Party for a statement made by Peter Hain on the subject. Writing to me on the 10th October, 1973, Short said, 'Thank you for your letter, which I read about in the press before I received it. I have probably suffered as much as anyone from innuendo in this matter, very largely because I tried to help Dan Smith pay for his defence at his last trial, in the same way as a few years ago when you had defamation damages awarded against you, I raised both the whole of the damages and your costs for you. It is a sad day when we are to be black-guarded for trying to help friends.'

It is not surprising that a little time later *Blackwood's Magazine* (July 1974) was to produce an item entitled 'The Smell of Corruption' which said:

The smell of corruption is unmistakable, pervasive but difficult to trace to its source. With other crimes there is an injured party who will complain, but neither the giver nor the receiver of a bribe is likely to do so, and the injured party is the general public which is either ignorant of what is going on or composed largely of friends and political sympathisers of the corrupt. This is particularly so in an area such as North-East England which has for a long time enjoyed one-party Labour rule. *For some years well-informed people and journals have alleged corruption in the North-East. But when Mr Milne spoke out he was hounded from the party and Mr Edward Short in particular pursued him with relentless animosity.*

With the pressure on Short, the Ashton disclosures and the back-wash from the party throughout the country, Underhill and the Transport House people around him were getting restive. I was told of numerous approaches to the party chiefs and to the Labour parliamentary leaders, asking why they had not acted on the Smith, Cunningham cantrips a long time ago. It was also not without the knowledge of Transport House that the tide was running strongly against them in the North-East, despite their protestations to the contrary, and the demands for an inquiry could not much longer be kept in check. Hayward and Underhill were of course also conscious that the Northern Regional Labour Party Conference was due to take place in the Guildhall of Newcastle on Saturday 18th May against the background of the stormiest buffeting the Party had ever received in a spell of just over four weeks, beginning with Millhench and Field at the beginning of April. Part of the year under review at this conference was the period covered by the chairmanship of Alderman Andrew Cunningham. The 1973 Report presented to the previous conference carried the signatures of Andy C. Cunningham as chairman, and Ron Evers as secretary. Underneath the signatures appeared the following.

> 'True eloquence consists of saying all
> that is necessary, and nothing more.'

It is only necessary to add that one of the direction posts facing the delegates on their way to the Guildhall, says quite simply 'Watergate.'

The pressure showed and resulted in a news release containing a statement issued by Mr Reg Underhill, National Agent of the Labour Party, on Monday 6th May, 1974. It was put out, not by the National Executive, not by Percy Clark, the Director of Information, nor by Hayward, but by Underhill. Somebody's slip was showing. It was the reaction to an article which I had written in the *Daily Express* that day, headed 'How the Party tried to gag me,' in which I outlined the efforts of people from Underhill downwards or upwards, to prevent any examination of the matters which were now clearly revealed in the Leeds trial reports and the clash between Dan Smith and Short on the cash payments made in 1963. Underhill's statement was a shortened version of the February Election advertisement. Milne had fallen foul of the party in Blyth, had never mentioned Poulson and had used the press and other media for constant attacks on the Blyth Labour Party officers and committees. He finished his statement by declaring, 'These [Milne's] assertions have no foundation whatever and such inaccuracies and untruths should not be repeated.' Again the point has to be made: supposing Eddie Milne had never existed, should not Underhill and others have been doing something about the state of affairs in the Northern Region and throughout the country.

But alas for the Underhills of this world, the facts kept coming to the surface. Four days before the regional conference, Geoffrey Rhodes, the Labour Member for Newcastle East and formerly Parliamentary Private Secretary to Dick Crossman at the Ministry of Housing and Local Government in the 1964–66 Labour Government, issued a statement in his constituency, claiming that in 1965 he was told by Dick Crossman to keep out of the situation in the North, because a dossier was being prepared which would arrive in the hands of the properly authorised body. He had reported to the Minister an invitation that was extended to him to see developments in Wandsworth, from a person involved in the South Battersea Labour Party when he had fought the seat in 1959. On accepting the invitation Rhodes was collected by car, and after the visit to the flats, he was taken to Carlton Towers Hotel and introduced to his host, Mr Dan Smith. Geoffrey Rhodes reported to his Minister, Dick Crossman, 'that something was rotten in the state of Denmark and the capital of it was located on the Tyne'. This was confirmed when a spokesman for the Department of the Environment said that the Chief Inspector of Audits had sent 'certain information relating to the Poulson affair' to the Director of Public Prosecutions as long ago as 1970. The magazine *Accountancy Age* of 24th May, 1974, reported that evidence had come forward which could corroborate the assertions of Geoffrey Rhodes. They went further than the Department of the Environment spokesman in stating that a report detailing evidence and suspicions of Poulson's and Dan Smith's corrupt dealings was given to the Director of Public Prosecutions by 1968. It had been prepared by the service responsible for auditing the accounts of those local authorities which had connections with Poulson and Smith. *Accountancy Age* claimed that Dick Crossman as Minister of Housing and Local Government from 1964–1966, was the titular head of the district audit service, and would have seen any report which was passed on to the DPP. The report had been compiled over a number of years and even if Crossman had left the Department he should have known of its existence.

As a branch of the Department of the Environment, the district audit service is regarded as one of the more anonymous public bodies. It is interesting to note, as reported by *Accountancy Age*, that although under the 1972 Local Government Act a greater number of the accounts of local authorities are open to external audit, the overwhelming majority remain in the hands of district auditors. Even at the distance of a year, the issue of *Accountancy Age* still makes fascinating reading, but the relevant officials at the Home Office, the Royal Courts of Justice and the Department of the Environment did not appear to think so, or at least did not appear to take much notice. It should have been compulsory reading for Transport House officials. The 1972 Act included new district auditing legislation for the first time in 39 years. As the magazine stated, District Auditors had the opportunity and responsibility to recognise the corruption that was instituted under the auspices of Poulson. It was an opportunity they did not miss and, as was stated at the time, it was the demands of creditors not the bribes and scandals, which provoked a full scale investigation. The auditors must have alerted the creditors. If there had been no bankruptcy, the whole merry game could still be going on, at the expense of the interests of the great mass of British people.

Yet *Accountancy Age* claimed that two years before, the creditors had demanded a full scale examination, and district auditors had summed up the situation as follows: certain public relations companies, pressing the interests of building contractors doing work on an extensive scale for local authorities, had a number of local authority members in their pay; that a very large firm of architects, linked in business with hospital boards and local authorities, had members in its pay. It was also likely that there was contact between the firm and the public relations companies. The conclusions were devastating, but no-one was prepared to take much notice. Those in control at Westminster and Whitehall chose to talk of 'smear campaigns' and 'character assassination', rather than have a close look at the substantial evidence provided by experts in the chosen field.

Certainly new legislation must arise from the present situation, for apart from the suspicion of a cover-up in certain quarters, the powers of the district auditors are to a large extent limited, and *Accountancy Age*'s paragraph graphically illustrates the point. 'The main drawback to efforts to expose corruption where it is suspected, or indicated, is that the district auditor is powerless unless corruption involves a direct loss to the local authority. If no loss is involved, the district auditor's only recourse is to pass his evidence to the local police or the Director of Public Prosecutions. The Poulson case has proved, that either this is an inadequate procedure, or that the police are themselves subject to heavy restrictions.' What solution will emerge to the problems posed is anybody's guess. But what hope would a district auditor have of getting complaints dealt with in the period of the Cunningham rule of police and local authority in the Durham area. If the freedom to bribe and influence, which Poulson, Smith and others enjoyed, is to be prevented in future, then steps must be taken to extend the powers of detection. Perhaps some of our top police officers in Scotland Yard and elsewhere could spare a little of the time they devote so readily to delivering lectures on the decadence of modern youth, and turn their attentions to the activities of the middle-aged and elderly in the realms of local government and associated fields, so that we could do something to improve the standards of public life throughout the United Kingdom.

The finding of the Redcliffe-Maud Committee on Local Government Rules of Conduct set up by Heath when he was Prime Minister may provide some of the answers. I have not had the opportunity to study closely the evidence that was given to the committee by the Chief Inspector of Audit and others in that field, but as the only back-bench MP who gave evidence, I am interested in what flows from the recommendations made. They appeared to be a bit timid when they said that the power to inspect financial records, including other records than bank accounts, is not to be contemplated lightly, but the importance of dealing firmly with suspected corruption justifies in my view the provision of such power, and the committee went on to recommend that power to proceed on these lines should be enacted at the earliest possible legislative opportunity. The Committee cautioned that it would represent a new measure of intrusion upon the liberty of the individual, but I feel that the risk is worth taking. Too often in the past, the liberty of the individual has protected the unscrupulous and the corrupt. Perhaps some of us will have the opportunity some time in the future, to ask what happened to the reports on corruption which were sent to the Director of Public Prosecutions in 1968 by the district audit service concerning the local authorities which had connections with Poulson and Smith. If so, it should make interesting reading.

Chapter Ten

The Regional Labour Party Conference was approaching. Thirk and Maldon's Constituency Labour Party, headed by Joan Maynard, a member of the Party's National Executive, had tabled a motion and received early support from her own Agricultural Workers' Union, the Transport and General Workers' Union and the Boilermakers of which John Chalmers, who had chaired the Blyth Inquiry and served on the Party's National and Regional Executives, was the General Secretary. Dan McGarvey, President of the Boilermakers, with Headquarters in Newcastle, made a blistering attack on Labour Party secrecy in a circular sent to union members. He wrote, 'The time has now surely arrived to stop the double talk by those within the Labour Party in the North-East and at national level. To those of us who live in the North-East, the position has reached farcical proportions—even the birds in the trees are talking about it. The decision to expel Eddie Milne from the Labour Party was one of the most stupid decisions that I can remember. The belief in the North-East is that this all happened because he was an "honest man", and I am inclined to agree with this. The most serious part of this whole issue is the question which is generally being asked: Is there a mafia in the North-East Labour Party? What really puzzles me on this whole issue is Harold Wilson. Who is advising him on the reactions and back lash on decent members and supporters of the Labour Party in the area?' McGarvey was strongly backed by David Shenton, Northern Region secretary of the T & GWU, who said that his Union's Executive wanted a full inquiry into Mr Milne's expulsion and the party's activities. Shenton said, 'The way he was expelled, and a lot else that has happened has been shabby, and the facts should be fully established. The Labour Party has a job to do.'

Tribune weighed in with loud demands by stating that too many echoes of the past remain in Labour Party circles. In the light of the recent revelations, they claimed that the warnings of Milne over the last two years had now become of first importance to the party. They pointed out to their readers that those who had studied my case will understand that from the very beginning it was the political aspect of the situation which caused me most concern. Indeed they said, I knew what damage it could do to the Labour Party should it be allowed to go unchecked. No one could now doubt how right I was. Jack Jones backed up his regional Transport Worker colleagues by adding his weight to the demand for an inquiry. Chalmers, McGarvey's colleague and secretary of the Boilermakers, was now making strong demands, resulting from the pressure being put on him, to make the Blyth Inquiry findings public. Underhill was strongly resisting these moves and building up, or he was hoping to build up, opposition to the growing demands for an inquiry.

Watching the moves and the manoeuvres from outside was a fascinating business. Underhill, who had spent most of the previous year attacking as lies my complaints that my expulsion from the party hinged on the attitude I had adopted to the Poulson case, and the connection of leading Labour figures with the corruption and conspiracy trials, was now engaged in efforts to defeat the demand for an inquiry from the Labour Party into, not my allegations, but the concrete facts of the situation emerging from the imprisonment of Smith and Cunningham. As far as one could make out, Short, Wilson and other Labour leaders were engaged in a similar exercise in the House of Commons. Speaking in my Blyth Constituency two weeks before the Regional Conference, I made the point that while an inquiry was still required, officials of the Labour Party at Transport House, the members of the National Executive and Parliamentary leaders, had all forfeited any right they might claim to have to conduct such an inquiry. 'They have shown they don't care about, and aren't up to the job.' What we need is a team of leading people from the movement, headed by someone like Gerald Gardiner, Lord Chancellor in the Wilson Government, or Vic Feather. Then maybe we'd get to the bottom of this mess.

So on the morning of 18th May, along the Newcastle quayside, by the Watergate sign, in the Guildhall, the Northern Regional Conference of the Labour Party opened. As one newspaper report put it, it was a kind of Hamlet without the Prince. It was the first Regional Conference of the Party, in any part of Britain, where I had been active for over thirty years, that I had been prevented from attending (this time even as a visitor). But the newspaper reports filled the gaps for me. Underhill made an impassioned speech, described to me later by a delegate who heard it, as an hysterical outburst. Underhill apparently got near to admitting that there was no basis in the report of the Blyth Inquiry, held just before the February General Election, for my expulsion. The report at this time had of course not been issued. Apart from Underhill, the Conference appeared to have produced a flood of recriminations, and uproar was reported as some of the 270 delegates shouted interruptions at speakers and tried to get an opportunity of speaking on the motion demanding an inquiry. Collier, the Blyth Party delegate, said that at Blyth they had been fighting a lone battle, not against corruption, it never entered into it, but against Edward Milne, the man who wanted to be a local dictator. Another delegate from Blyth, Murray of the Colliery Mechanics, who just prior to Conference had been facing problems in his own organisation, declared that no other politician had found easier access to the Conservative press than Mr Milne during the past eighteen months. He pointed out that I had gained this access by pulling the Labour Party to bits. One report claimed that Underhill's speech lasted for '20 blistering minutes and never once mentioned Smith or Cunningham'. Evidently to his way of thinking, the problems of the Labour Party stemmed from the activities of Milne and no-one else. But Underhill's pyrotechnics were of no avail. Following a savaging of his viewpoint and argument by no less a person than Bill Ricklington, who had succeeded Andy Cunningham as the regional secretary of the General and Municipal Workers' Union, who dismissed Underhill's argument that the strict operation of the Labour Party rules was sufficient to prevent corruption in local councils, and said 'Let us be honest with ourselves and say that the machinery of our party is wrong.' He continued, 'Too often the man who exercises power in the local authority is the man who exercises power as chairman of the local Labour Party. He also happens to be the chairman of the Labour group.' Ricklington criticised the Northern group of Labour MPs for their lack of action over Dan Smith and Cunningham. 'Did they ever question how these individuals had direct access to Cabinet Ministers, and did they ever ask what went on between the ministers and these two ?' he asked.

There was a massive vote in favour of the inquiry demand: 306,000 against 166,000. Immediately after the conference I wrote to the Attorney General, Sam Silkin, and asked him to obtain a transcript of the conference proceedings with a view to securing information about the Poulson affair. The reason for this arose from a speech, opposing the need for an inquiry, by the Treasurer of the Regional Party, Councillor Colin Gray of Newcastle, who argued that the Regional Executive had opposed Dan Smith's appointment by George Brown, as chairman of the Northern Economic Planning Council, and that the party chiefs in the North-East had at different times tried to stop the award of party public relations contracts to the Dan Smith companies. I pointed out to Silkin that we should have heard more of this before, and asked what evidence existed of the reasons for the action taken against Smith. In my letter, the suggestion was made to the Attorney General, that in view of the conference decisions and the speeches, a stage had been reached where we should go beyond the Royal Commission and have a Tribunal of Inquiry with the force of law behind it. A jarring note from the meeting was reported to me later. Arthur Hamilton, an USDAW delegate to the conference and its representative on the Regional Executive, said he had come to the rostrum because his brother Tom, also an USDAW official, now deceased, had introduced me to the Blyth Constituency in 1960. He said, 'And it's by way of apology for that, for Tom, that I come to this rostrum to-day.' Some months later I had to take legal action against Arthur Hamilton for character assassination, because he claimed that I had been a party to illegally and corruptly claiming election expenses. The various hints and remarks that were being spread privately by him, were to the effect that in the 1960 by-election, when I was first elected, I had over-claimed my expenses. To this scurrilous lie, I can only say this. First of all, I had neither the occasion or the thought to get any financial advantage from expenses that were well below the legal allowable limit and certainly offered no scope for personal extravagance—in fact we were all out-of-pocket, but I had no need as I was a sponsored candidate. Moneys went to the agent and the constituency organization, not to the candidate. Secondly, no suggestion of any financial irregularity had ever been made about me, and the motive of my enemies for trying to smear me with that particular type of accusation, is clear enough, but hardly credible after fourteen years, and then never made in public, where some evidence would be required. Arthur Hamilton is a brother of Willie Hamilton, MP for West Fife. I did get satisfaction however in October 1975, when my legal action against Willie Hamilton culminated in a settlement for damages of one thousand five hundred pounds to me from Willie Hamilton and a similar sum from the *Northern Echo*, together with a full apology and retraction of the allegations for any distress and embarrassment they caused. Willie Hamilton has since been very silent where I am concerned.

Then Ron Hayward, the Party's General Secretary, the democrat who argues that conference decisions are sacrosanct, the keeper of the party conscience, immediately declared that a vote at a Regional Conference, even about its own area, could not be regarded as an instruction to the National Executive. Time was to prove him right. The National Executive, which moved so quickly at Blyth, decided to do nothing about the problems created by the imprisonment of two of the North's leading figures. They did play around with the pretence of a national inquiry, including the North-East, and some time later a deputation from the National Executive Committee, which included *Tribune* leading light Ian Mikardo, came for two days, saw, and returned to London to report that they were satisfied with what they saw. Of such stuff are Transport House inquiries made. It was left to Denis Healey to mop up the pieces. In June he travelled north to address the Durham

Labour Women's Gala and stoutly declared that an inquiry into the North-East Labour Party was essential. He and Hayward must get together sometime. It is a pity that Healey did not do more to persuade his colleagues on the National Executive to follow his lead. Or was this another example by the Labour leadership of saying what suited the area they were visiting, and then returning to London and covering up the whole matter?

But suspected irregularities continued to erupt in the North-East. In early June an investigation was being made in County Durham into the sale of houses by a Birtley builder to two officers in the Durham Police. The houses were luxury split-level bungalows in Chester-le-Street. Along with the house which lay between, they occupied a site in Newcastle Road. Where the similarity ended was that the houses occupied by the police officers cost some £4,000 less than the third one sold for £9,121. The documents in connection with the sale of the houses, and other matters concerning planning and development projects in County Durham, had been passed on to me one Monday at Newcastle Airport on my way to London, and I arranged for the Attorney General's staff to collect them from me in my desk room at the House of Commons. There were a number of unsatisfactory features about the whole case. A television interviewer visiting the builder after the matter had been reported in the press was subjected to considerable police harassment despite the fact that matters affecting a police force should only be dealt with by members of an outside police squad. The man leading the investigations into the sale of the houses to the police was Detective Superintendent Terence Light, of the West Midlands Police stationed at Birmingham, who was brought in at the request of Durham Deputy Chief Constable Mr John Hallett.

I was telephoned by Detective Superintendent Light one Sunday at home and asked if I would meet him, and I arranged to see him in the House of Commons the following week. On his arrival in the House we went for coffee on the Terrace, and he immediately asked if I was aware that I had been handling stolen property, the documents mentioned in the foregoing paragraph. I told him that anybody who received information in the way I did must consider the possibility of this having happened, but in view of the fact that everyone from the Prime Minister downwards was counselling all of us to forward to the authorities any information that came to hand on the subject of likely corruption, I had done just that. I also said that I was prepared to sign a statement if they wanted one. This I subsequently did in a Committee Room of the House. I got the impression from the whole police approach, that they were more concerned about proving that the documents had been stolen, than they were in examining the evidence they contained. And as will be shown later, this feeling prevailed throughout my connection with the case. I had already forwarded a request for a meeting with the Attorney General, which was to be my first meeting since Sam Silkin was appointed by Wilson to the post. On the day I went to the Royal Courts of Justice, the headquarters of the Crown's Law Officers, I learned that two Scotland Yard detectives had flown to Malta, as new evidence had appeared in connection with the planned payment of a £5,000 bribe for a hospital contract. As had already been revealed, Maudling and Roberts, the Labour MP for Normanton, had strongly recommended Poulson for the Malta job. The contract was for the over £1,500,000 Gozo Island hospital. This project, financed by the Department for Overseas Development in the period during which Reg Prentice was Minister, was a profitable venture for Poulson yielding it is believed, close on £200,000 (Two hundred thousand pounds). Whilst attending a seminar on the international aspects of corruption at Sussex University in connection with the Institute of Development Studies in March last year (1975), I was told by a member of the Malta Attorney's staff that further developments were likely in the case, arising from the activities of Caruana (Dr I believe) who was Malta's Minister of Works when the Nationalist Party held power in Malta.

The meeting with Silkin was a dull affair. I had the feeling he either wasn't interested, or did not intend doing anything about the points I raised. We went again over most of the matters I had previously discussed with Sir Peter Rawlinson when in Office, and I requested information about the activities of McCullough, the builder connected with the police house sale, and expressed the concern felt in Blyth and elsewhere that matters were dragging on far too long in this case. I also pointed out to him that all the evidence of corruption I had received in the course of the years had been handed to his predecessor, which was in accordance with my handling of Parliamentary matters. All my cases went in the first instance to the Minister responsible for dealing with them. Only one new point was raised. I passed on to Silkin a letter received by me after the details of the sale of police houses had been made known. This was an anonymous letter. Normally I do not deal with this type of correspondence, as anonymous letters are always suspect, but matters were at such a pitch in the North-East that everything went. The letter was dated 14th June, 1974.

Dear Sir,

Perhaps the good work you have initiated in causing the investigation as set out on the attached press cutting may have good results, but should not the question of the purchase and resale by Alderman Cunningham to the Durham Police Authority of the house situated next to his and into which the Deputy Chief Constable Mr Hallett then moved. What were the terms of purchase and what was the inducement for this officer to move?

Yours faithfully,
An admirer of your stand.

Before leaving, I had a talk with the Legal Secretary to the Attorney General and the following joint statement about our visit was released to the press.

PRESS STATEMENT

The Attorney General had a meeting this morning with Mr Edward Milne MP about affairs in the North-East. The meeting was a continuation of a series of meetings which began under the previous administration. They discussed the question of allegations about police houses in the North-East and matters arising out of the annual meeting of the Northern Region of the Labour Party. It was agreed that they would meet again whenever there were other matters to discuss.

It was only some time after McCullough had started his prison term that the corruption case involving the two police officers Bains and Young came to court, and the case only ended in May 1976. The result has created much local comment. Judge Jones, after the jury had returned their verdict, sentenced McCullough to three years imprisonment, but this would hardly affect him as he was already serving a longer term than that. The two policemen were however completely cleared! Many people are still trying to work out how a man can be guilty of corruption if no-one is guilty of being corrupted, but then the North-East has a logic all its own.

Chapter Eleven

But there were to be no further meetings with the Attorney General, Sam Silkin. The Summer Recess was fast approaching and there was to be no return to parliament for me after the General Election of October. There was no evidence of anything tangible being done by the Attorney General following my visit to him. The Labour leadership was certainly not inclined to take a major part in clearing up the issues I had raised, because the corruption disclosures lay too close to leading figures within their own ranks. As I have shown earlier, my attitude to the Attorney General's role led to a clash with Silkin about a speech he had made at Oxford on the Poulson case. But, as I was to discover in a number of different ways, the pressures from police and parliament were increasing and the 'relentless animosity' which Short had shown towards me, was surfacing in many ways. Despite numerous press reports and television and radio appearances on the subject of corrupt activities, no approach had ever been made to me by the police for evidence. I, of course, had tackled the matters which came to my notice, by passing the information to the Cabinet Minister responsible for dealing with them, mainly the Attorney General and the Home Secretary. On occasions I had approached Wilson and Short directly, as Leader and Deputy Leader of the Labour Party. I had also approached Callaghan in his term of office as chairman of the Labour Party. Most of the members of the Party's National Executive had discussed the position in the North-East with me in one way or another, and my wife had written to both Frank Allaun and John Chalmers or Alf Allen of USDAW giving some of the background details to what was going on in Labour Party circles in Blyth and throughout the Northern Region. There was no excuse for anyone in authority in any of these quarters not to be aware that investigation was needed.

The first police approach to me for information came after the 1974 February General Election from Detective Superintendent Connor, later to become head of the Durham Fraud Squad. He 'phoned me after the result was declared and said he would appreciate a talk. This I arranged following my return from a few days break with my wife in Allendale. One point in the conversation stuck with me. When Connor asked me where we should meet, I suggested Blyth Police Station, and he said, 'Preferably not Blyth, let's make it Seaton Delaval Police Station.' At the meeting we discussed in detail the various activities of the builder, McCullough, and his housebuilding contracts for a number of leading local authority figures.

But Ted Short could not keep out of the news. On Tuesday, 4th June, he turned up with Mrs Short in St Andrew's Parish Rooms in Penrith to purchase for the sum of £15,000 Crag Close, Glenridding in the Lake District. There was nothing wrong in this, but what raised a number of eyebrows was that during an acute housing shortage, he had bought this house, that stood next door to Bank House, Glenridding, already occupied by the Shorts as a second home, which he had purchased some nine years previously in order to knock it down. The former Blyth Headmaster, in his usual insensitive way, declared to the press men who approached him on the matter, 'I don't want the cottage.' He never intended to keep it, he said, for all he wanted was part of the land on which the house stood, to ensure the privacy of the other house. Not for the first time, Labour's deputy leader ran into a storm of criticism from a number of quarters. The problem of house improvement grants and the controversy created by them was still in the public mind. The occupancy of second homes in Lakeland at the expense of local people looking for accommodation, was also a sore point, because the Shorts had their home in Newcastle. The local council viewpoint was expressed in forthright terms on the 8th June, 1974 in the *Penrith Herald*, 'Mr Short is rubbing in the mud the faces of those working to ease this second house problem. It is an arrogant contempt for public concern about these homes being used for holidays and week-ends. The attitude taken by Labour people locally was that the action of a Socialist leader was depriving the community of a family house and that it must cast doubts on the integrity of the MP for Newcastle Central who claims so much to be working for a system of equality in the country and yet privately seeking the things that he scorns and condemns in others.'

Short countered by claiming that he had never intended to keep the cottage, and once he had the privacy he sought, he would be selling it with the rest of the garden as soon as possible. He went on to say, "After an independent valuation has been made of the part of the land I wish to retain, I am quite prepared to sell the rest, and the cottage, to the county council or anyone else at a price that will show me no profit on the original price I paid." The house, built of Lakeland stone with ground floor living room, sitting room, breakfast-room, kitchen, bathroom and storeroom. The first floor has three bedrooms, a toilet and a storeroom and outside are what the description gives as some rather dilapidated buildings.' But it did not end there, and the purchase figured in the October General Election discussions on a fairly wide scale. Murray Taylor, the Labour Candidate for Westmorland, obviously reacting to the political damage done to the Labour Party by Short's action and the storms arising from it, said in his election address, 'The buying up of available property for second homes must be stopped.' In the case of Short, it was at least the third home, the fourth if a London flat is included. Interviewed by the *Evening Chronicle*, Murray Taylor expanded on his viewpoint.

'I am very sorry, but I feel that Mr Short should not have a holiday home anywhere. That is, not until each family in Britain has one home. We cannot go on allowing people to have two or even three, as is the case with the Conservative candidate here in Westmorland. We have got a large waiting list in the constituency of people wanting mortgages and council property. We have got to cater for local people. I am very sorry for Mr Short, but if we are going to bring in rules to ban second homes in the Lake District, then it applies to Mr Short as much as anyone else.'

When interviewed Short responded in typical fashion. 'I don't want to make any comment. It's just the sort of rubbish that gets kicked about in elections.' It was a remark that must have endeared him to his Newcastle Central voters, struggling to bring up families in the twilight, slum and overcrowded areas of his constituency, an area he represented on the Newcastle City Council along with Dan Smith, at the time that *Crudens* was being peddled by Smith as having the answer to the dreams of the City's homeless thousands.

It was now obvious, as event came crowding in on event, that Short was to keep on playing an important part in my future, or lack of it, as Member of Parliament for the Blyth Constituency. Heartened by my success in securing the setting up of a Royal Commission, I now decided in the light of subsequent events to test out the Government's, and particularly the Prime Minister's, attitude to a Tribunal of Inquiry to look into some selected sections of the Poulson case. I went ahead and tabled a question for Tuesday, 25th June, 1974. It appeared on the House of Commons Order Paper thus:

Mr Edward Milne (Blyth). To ask the Prime Minister, if he will set up a tribunal of inquiry to examine the cases of corruption arising from the Poulson trial and associated matters.

The fates conspired that day for Wilson to be in Brussels and his questions to be answered by no less a person than the Lord President of the Council, The Rt. Hon. Mr Edward Short. Tersely he replied, 'No, Sir. Specific allegations of corruption are a matter for the police.' In the supplementary questioning which ensued, Willie Hamilton stepped into the fray by asking Short, that if there were to be inquiries into this matter, would they include inquiries into what Hamilton told the House were 'the illegal or corrupt claiming of election expenses in by-elections in the North-East and make it retrospective.' This was a veiled allusion by Hamilton to the stories that had been circulated recently by his brother Arthur in the North-East, to which I have already alluded. Willie Hamilton made the mistake of raising the matter outside the House, in what for all the world had the appearance of a stage-managed affair. When he emerged from the Chamber a number of press men were waiting for him. This was unusual in the context of the questioning, for it was a supplementary question he had raised on the last item dealt with before the end of questions, and the press could have had no inkling of what was to emerge, unless told in advance. The Member for West Fife told the waiting press men, as reported in the *Northern Echo* of 26th June, 'Ask Mr Milne what he thinks I and my family know about his activities in Blyth. The sooner he gets out of his shining armour the better for his own good. He knows exactly what I mean.' As I stated earlier, my election expenses had never been questioned at any election and I had almost certainly been out of pocket in the 1960 by-election, especially as my wife and family had to travel occasionally from Falkirk in Scotland to Blyth to take part in the campaign, and although they were good helpers, they were my own financial responsibility. I naturally assumed that the Hamilton brothers had talked to each other, but I have always wondered how much parliamentary collusion there was between Willie Hamilton and Short on that day.

My first telephone call from London after my defeat at the October election was Commander Morrison of Scotland Yard. When would I be in London, and would it be possible for him to have a talk with me? I told him it would be some time before I could come to London, as I was leaving for a visit to Aberdeen where my mother was ill in hospital. Could he come to see me in Northumberland? And so the visit was arranged for the following week. The background to this request by Morrison for an interview goes back to a morning in the House of Commons before the Summer recess. A number of members, including myself, had received copies of Swiss Bank documents in the name of Mr Edward W. Short, Account No. 312'596 of the Swiss Bank Corporation of Zurich. The *Sunday Express* dealt with the matter this way.

What is to happen about the mysterious affair with the Swiss Bank Corporation? Was it a total forgery conceived in a deliberate attempt to smear Labour's deputy leader, Mr

196

Edward Short, and so harm his party's prospects at the next General Election? Or does such an account really exist in someone else's name? And if so, whose account is it? (21.7.74.)

Harold Wilson, on whose behalf Downing Street was later to issue a statement, explaining that two accounts had been opened for him at a Swiss Bank in London, ordered Commander Morrison to Zurich to investigate the whole matter.

I tried to get some information from the Attorney General prior to the Summer Recess, by tabling two questions on July 25 asking the Government's chief law officer if he would arrange to make a progress report before MPs left for their summer holidays, and in this case, the General Election as well. But the Attorney could tell us nothing. However Commander Morrison did. When in Zurich, Morrison is reported, on 1st August, as having received confirmation that the papers, which indicated Labour Deputy Leader Mr Edward Short had a Swiss bank account, were forged. But two key questions went unanswered. Firstly, had someone else opened an account in Edward Short's name using a forged passport? Secondly, and the more important of the two, how is it possible to obtain, if at all, the stationery of the Swiss Bank? In order that these two matters be kept secret, it was reported that Commander Morrison had arranged with Scotland Yard chiefs that the answers would not be relayed back to London by telephone in case of an accidental crossed line. Instead the commander would report fully on his return, but his Swiss discoveries might be kept secret as he would now concentrate on hunting the forger. So far no one has been named as being sought to assist the police with their enquiries.

My earlier conversation with Detective Superintendent Wood, and his colleague Marsden at the House of Commons, came to recollection in my talks with Morrison, and while I am jumping a little ahead at the moment I want to deal with the visit of the Commander from Scotland Yard to my home in Northumberland after the election in November 1974. As I was not, at the time of Morrison's visit a Member of Parliament, I was reluctant to meet him on my own, and in talking the matter over with my wife it was decided that we would both be present when Morrison, and as it turned out, another colleague of his called at our home. We also arranged that Councillor Mrs Yellowley, a local magistrate, and my agent at the General Election would be present at the interview. Morrison and his colleague arrived. We had coffee together. All of us went upstairs to my study, although the Scotland Yard officers did not seem too keen at my being accompanied. When we sat down Commander Morrison said to me, '*What did you want to see me about Mr Milne?*' I told him to 'come off it.' It was he who wanted to see me. Why else telephone me in the first instance from London, and be so keen to come North when he could have waited till my return from Aberdeen. In any case, as I reminded him, I had already given a full statement to and had met Detective Superintendent Wood and Detective Inspector Marsden on three occasions at the House of Commons, following receipt of the Swiss Bank documents, now described as forged. All the press and MPs who had received the documents had had their fingerprints taken, and as I was unable to arrange this before the House rose, I gave them to the police officer accompanying Morrison to my home on that occasion. That was the visit over, although we sat and chatted in our home for over an hour. I am still puzzled as to why a top Scotland Yard Officer would 'phone me, arrange a visit, find it necessary to come up almost immediately to see me and then, on finding that others were to be in on the conversation and discussion, in effect call the whole thing off. I have experienced a great number of strange events since embarking on an investigatory course into corruption and related matters, but the Morrison episode will rank amongst the strangest. Equally strange was the way in which the Swiss Bank documents alleged forgery featured amongst the first of the matters touched upon by the Labour Candidate for the Blyth Constituency, following his selection for the forthcoming General Election. But that is another story which must await its telling. We said good-bye to the Commander who set out on his return road trip to London with a lot of unanswered questions buzzing around.

This brings me back to the *Sunday Express* editorial of 21st July. Its querying note intrigued me.

But there are other questions raised by Mr Short's own remarks.

He talks of the operation of 'one or more dirty tricks departments', of attempts to implicate other senior politicians in engineered scandals. What exactly is Mr Short saying? Whom can he be accusing? Is he suggesting that the Tories may be implicated?

If Mr Short really does know of other forgeries, of other attempts to frame politicians, then does he not have a public duty to reveal them? The British people will require an answer to every one of these questions before the election.

This was the theme I touched on in addressing a public meeting in my constituency on 1st August before leaving for holidays in France with my wife. We were on the hard run-up to the most strenuous of General Elections, although the date was not yet known and some prior relaxation was required. At the Market Hotel in Blyth I said, 'The Leader of the House of Commons has spoken about the existence of a dirty tricks department operating against himself and other leading figures in the Labour Party. More proof of the existence of such activity must now be provided by the persons making the accusations. People are entitled to know what their leaders are doing and if awkward questions are asked of us, this is no more than public life demands. But I would have more sympathy with the attitude of Mr Short if he himself had listened more sympathetically to the evidence I have given him in the past about a dirty tricks department operating against myself during at least the last four years.' As the *New Statesman* summed it up, in dealing with Mr Short's role as a public figure over a period of time:

What of Mr Short's position in all this? We have every reason to believe that he is an honest man. But, given that he is the leading Labour MP from the area, his own record of silence on all the issues involved over the last 12 years inevitably makes his present position an awkward one. Might he not, for the time being at least, feel more at home on the back benches? (3rd May, 1974)

But of course Mr Short was not the only one to be troubled by forged Swiss Bank documents. The Treasury had to admit in 1972 that they had paid out £50,000 to Swiss Bank Officers for a list of British citizens with accounts in banks in Switzerland. It would not be a bad idea for the Government Departments concerned to go ahead with a further move in this direction. The matter of Swiss bank accounts also surfaced in the wake of the imprisonment of Dan Smith and Andrew Cunningham. Tremendous mystery still surrounds the disposal of the vast sums paid by Poulson to Smith and others. The bankruptcy hearings, and the Leeds Crown Court trial, showed what happened to only a small proportion of the monies involved in the complicated network of arrangements between interlocking companies and individuals. It is believed that something less than a quarter of the cash has been accounted for. The bankruptcy trustees have never succeeded in recovering any of the balance from Smith. The police, and I do not know if Commander Morrison was involved in the enquiries, made intensive examination of all the books and visited Switzerland to make special investigations but all to no avail. In this context, Mr Peter Taylor's comments at Leeds Crown Court are worth recalling. The QC described the Smith company set-up as an organisation of extreme complexity 'designed to make the whole operation difficult to understand by anyone who did not have the whole picture,' and certainly not the operation of someone who lacked friends and business associates in the right places. Later on in the year we were to learn of the loss of around thirty-five million pounds suffered by Lloyds Bank, due to unauthorised foreign exchange dealings in one of their small branches in Lugano, Switzerland. The matter only came to light during a telephone call from Lugano to London. It was believed at the time that the deals in Lugano were enormous in relation to the branch's normal turnover and large in the context of the total Swiss business of Lloyds Bank, which should sufficiently demonstrate that solving the problems of the Swiss banking system, and its ramifications in the international currency field, is not a job for amateurs.

It needed two selection conferences to get my opponent for the next General Election chosen at Blyth. On the 14th July, the

Blyth Constituency Management Committee of the Labour Party again picked a London barrister as their standard bearer. Somebody around Blyth and the North-East must have been feeling the need of legal protection. This, of course, was an occasion when Transport House did take action on the matter. They ordered a second selection conference because, so it was claimed, Mr John Ryman, the London Barrister, had claimed at the first meeting that he had been a former personal assistant to the Prime Minister, Mr Harold Wilson. This Mr Wilson had denied.

The instruction from Transport House meant little to the officials of the Blyth Party. Between the two conferences the London Barrister was accompanied around the constituency by the secretary-agent, to the exclusion of the others still on the short list, and Councillor Collier of Seaton Valley claimed that despite the National Executive ruling he was still the candidate. According to Collier the NEC decision 'appears to me to be, once more, someone trying to split the party from within. Eddie Milne still has supporters in the party.' And so the merry circus went on. So much so, that Ryman was able to appear on Independent Broadcasting's Local Radio Station, *Metro*, as the prospective candidate before the NEC had considered his appointment. Even the National Executive Committee seemed determined to prove that rules and constitution mean little to the Blyth Labour Party.

But the bombshell was to come in the *Metro* interview. Ryman kicked off well by saying, 'This man Milne, in our opinion, is simply using the corruption issue to distract the attention of the electorate from the real issues.' In answer to a question from the Station's political broadcaster, Michael Chrisman, who asked, 'What about the files Mr Milne has in his possession and turned over to Scotland Yard concerning a Swiss bank account?' Ryman replied, 'Oh I don't know, he may well have fabricated it himself. Mr Milne is a very malicious person in my view, has been carrying on some sort of vendetta against Mr Short and Mr Wilson for some time.' In response to a further question from Mike Chrisman, about how much corruption he believed existed in the North-East and the Labour Party, Ryman replied, 'Very little . . . What I am saying is this issue of corruption has been exaggerated beyond all recognition for individual career purposes by Milne.' Going on to deal with the question of how big a part corruption would play in the General Election, the still to be selected Labour candidate said, 'I think Mr Milne will raise it a great deal, because he has a fetish for publicity and I think at the moment he is abusing his position as a Member of Parliament, in order to gain attention to himself by raising these matters.'

All this must be puzzling to those not familiar with the North-East scene. A re-selection had been ordered, with no decision given by the NEC as to the reasons. The still unadopted candidate was invited to appear on a radio programme run weekly from *Metro*, on which up to that time I had not been given an opportunity to appear, even as the sitting member for the Blyth Constituency. Also, not unusually for the Northern Regional Labour Party, the Assistant Regional Organiser of the Northern Regional Labour Party, Mr David Hughes, the same who had acted at Blyth in February, witnessed the selection conference and reported no irregularities.

During the summer, the Labour Party activity at Blyth had all the appearance of being conducted from a public relations source. Two local reports in the press caused wide-spread discussion. It arose from a paper given to the Society of Labour Lawyers by Barry Payton, who it will be recollected was sacked from his Wandsworth post as Town Clerk, for demanding action against corruption. In his speech Mr Payton had talked about the way in which freemasons were uniting to influence decisions in town halls throughout Britain. The *Newcastle Journal* fully reported the speech in a double column, front page, news item and continued inside with an 11-inch single column. I had made no speech during the week-end, but in five lines at the end of the inside column, the reporter wrote, 'Mr Milne said last night (I was not contacted by the reporter on this matter at all), while welcoming any moves to expose corruption, he would continue with his campaign for top level party and Government inquiries into the issue.' That was all my share of the report. But on the front page under a banner headline, 'Masons at Work in Town Halls' appeared a largish photo of myself captioned 'Mr Milne's campaign continues.' Aside from the lie, to imply my criticism of Freemasons was inaccurate. What made the matter worse, was that I had had to complain during the February election about the same reporter and the same newspaper. Ivor Richard, the Labour candidate had come in for some severe heckling in Blyth Market Place, whilst addressing an outdoor meeting. The *Journal* headline read, 'Police Stop Hecklers at Blyth,' underneath a large photo of myself, captioned, 'Mr Milne addressing the crowd yesterday.' Then there was the planned march of the Orangemen through the streets of Hebburn. The master of the Hebburn Orange Lodge was called Mr Edward Milne, and readers should need no telling of the use made of that one. What was disappointing was that in numerous reports of the march and the arrangements for it, only once was an explanation given, and that in the *Journal* of 14 June, when Sir William Elliott, Tory MP for Newcastle North, urged the Hebburn Orange Lodge to call off their march on 22nd June. He fully understood, he said, the anger being felt, and, 'I publicly suggest to Mr Eddie Milne, chairman of the Tyne Orange Action Committee, and the other organisers of the proposed march, that nothing can be gained by demonstrations of this kind at the present time. A great deal of damage could result.' Only on this occasion was a footnote added saying that the Eddie Milne of the Tyne Orange Action Committee, had no connection with Eddie Milne, the Independent Labour MP for Blyth. But I had numerous approaches over a wide area of the constituency about my role in this event, and at the nearby Eccles NUM branch the matter was used against us and details taken from the press cuttings were circulated in areas of the constituency. To some extent there may not appear to be anything untoward in these happenings, but in the highly pressurised atmosphere in Blyth at this time, every incident and event loomed larger than large, and character assassination, true or false, was the order of the day. Every form of popular emotive prejudice that could be exploited against me was used. For instance, Catholic voters, mainly in the Cramlington area, which had a strong anti-abortion lobby operating, were told that I, in common with most other Labour MPs who had bothered, or had the courage to vote on this difficult conscience issue, had supported the David Steel Abortion Bill. It was a nasty, dirty election.

The next moves came from the Blyth Valley Council and its branch of NALGO. The Council move was to set up a committee to check on allegations of corruption in the area. They engaged a solicitor and appointed Councillor George Adams as chairman. I was rather annoyed to learn that on the night the committee was set, Councillor Adams told the press that I had been invited to meet the committee, but no word had been received from me. This was hardly surprising, since the decision had only been taken that night, and no-one, least of all myself, had been approached on the matter. I met the Inquiry committee later at what was a rather abortive meeting, and pointed out to them the methods I used in dealing with any evidence or information which came to hand. Some weeks later the secretary of NALGO wrote, making the same request for information. I replied that I would be prepared to meet them, and got the reply that a meeting would serve no useful purpose, as it would appear I had no information to give the branch. I pointed out to them that while they could decide whether to meet me or not as they liked, they were certainly in no position to decide whether I would have information for them or not.

Chapter Twelve

10th October. General Election. The Returning Officer was Mr Peter Ferry, Chief Executive Officer of Blyth Valley Council, and a long, hard three weeks the election proved to be. The Labour Party mounted a massive machine, and as was said in the context of a previous council election, one could not get moved for builders' men. Added to local councillors from a wide area of the North-East, there were others, and with NUM and other Trade Union officials, it made up a formidable fighting force. I have of course no complaints about that, organisation and manpower are what elections are all about. Books have been written about elections, and certainly a book could be written about the Blyth Constituency General Election in October 1974, and as in so many other events described in this book, it was the Right Honourable Edward Short who set the tone and the standard. Chairing the demonstration in Newcastle, which welcomed Harold Wilson to the North-East, he introduced the Labour candidate for Blyth, the only Northern candidate to speak with Wilson, as the person who was to defeat 'that squalid little man at Blyth.' Things got worse as time went on. And then the police stepped in. During one afternoon in the campaign, Detective Superintendent Connor visited my committee rooms, accompanied by another police officer. He told me that the DPP wanted some further information, in order to make a prosecution in regard to the police houses bought from a man he called McCullough. I could not understand this, as I knew this matter was being dealt with by the West Midlands Police, operating from Birmingham. They then visited the home of one of my party workers, and adopted such a threatening attitude to him, that his son left the room in great distress. On hearing about this, I telephoned the Home Secretary's constituency, and reported the matter to his secretary, and the following morning visited the police headquarters in Newcastle with the colleague who had been subject to harassment the day before, seeing Connor. On leaving the police officer's room, he said to the two of us, that he appreciated very much the things we were doing and that nothing further would be done on the matter.

Ron Hayward, Labour's General Secretary, had circulated Labour agents about the conduct of the party during the election. He wrote: 'The Prime Minister has drawn attention to the likelihood of a smear campaign. Smears and character assassination must be left to the opposition. Let us fight a clean fight.' My daughter Edna, incensed by this latest example of Transport House double talk, and the Prime Minister's as well, wrote as follows to Hayward:

Dear Colleague,

I am not writing as the Pentlands (Edinburgh) Constituency Labour Party Secretary, but as an ordinary Labour Party member. I have just spent a day in Blyth visiting my father. You may remember that he has been Member of Parliament for Blyth for 14 years and is now the Independent Labour candidate.

In view of the fact that you sent out an excellent letter to all candidates asking for a clean campaign, I am appalled by the way the Labour Party is behaving in Blyth. Whilst I was there I met another party member from Wandsworth, a London barrister who was helping father. On his advice the Independent Labour agent Mrs Yellowley, JP, made an official complaint to the police about the Labour agent, Mr Mortakis, personally defacing her candidate's posters. The party workers are also insinuating that my father has been voting against the Labour Party in the House since February. As we both know, this is untrue and amounts to the character assassination you asked our candidates to steer clear of in your letter.

Having worked in Pentlands for the last two campaigns, and seen the candidates every day of the campaign, I have been most impressed by the dignified way the campaigns have been conducted in Edinburgh. I find it hard to believe that the Blyth Labour Party is the same party as I am working for in Pentlands and feel it should be brought to your notice.

Yours fraternally,

Edna Bryce.

As the campaign neared its close the Returning Officer became increasingly awkward and difficult. My agent, Mrs Yellowley JP, and myself, along with other officials of our organisation, tried to get a meeting with the Mayor of Blyth Valley Council, Councillor Jack Patterson, BEM, JP, who as the titular Returning Officer would be present at the count and announce the declaration. In my period in the Blyth Constituency, I had clashed with Patterson on a number of occasions. Patterson, a rather grim-visaged individual, had been particularly annoyed at our intervention in the New Hartley Residents Association's dispute with the Council, during the time the decisions were being taken about the grants given to the *London and Tyneside Property Company*. Patterson sheltered behind Ferry as Ferry did behind him.

As polling day drew nearer, tension mounted in the constituency. Ferry proved more and more difficult to contact, and on the eve of the poll, following failure to respond to complaints about wrongly-sited polling stations, it was necessary for my agent and myself to visit Blyth Police Station in an attempt to contact Ferry, whose wife had refused to pass on a telephone message from me to him at 10 p.m., saying that she was not an employee of Blyth Valley Council. I reminded her that I was not phoning to the council official but to the Returning Officer in an election at which people would be turning up to vote in some nine hours' time, where the officials entrusted with the arrangements had fallen down on the job. The visit to the Blyth Police Headquarters proved of no avail. They could not help. This was the attitude of the police during this strange election, one of subdued hostility. During the course of the count, along with others I had occasion to draw the attention of the officer in charge to complaints from people supervising the count, that one Labour checker had brought a whisky bottle into the hall and was showing the effects of it. The Blyth Police Chief then roundly accused me in a hectoring tone of telling him how to do his job.

Confident predictions were now being made by the Labour camp that the Liberals would come second in the election and Milne would be pushed into third place well down the field. As late as polling day, changes had still to be made in the polling arrangements, and these had been pointed out to Ferry and his other election officials, some days before. At 8.20 a.m. when visiting a Shiremoor polling station, I met Ned Murray, a local NUM colliery mechanics official, with two large cars carrying Labour posters parked outside the immediate voting area. He had been notified of a change in the polling station by one of Ferry's staff. Labour voters were being taken to the correct station, others had to walk, and it was only after protest that an announcement was made in the district affected by the Returning Officer's mistake, and after many electors had gone to work. The *Evening Chronicle* of polling day reported the position thus:

POLLING BOOTH SLIP-UP COULD LOSE VOTES
More than a thousand people in marginal Blyth were in danger of losing their vote to-day through being told to go to the wrong polling station.

Deputy returning officer, Mr Peter Ferry, sent out an emergency squad of helpers with a loudspeaker car and letters to be delivered by hand as soon as he heard of the slip up which affects 1,272 residents of the South Beach area.

Mrs Winnie Yellowley, agent for the Independent Labour Candidate, Mr Eddie Milne, said she discovered the error several days ago, reported it and presumed it had been corrected.

She said: 'Last week I heard that South Beach had been told to go to Dent Street, instead of their usual polling station and I personally contacted Mr Ferry to put it right.

'That wasn't the only mistake. People in the Beacon Hill, Cramlington area, had been told to go to Whitelaw School to vote, instead of Beacon Hill School and some residents in Shiremoor had also been given the wrong address.

'This could affect the result of the election. I am not very impressed with the organisation.'

Mr Ferry said, 'I understand the difficulties in Beacon Hill and Shiremoor were cleared up last week, but I learned this morning that the corrections have not been sent out to part of South Beach. Some residents have been told to go to the wrong polling station. Now letters are being taken out by hand and a public address car will go out, announcing the change.

'This is a legacy from February. With reorganisation, we have had constant staff changes and it's very unfortunate, but everyone should be informed within three hours of polling opening.

'I am very grateful to Mrs Yellowley for pointing it out to us.'

All this from a returning officer, well paid for the job, who could not be contacted at a vital period in the election, even with the help of the police. The excuse of the nearness to February was lame, for no big changes had taken place in the area in the eight months concerned.

A letter to the press from a party member in London E5 was forwarded to me and summed up the Blyth situation perfectly.

Voters in Blyth are currently being amazed by the des-proportionate amount of time and money being poured by the North-East Labour Party into the campaign to unseat Eddie Milne at the General Election. One gets the impression that Eddie Milne, rather than the Tories or Liberals, is regarded as the principal enemy in the region by the powers that be. Is this what our party annual subscriptions were intended for?

Certainly, the paranoiac fervour which characterises the hordes of incoming canvassers, mostly right-wing Labour councillors, is indicative of the moral collapse of the party in the North-East.

In a sense, these desperate people are right. If Eddie Milne wins . . . the call for a party inquiry into corruption, the rooting out of corruption in the Labour Party, both at Westminster and in local government will gather momentum.

But if Eddie Milne loses there will be a deep sigh of relief in the Labour Government: things can be got back under control, as during the 1964–70 period, when corruption could generally be guaranteed immunity against prosecution.

The polls closed and we came to the count, with two recounts, until in the grey dawn of an October morning, after 5 a.m., we received the result. I was out by 78. Our small band of workers, who had spared no effort for the second time inside a year, had almost pulled off the impossible. My spell as MP for Blyth was over.

The final result was as follows:

J. Ryman (Lab)	20,308
E. Milne (Ind Lab)	20,230
J. Shipley (Lib)	8,177
B. Griffiths (Con)	6,590

Majority 78 (0.1%)
Electorate 74,449

After the first count, Ferry decided to have a recount of the first two candidates only, and when this produced a similar result, we asked for a recount of all votes cast. John Shipley and Brian Griffiths and their agents, once they were out of the ring, showed a lively interest in checking the complete vote to get an accurate result, and were not only aware of the strange conduct of the election, but concerned at Ferry's inefficiency.

There remained the speeches. Ryman made a rude, ill-tempered attack on myself, and for the first time in my long election experience, I heard a winning candidate being booed by some of his own supporters.

So much had happened in the election, and the Returning Officer's actions were such, that we decided we would ask for an examination of the whole manner in which the contest had been handled by Mr Ferry, particularly as the count, which was handled entirely by Blyth Valley officials, was headed by a former secretary of the Blyth Labour Women's Federation in the Robens era. Amongst the people we met during the round of polling stations, and at the count, was a top officer of one of the property companies operating in the Blyth Valley area, and many others who were associated with the issues which had caused controversy in the Blyth area, while I was the Member.

It was not possible to collect all the evidence in the three weeks allowed by law, nor to gather the £2,000 or £3,000 needed to finance a petition. But a comprehensive report was drawn up and forwarded to the Home Secretary, the Speaker of the House of Commons and the Clerk of the Crown in Chancery at the Crown Office, the Government Department concerned with the running of elections. From the Speaker of the House of Commons we received the reply that while nothing could be done at the time, he would see that the documents we had forwarded to him would be made available to a future Speakers Conference on Electoral Reform.

But evidence continued to come in. Numerous people were denied their vote in one way or another, and in many cases in dubious circumstances. Two incidents, under examination at the moment, concerned the return of election expenses submitted to the Returning Officer. It cost the Labour Party £1,622.98 to take the seat from us, only £12.35 inside the legal maximum candidates were allowed to spend. In that, no charge was shown for the services of the agent, Mortakis, although there is a Transport House recommendation of a sum around £75. The sum spent by the Liberals, Tories and ourselves was respectively £899.10, £766.40 and £951.37. When, on two separate occasions, my agent Mrs Yellowley, and Councillor McManus, the chairman of our Election Committee, visited the council offices it was necessary to draw the attention of the Returning Officer to the money spent by the Labour Party on printed work used in the election.

This particularly referred to printing work, listed as over £761 paid to *Hartley Display Crafts* of Blyth. During the election campaign, one of our helpers, familiar with the printing trade, estimated that the Labour Party had exceeded their legal maximum on printing alone. When Mrs Yellowley raised the matter with Mr Ferry, at a meeting with myself and another council official present, he said it was no responsibility of his to act on complaints of that nature, nor to check on the financial returns of candidates. It has now transpired according to reports received, that at the time of the declaration of the result at Blyth, an unpaid printing account from the Labour Party to *Hartley Display Crafts* was being discussed. The amount was in the region of £1,100 and arrangements had been made to suspend payment for a period and pay an interest charge of 15% on the outstanding amount. A sum of approximately £400 was paid in April, and the remainder during May. I understand that the negotiations for the payment of the account in the manner described were undertaken by Mr John Ryman, the new MP himself. Some of this printing was included in a transfer item on the election accounts, listed as Blyth Constituency Labour Party, and not election funds, for 17,000 *Labour Express* leaflets at a cost of £204 which was receipted by Mr J. T. Fulthorpe, Treasurer of the Party.

The other matter being investigated at the moment concerns a packet of postal votes handed to us with the election returns during a visit to the council offices. Apparently these postal ballot papers should have been returned to the Clerk of the Crown in Chancery. Whether they were late in being received, or had been returned in time for the ballot but not included, will never be known, for on coming across them in the papers presented to me, I passed them over to a clerk to be returned to Mr Ferry. Some weeks later, I reminded Mr Ferry that I had not been notified about the postal ballot papers, and he seemed very vague on the matter and could not recollect them. I wrote him on the 2nd April on this, but received no reply. I sent a recorded delivery letter two weeks later, and received the following reply:

Dear Mr Milne,
    Please accept my apologies for the delay in replying to your letter of 5th April, and I acknowledge receipt of your reminder of the 24th received yesterday (28th April). Mr Colwell certainly recalls the conversation you refer to and he checked immediately afterwards to confirm that the packet had been despatched. He cannot however pin down the precise date. You will know that the packets to send these documents on for storage are pre-printed and do not need a covering letter. All documents are sent to 'The Clerk of the Crown in Chancery'. I am sorry it is not possible to be more specific or helpful—you may wish to note that there does not appear to be any definite instruction or ruling on dealing

with postal vote packets which continue to be returned many weeks and even months after polling day.

Yours sincerely,
Ferry
Returning Officer

The mystery heightened, when on 23rd April, 1975, Mr David Butler of Nuffield College, Oxford despatched the following letter to me.

Dear Mr Milne,

In a draft footnote to my book on *The British General Election of October* 1974, I have just written, 'The defeat of the independent Mr Milne by 78 votes may be attributable to the 750 postal votes recorded in Blyth.' In fact, Blyth is one of the few seats that has not sent in a record of valid postal votes to the Home Office, so I cannot check that 750 is an exact figure (it assumes that there was the same return of postal ballots as in other seats). And, of course, I was not at the count so I have no confirmation about how the postal votes divided in Blyth. I would be most grateful if you could throw any light on the subject.

Yours sincerely,
David Butler

Efforts are still being made to throw some light on the mysteries, one on the payment of accounts and the other on the postal ballot papers. The answer may be more innocent than appears to be the case, but all the evidence goes to show that the General Election of October 1974 in the Blyth Constituency in the County of Northumberland was quite an event. Perhaps the Nuffield College election psephologist might come one day and have a look at this area where happenings are never quite the same as elsewhere.

Possibly the most disappointing feature of the October election was the attitude of the NUM. In the period of heavy pit-closures in Northumberland, we worked closely with the local branches of the Union, and in a number of instances managed to get concessions for the local collieries when the

213

officials of the Union at Burt Hall had thrown in the sponge. It was difficult at Parliamentary level to interest the official NUM MPs on the closure issues, with one or two honourable exceptions, and even in the three debates which followed the Wilberforce Report, compiled in the wake of the 1972 strike in the mining industry, many NUM MPs, including Grant, the Member for Morpeth, failed to take part in the parliamentary proceedings. Support still came from the Bates Colliery at Blyth, but even there attempts were made to smear me in a number of ways, and communist leaflets supporting Eddie Milne were distributed, although no approach had been made to my agent at the election for permission to do so according to election law, and we were not aware of the distribution until after it took place.

One pit which secured a reprieve, on a closure decision, some years ago was the Eccles Colliery at Backworth. At this colliery, the items concerned the Orange March led by another Edward Milne were distributed, and steps were taken to remove officials and supporters of mine in the February election from office. Prior to the election, a request to address an Eccles NUM branch meeting was refused, and it was the only colliery in the area to display Labour posters, although this is contrary to NCB agreement. Local interest was therefore aroused when Jack Amos, the *Evening Chronicle*'s industrial reporter, issued details of what was described as ballot rigging at Eccles colliery. So angered was the branch chairman that he threatened legal action, and said, 'I'm sick and tired of it. If I can find out who is spreading these malicious rumours, I'll take legal action.' The fact remains that irregularities were discovered in the Eccles Lodge votes, in the ballot for the county executive, and the Eccles vote was rendered null and void. The rumours arose because the chairman had taken the ballot box home, to be picked up by an official from NUM headquarters, after the votes had been cast. The Eccles officials claimed it was a domestic issue and in no way connected with any national matter and they did not want to comment about it. NUM General Secretary Main reported that he would not go so far as to say there had been vote rigging. Possibly this was a storm in a tea cup, but it is strange that all these seemingly unrelated matters around election time have a thread running through the Blyth Constituency connecting them. Many of us would have been more reconciled to the efforts of the NUM and their one Northumberland MP, George Grant of Morpeth, to return a London barrister as the official Labour representative for the area, if they themselves had done some more battling on issues like the threatened New Hartley eviction of NUM members.

The police came back on the scene in two ways: first in connection with the resurrection of the issue of the houses built for police officers in County Durham, and the documents containing evidence on the matter; and secondly over the dismissal of my son-in-law from his post with the new Trafford Authority's Youth Department.

On the Sunday afternoon of 15th December, at around 3 p.m., a Detective Superintendent Elliott with a colleague of his, arrived unannounced. As is usual with visitors, my wife invited them in. Elliott said to Em that she might not have been so willing to ask them in if she had known who they were. My wife remarked that would have made no difference anyway. After the police officers had introduced themselves, Elliott laid great stress on the fact that he had not called to deal with any of the corruption issues about which I had been calling for an inquiry, but concerning the letters and documents which I had handed over to the Attorney General in May 1974 in my desk room at the House of Commons. The police action in this matter was again puzzling, for it seemed to cut across the investigations being conducted by the outside force, in this case West Midlands, under police regulations. As with other officers in the past, I pointed out to Elliott that he appeared to be attaching more importance to the fact that the papers appeared to have been stolen, than to the facts they contained. The police officers were very ill at ease, and the junior officer kept interjecting, that it was not they who had ordered the visit but 'someone higher up'. Elliott then said he wanted to ask me two questions, and the complicated wording he used, prompted me to ask him if he was cautioning me on the case. He said he was, and I told him to go ahead. Did I know the documents had been stolen? I pointed out to him that the same question had been asked and answered on the Terrace of the House of

Commons in an interview with Detective Superintendent Light of the West Midlands Police. Then came the question which seemed to cause Elliott some embarrassment. 'Did you (Milne) pay to get the documents?' I angrily told the police officers that I had never paid for these or for any documents ever received by me on any matter. As with the Morrison visit regarding the Swiss bank documents, I was dubious about the role of the police, particularly as both visits had a similar ring about them, and both were conducted against the background of my election defeat. I asked the police officers to await the arrival of two of our party members, whom I had phoned in conjunction with their visit.

Although the police had arrived unannounced, and had spent nearly two hours with us, they said they could not wait when I asked them to stay until Ray Green, one of our Party members who had been subjected to police harassment during the election, and my agent Mrs Yellowley, had arrived. I told the police I was making a telephone call to them and they heard me doing so. Both friends lived only a matter of ten minutes from our home, but the police officers were gone by the time they arrived.

But attempts were made to strike at our family as well. Following the reorganisation of local government areas, our daughter's husband Brian, who had been employed as a youth leader with Lancashire County Council, was appointed to the Youth Department of the new Trafford Authority. Not long after taking up the post, he noticed that the head of the department, Mr Martin J. White, had on his desk a copy of an article referring to my anti-corruption activities, and after a few days White approached Brian and asked him if he was in favour of what his father-in-law was doing. It was only a matter of days before Brian was suspended from his post and later dismissed. The police investigation, which was started against him, was conducted by Detective Inspector McRoberts of the Fraud Squad on supposed financial irregularities committed by Brian while employed at Flixton Youth Club. Immediately following the October election, Brian was charged with the supposed mispayment of a cheque for £27. This was the only one of a list of eight supposed misdemeanours which McRoberts was

216

investigating. Kathleen and Brian decided to fight the issue right through, and made a number of visits to other parts of the country to check on the allegations, which were all in connection with Youth Club activities. The case went to Manchester Crown Court on 6th May this year. It was then withdrawn by the prosecution on the grounds that the Treasurer of the Council was too ill to give evidence, and Brian was able to leave the court, following a statement of the judge that he did so without a stain on his character. This still prompts the question of why a family should be deprived of its income for twelve months on a charge of this description, why a local authority could dismiss an employee while investigations were being made, with charges later withdrawn? How far did my article lead to Brian's dismissal by his senior officer, and would there have been police charges had I won the election at Blyth by 78 votes instead of the other way round? In my view it adds up to the conclusion that the casualty list is longer for those who oppose corruption than for those who practice it. It also indicates that our police forces are needing much more stringent examination and inquiry than has been the case up to now. It is not without significance to me, that my last interview with a Cabinet Minister in the House of Commons was with the Home Secretary Roy Jenkins, in his room to ask, in his case, for the third time, for an inquiry to be set up into the Durham Police Force for the period in which Cunningham was chairman of the authority. Neither Jenkins, nor the Government of which he is a member, can talk about the principles of open government until such an inquiry takes place.

Chapter Thirteen

As can be imagined, my post-bag from all over Britain and indeed from many parts of the world, has been a heavy one in the last three or four years, and it is a tribute to my secretaries that they have kept pace with it. My wife has also been besieged with calls at home in that period of time. What has impressed all of us dealing with the problem, is the evidence available from all sources and the indifference of authority to tackle it. Let me give only a very small cross-section of what came to our knowledge in that period.

The story of Alan Grimshaw is now a national one. It has figured in a Select Committee Report to the House of Commons concerning the National Coal Board. Grimshaw was Regional Stores Officer, General Adminstrative Grade 1, at NCB Northern Regional Headquarters, and he was transferred to the Doncaster Headquarters of the Coal Board's Purchasing and Stores Department in 1968. He has recently been declared redundant by the NCB. In between, lies the story of the House of Commons Select Committee on Nationalised Industries and its report No. 129 of 14th May, 1974. It was a report that almost became a casualty of the February 1974 General Election, for the committee had completed its findings and was preparing to report, when Heath went to the country. Its chairman was Sir John Hall and members included Sir Donald Kaberry and Mr Russell Kerr. Its specific task was to inquire into the purchasing by the National Coal Board of powered roof supports and spare parts for such supports. The report and appendices, with evidence given to the committee, covers over 500 pages, although some written evidence to the committee is not included in the report.

Amongst those who gave evidence to the Committee were included Dr R. D. Leigh and Mr W. A. Grimshaw. Alan Grimshaw as stated is now declared redundant by the Coal Board and Dr Leigh is in other employment. In the section of the report dealing with the specific criticisms of Dr Leigh and Mr Grimshaw, the committee had this to say: 'We judge that the main assertion made by Mr Grimshaw and Dr Leigh was that suppliers, by some kind of deception, induced the Board to buy too many spare parts at too high prices. We are fully satisfied from our enquiries that this assertion is not justified.' What indeed were the claims made by the two Coal Board employees in their evidence to the Select Committee? Dr Leigh, in one instance, first compared the price of hand-set props with the price of power-support legs, and he further compared the prices of *Gullick Dobson* legs with those from *Dowty*. He concluded from both these comparisons that the *Gullick Dobson* legs were overpriced by £10 each and that this was costing the Board £500,000 per year. Another estimate of the two Coal Board employees in their Select Committee evidence was, 'On the assumption that 50 *Gullick* installations will be bought each year, that each installation consists of 200 powered supports and the price differential between *Gullick* and other manufacturers' valve gear is £100, then the Board could be paying up to £1,000,000 per year more than it need for valve gear.' Again the Committee came to the conclusion that they could not agree with the Grimshaw and Leigh assessment of the position.

The Committee did however conclude in its findings that the NCB's pricing arrangements have been only partly effective in recent years in restricting the suppliers to a reasonable level of profitability. It also stated, that the evidence given to them showed clearly that after *Gullick* changed their name to *Gullick Dobson*, and began to sell powered supports and spares (in addition to their own products) made by *W. E. and F. Dobson*, the NCB failed to appreciate that a proportion of Dobson's profits should be added to those of *Gullick Dobson* for the purpose of assessing the true profit margin on the joint sales. In your Committee's view this was a major oversight on the part of the NCB. From reading that viewpoint, based on what actually could be deduced from the evidence given by Mr

219

Grimshaw and Dr Leigh, one would have thought that the NCB might have thought up a more fitting reward for the two employees concerned, than redundancy on the one hand and the need to seek alternative employment on the other! The publicly-owned industries of this country are not all that well endowed with employees at top level devoting so much to the industries they serve, that they can afford the departure of employees of this calibre and loyalty. Nor can I say, in conclusion, that the committee and other Members of Parliament, were so impressed that they raised the matter in the House of Commons, for I was no longer there to see it happen, if it did.

But should not the Select Committee take another look at the fate of those who gave evidence to it, for the National Coal Board itself has surely been made aware of its short-comings by the Nationalised Industries Report. I instance the *Doncaster Evening Post* of 9th May, 1975.

> A shake-up of the National Coal Board's audit department has just been announced. This follows an independent committee of inquiry into the board's spending procedure. A NEW AUDIT DEPARTMENT HAS BEEN CREATED

Following a letter in *The Times* in early 1975, I received a letter from Alan Ellis, the ex-police inspector who had campaigned against organised police and administrative corruption in the Hong Kong Government, and what he described as the protection supplied to it by both major parties in the UK, whether in Government or Opposition. He wrote, 'I doubt you need any encouragement yourself, but as one of the biggest enemies I have had to face is public indifference, I write to let you know that your efforts are certainly appreciated by myself.'

Around this time the Stonehouse affair was beginning to gather momentum, and the Leader of the House of Commons was setting up a committee to see what could be done about the matter. Following a letter from the Reverend Michael Scott, I wrote to Wilson, asking for a Tribunal of Inquiry to be set up, and received the usual long-winded reply that the matter was being actively pursued. The letter may have sounded all right, had I not known that Michael Scott had tried for over a year to have the Ombudsman or the Charity Commissioners look into the activities of Stonehouse. A few weeks later I spent a few hours in London with Michael Scott and Mr Fazlul Huq, and even in that short space of time was appalled at the extent of the mishandling of the Bangla Desh fund-raising efforts. The delay in the Government's handling of the Stonehouse affair has, of course, its repercussions in other matters of police investigation relating to the Poulson case, and other matters. It was reported at the end of January that Fraud Squad detective Etheridge had to take time off from his probe in County Durham to handle more urgent inquiries into runaway MP John Stonehouse. This was at a time when both the Attorney General and the Director of Public Prosecutions were asking for more detailed reports on public figures linked with Poulson. Indeed I had a letter at this time from Sam Silkin, Attorney General, chiding me for suggesting that there might be a cover-up on the way in the Poulson case. At the same time, the Attorney General's department had issued a statement, that the further report on public figures would have to wait until senior detectives leading the Poulson inquiries were free to return to the North-East. One of the matters apparently having to lie in cold storage is Poulson's connections with *Peterlee Development Corporation*. This has been referred to in the earlier stages of the book. At least some people in the North-East will be pleased to learn of the delay, caused by the investigations into Stonehouse and the lessening of pressure on the Poulson case. Comparison with Watergate and events in Britain may not be so wide of the mark after all.

Action within the party was slow to get off the ground. No-one at national level on the Executive Council did anything to get an inquiry going in the North-East and in the *Tribune* Group Mikardo managed to keep the others quiet. Staunch self-styled democrats like Frank Allaun, and others, ran for cover when the first signs of trouble showed itself. The 'Campaign for Democracy' in the Labour Party asked me for a memorandum on my case, which I provided, but there was still no action. Like one or two of my USDAW colleagues, they consider that my action in standing against an official Labour candidate was the crime of crimes, and they now refuse to examine the circumstances of my removal from the Blyth seat. What they were asking me to do in February 1974 was to go into political oblivion and let the official candidate have a walk-over at Blyth, so that everything in the garden would be lovely. It is not surprising, that since that February in 1974, the Government formed after the election, and the Labour Movement throughout the country, has been in a state of decline, and all the blame cannot be attributed to the dispute on the Common Market which first broke out at Cabinet level and then spread throughout the wider Labour Movement.

One area and one person did try to find out the facts of the Blyth situation. I was invited to address a meeting of Labour Party supporters in Nottingham. It was arranged and chaired by Dieter Pietz, a lecturer in the Department of Philosophy at the local University, who was formerly active in the Labour Party in Edinburgh. The Nottingham Labour Party afterwards expelled Dieter Pietz and one or two others in the city, and the National Executive upheld the decision. The meeting, addressed by myself and chaired by Dieter Pietz, was given as the reason for the action taken, but matters had been moving to a head in Nottingham for some time. Many party members had been critical of one of the local MPs, Mr Jack Dunnett. It was claimed by party members that his investment and land deal activities were contrary to the spirit and principles of the Labour Movement. There had been widespread discontent amongst party workers at the reports of the activities of leading local figures around Dunnett, and demands had been made for an inquiry into the property holdings of Dunnett in London. These are of course matters for the local party in Nottingham, but one could not fail to notice in visiting Nottingham, the similarity of the Labour Party set-up to that of Newcastle and the North-East of England. In any case the Nottingham Labour Party considered the chairing of a meeting for Eddie Milne strong enough grounds for expelling members with a long record of service to the Labour Movement.

With the election over, the next step for the Labour Party was the Annual Conference in November, postponed and shortened because of election year. Up pops Ian Mikardo for the Executive, to oppose a motion calling for MPs to resubmit themselves for re-selection between elections. In a speech which was described by *Labour Weekly* as a tour-de-force of good-humoured Cockney humour, Mikardo, and Labour's National Executive, rejected the motion. He denied a suggestion from one delegate that a safe Labour seat was a meal ticket for life. 'We want', said Mikardo, 'selection of candidates to stay with the people who do the day-to-day, week-to-week, month-to-month work, not with those who turn up for selection conferences and ceremonial occasions.'

There is no report to show if the Blyth delegate went to the rostrum on this item on the agenda, or if Mikardo used, as an illustration of a ceremonial occasion, the issuing of credentials by a former chairman of Blyth CLP, an official of the Constructional Engineering Union, to a local taxi owner who was not a member of that union, and if at all a member of the Blyth Labour Party, had only been so for a matter of two to three weeks. All this, of course, was brought to the notice of Transport House, but no action was taken. Mikardo himself was under fire at this time on the question of the declaration of members' interests, the matter that had and has been so skilfully delayed by the Leader of the House for so long.

A member of the Labour Party in Wembley took Mikardo to task for having expressed himself against an inquiry into the affairs of the Labour Party in the North-East. Mikardo's decision on this was vital, for the others on the NEC would have followed his lead. In a reference to myself, the party member said, 'If Eddie Milne's sin was that he rocked the boat of complacency and plain stupidity and has been proved right, so the party will be most unforgiving.' He referred to Mikardo's business interests, particularly *Ian Mikardo Ltd*, formed in 1946 as 'agents for overseas exporters', which in its last available return in 1971, showed Mrs Mikardo and Labour MP Miss Jo Richardson as co-directors, receiving total payments of £16,300. This £300 private company made a pre-tax profit of only £400 in 1971. He stated, 'What has been reported about your business interests is in no way illegal, but since you have for so long pontificated about a true Socialist philosophy, it most certainly leaves a sour taste in the mouth. There are moments,' said the writer, 'when I feel that "Labour" has more to fear from its own leadership than it ever has from the capitalist class.'

For a brief spell following the October election, the spotlight descended on Blyth's new MP. On his selection, he had notified his legal colleagues that the reason for his being chosen was that he had told the Blyth Party he was the only man who 'could beat Milne'. Full marks for that prediction anyway. Apparently he joked in the Robing Room of a court that he was not too keen on the seat, as champagne was not served on the 'plane to Newcastle, but the wine at the Railway Hotel passed muster. In November he appeared at the Old Bailey, his head in bandages, stating that he had fallen off his horse whilst fox-hunting, and the same week the *Blyth News* carried the story that the Blyth MP had been injured in a car crash in Derbyshire, had narrowly escaped death, and suffered broken ribs, a broken nose, two black eyes and had to have 30 stitches in his head. This resulted from a head-on crash in Derbyshire while he was travelling from Blyth to London. He was kept in hospital for three days, but was officially sworn in as MP that week and managed to attend the State opening of Parliament. Blyth's new MP referred to the accident in his maiden speech in the House on 4th December. 'I apologise for making my maiden speech rather late in the day, because I understand that I am the last Government supporter to do so. Soon after the General Election, I was a passenger in a motor-car that was involved in an accident, and I was in hospital for some time. As a result, I arrived somewhat late at the beginning of this Session.' A knock on the head can be a disturbing thing and have repercussions, but the Member for Blyth must take steps to clear up a matter that has been puzzling many of his constituents for months now. I was questioned about this at a meeting, and replied that I had no idea what the real story was, but if it had been a hunting accident, then as I saw it, the Blyth representative must be the first man in history to be thrown through the windscreen of a horse. Little wonder that the *Daily Mirror* of 6th December carried an article headed:

THE RYMAN FOLLIES

What are we to make of John Ryman, the new boy Labour MP for Blyth?

Since he was elected in October he has attacked the 'rich, idle, wet ladies of Belgravia' for promiscuity, labelled estate agents as 'thieves and robbers', and described Coal Board deputy-chairman Norman Siddall as 'a pin-striped twit'.

Last week-end he accused West German Chancellor Helmut Schmidt of being an impertinent and patronising Hun.

I heard Chancellor Schmidt at the Labour Conference. And impertinent and patronising he was not.

He was urbane, civilised, self-deprecating, amusing and amiable—everything which a real Hun could never be.

If Mr Ryman was as far off his targets as he was with Herr Schmidt, then I'm all for Mr Siddall and the estate agents, not to mention the ladies of Belgravia.

Before he was elected, Mr Ryman's only claim to fame was that he was the former husband of gifted Shirley Summerskill.

Now Mr Ryman, who hunts with the Meynell, has another claim. He's the only Labour MP who puts his riding boot into his mouth every time he opens it.

Chapter Fourteen

Now we are at the end of a period which started in an Aberdeen tenement and came to a temporary halt in a Northumberland town at the declaration of the result in the General Election of October 1974. More than four decades of ups and downs, indeed I believe it saw the rise and fall of a great Labour movement. It is rather strange that in my introduction to direct election campaigning it was the senior Benn who was in the limelight, having newly entered Labour's ranks from the Liberal Party. In June 1975, his son, having renounced the title taken by his father on leaving the House of Commons, and creating constitutional and legislative history in the process, was awaiting the result of a referendum on the Common Market to learn what the legislative and constitutional future held for one of the world's oldest Parliaments. And at the same time the younger Benn was facing a hostile Labour leadership with Wilson and Callaghan in the van, desperately trying to hide their anti-market speeches of the past, in order to lead the British people into the Europe of the future. I was writing these words during the referendum campaign. Afterwards, with Wilson again on the winning side, Benn was still in the Cabinet, but the question of his future still loomed large on the horizon.

The term 'crossroads of history' has often been used in our long island story but was never more applicable than at this moment of time. So often in the past, we have, as a people, had to make decisions largely decided and determined for us by others. This time the decision is ours. Will the Labour Movement as we have known it survive? Has it indeed the will and the capacity to survive? Beset by dissension, torn in its policies and its programmes by those who pay lip service to its hopes and aspirations, deserted by leaders who decided that self-aggrandisement and advancement were more important than the progress to a better life of the people they had promised to serve. Once again a quote from Wilson's Shildon speech comes to mind, cynically and hypocritically delivered, more with the intention of deceiving than leading, but carrying the truth in it nevertheless: 'Men and women of all parties who have given their whole lives to community service find their efforts greeted by cynicism. The dedication which inspires them no longer appears to their constituents to be the crusade which was proclaimed.'

But the Labour Movement needs not only big men and women, dedicated men and women, but men and women equipped with the moral fibre to face the challenge of the closing years of the 20th century. They must emerge, they *will* emerge. The failures of the Wilson Governments are now being felt, but the lessons can and will be learned.

In 1967 a period of 117 years of newspaper history ended. 18th June was the end of the road for the *Sunday Citizen*, formerly *Reynolds News*. A little bit of many of us died on that June Sunday morning. In 1850 George William McArthur Reynolds created the *Reynolds Sunday News* to support the People's Charter to campaign for many rights we to-day consider elementary. Reynolds was one of a great number of people in his day who rebelled against a system that multiplied wealth but destroyed people. In its last issue, Bill Richardson, its editor, had this to say to Wilson:

The *Sunday Citizen*'s voice will not be heard again after to-day. So we give this message to Mr Wilson and his colleagues. 'You compromise too much and it is hard to detect distinctively Socialist principles in many of your policies; even after making the most generous allowance for the compromise that life imposes on any government . . . you ask for sacrifices and they have been made, because you are our Government and we will strain loyalty to the uttermost limit to help you. But we want to glimpse the new Jerusalem as well as contemplate the import-export figures. We were inspired by Harold Wilson's vision of a great, new, humane,

227

efficient, self-confident, high technology society. WHERE IS IT . . .?

Bill Richards concluded by saying:

Now it is a story that has been told. But liberty, democracy, equality, social justice, the brotherhood of man, they are eternal ideals, and other newspapers will yet be born to speak out for them. Success was not to be ours, but we did the best we could. Something good in British democracy dies to-day. But the torch will be picked up again.

When that is done it will place even heavier responsibilities on the shoulders of all of us. There are siren voices sounding, because of the betrayal of groups of people in our movement, that democracy has failed. This is not so, but it places a responsibility on all of us. Part of that battle for democracy has had to be waged against the corrupt forces inside and outside our movement, all people have to be harnessed for the fight. As Professor Ralf Dahrendorf said in the 1974 Reith Lectures, 'As well as open government, we need open political parties and there will have first of all to be active, animated and truly democratic local Labour Parties.' I make no apologies for closing with my speech at the declaration of the count in Blyth in October 1974.

I want first of all to thank each and every one who took part in this election for the contribution that they made to it, to the police, to the helpers, to those who counted the votes, to those who received my wife and I so courteously when we moved round the polling stations to-day. I want particularly to thank the folk of the Blyth constituency whom I have had the pleasure and privilege of representing for the past fourteen years, for the kindness and the courtesy and the warmth of friendship that they have shown to my wife and my family since we came to live in this area. All I can say about my fourteen years record in the House of Commons is that I have tried to serve. For the past four or five years we know, in this constituency what has been going on, and we also know why, but my political career is ended to-night. I have no regrets whatsoever. Against an enormous machine, against an influx of Labour councillors from almost every part of the Northern Region, against a combination of Transport House and the Northern Regional Labour Party, and the leaders of the National Union of Mineworkers, we almost once again pulled off the impossible. We said to you on the occasion of the decision in February that the people of Blyth by their decision had lit a beacon, and I still think that represented on that table, at this moment, lies a magnificent achievement on the part of the people of this constituency, in demonstrating that they wanted things done differently. Powerful machines are difficult to fight. With limited resources we did just that. I am not going to make any promises about returning to political life in this constituency or anywhere else, but I do know that the standards that we set and the job that we set out to do has still to be done and that job will be done.

I want to pay two other tributes, I want to pay a tribute to my agent, Mrs Winnie Yellowley, who performed miracles with limited resources, and I also want to pay a tribute to my wife and family, who have been subjected during the last five years to actions and activities that have been mean, dirty and despicable, and which no family should have had to put up with, while the breadwinner of that family was earning his livelihood in the service of the community. My family suffered more than I did in the actions and activities of those years.

The successful Labour candidate was careful to point in his tribute to Brian Griffiths and John Shipley. This is the second occasion that I have had to thank my opponents and to omit mentioning the Labour candidate at all. I want to thank again, as I did in February, John Shipley and Brian Griffiths and those who worked and moved around them during the course of the campaign, for keeping some sort of standards that belong to this constituency in the political campaign, and refusing to depart from those standards in that period of time, and John and Brian, I would ask you to convey that thanks to those of the people who worked with you and are not here to-night to hear that particular statement. So I say once again thank you to the good folk of Blyth for having in 1960 allowed me to turn a childhood dream into a reality, a dream that has ended to-night, but one about which I have no regrets at all because to have been privileged to serve the people of this corner of South-East Northumberland for the past 14 years has been a fitting reward for any of the injustices we have had to suffer.

Chapter Fifteen

It is now possible to look at the events of the General Election of 1974, eighteen months later. I realise that I have not missed the Palace of Westminster as much as I thought I would. The year and a half since October have given me a tremendous opportunity to see the problems of the last twelve years, and particularly those of the years since 1970, in a new and different context. In that time growing national economic and industrial problems have demonstrated clearly the inability of the Government, and indeed of the opposition, to measure up to the challenges that face Britain and the world today. The much vaunted benefits, claimed by Wilson, Heath, Short and others, that would flow from the referendum decision of the British people in June 1975, have failed to materialise and the manna from Brussels is as meaningless in the light of Britain's present day problems as were the promises to the British people in the October of 1974 that the return of a Labour Government would set us on the road to recovery.

But the October Election still dominates the House of Commons. Wilson's slender majority has disappeared. It is a measure of Labour's shame, and its betrayal of the principles on which the movement was founded, that the Government of a once great nation, facing the most serious crisis in its long history, should have been dependent on the votes of two MPs, Ryman and Stonehouse, facing criminal charges in the law courts of England, and the Labour majority has disappeared with their defection.

On the local front the period has been marked by an insistent demand by constituents to have from the local Labour Party leaders the facts on the corruption issue and the names of those responsible. There was a significant silence, and certainly no protest from the Labour hierarchy, nor from Short or Wilson, when the following item appeared in the *Sunday Sun* of 12 October 1975.

> The Milne file and why we must postpone publication. The *Sunday Sun* is at the centre of a top-level legal wrangle. Three articles by former Blyth MP Eddie Milne, are the cause of the trouble.
>
> The Director of Public Prosecutions in London warned the *Sunday Sun* that the articles—the first of which was scheduled to appear in to-day's issue—could break the law. In an urgent letter to the paper's editor, Mr. Malcolm Armstrong, he appealed for publication of the articles to be postponed.

What then were the factors which lay behind the speedy moves by the DPP to prevent publication of matters vitally affecting the North-East and the country. Wilson had repeatedly said that nothing should stand in the way of the truth being revealed. But once again it was his old friend Cunningham who came to the rescue. The arrest of Cunningham in 1973 had led to the premature ending of the Poulson bankruptcy hearings in public, and in the days that followed, at Leeds Crown Court the details of the parliamentary file promised by Muir Hunter was only heard behind closed doors. This time the reason for secrecy was the proceedings pending against Cunningham and the builder McCullough, Mathew Allon, Cunningham's brother-in-law, and two Durham Councillors Bob Urwin and Sidney Docking. Their trial was held over till February. There was growing concern in the North-East at the way these trials were being dragged out. I must again quote Wilson from the Shildon speech of July 1973. 'Equally the press should not be inhibited by the existence of court proceedings which for *whatever reason* have dragged on for so long as to be *virtually moribund*, and which through the sheer passage of time may relate to a world or to a state of affairs which has changed almost out of recognition.'

In its editorial the *Sunday Sun* then went on to give a fitting reply to the Poulson and McCullough beneficiaries in the council offices and chambers of South-East Northumberland who have been reluctant to face the facts of corruption in the area.

WE WILL PUBLISH

The *Sunday Sun* is sorry to disappoint the many thousands of people who were looking forward to reading the first of three articles by Eddie Milne this week. We asked him to write about his forthcoming autobiography because, having seen its contents, we felt they were of vital importance to the people of this region.

This week's intervention by the Director of Public Prosecutions has done nothing to alter that view. The *Sunday Sun* will publish the Milne articles as soon as it is legally practicable to do so. Of course we would not wish to prejudice a fair trial of the five local men facing corruption charges, nor would we want to publish a watered-down version of the Milne articles.

We reiterate: THE *SUNDAY SUN* WILL publish the *MILNE FILE*.

We were learning the harsh lesson of anyone who clashes with the establishment, particularly the one then headed by Short and Wilson, with the 'relentless animosity' that the then Deputy Leader of the House of Commons revealed in *Blackwoods Magazine* of July 1974, now that I no longer had the limited protection of belonging to the House of Commons. One appreciates the apprehension of establishment circles in and around the North-East, when despite the October Election result—or maybe because of it—our support and influence in the area continued to grow. The antics of my successor played a very significant part in that development.

Both John Ryman and the Blyth Constituency Labour Party were running into troubled waters. Due to lack of finance the services of the full-time agent Mortakis had to be terminated. An urgent, special appeal for funds went out to the Unions and other affiliated organisations to save the situation. The net result was thirty pounds! Mortakis finished his job on 30th November, 1975. Neither Regional Office nor Labour Head-quarters at Transport House stepped in to save the situation, despite the past services given to them by the Blyth Labour Agent in 'Getting Rid of Milne'. It certainly confirmed the details given in an eve of poll leaflet issued by my campaign committee in the October election.

YOUR CHOICE ON THURSDAY

An absentee London Barrister who will be seen very little in the Blyth Constituency or in Parliament, but in the law courts of London. The affairs of Blyth and district will be run by the Labour Club Secretary . . . and all of us know what that means.

OR RETURN
EDDIE MILNE.

Our people would not claim the gift of prophesy, but follow-ing the termination of his employment as agent and secretary to Ryman and the Blyth CLP, Mortakis took over as full-time steward at the Blyth Labour Club. The *Newcastle Journal* of 10th December, 1975 reports:

Yesterday Mr Mortakis who has been connected with the club since it was founded in 1968, said there would be a readjustment of part-time staff as result of his appointment.

In addition to becoming full-time steward, Mr Mortakis will be a voluntary worker for the party and says he will be ready to help anyone, including local MP John Ryman.

Help was certainly needed in that quarter. On Saturday 23rd August, 1975, Mike Chrisman, the political reporter of local radio station *Metro*, visited the Labour Club and inter-viewed the then secretary-agent about election expenses in the October campaign. Previously he had visited the Labour Party printer and had received confirmation of dealings which were not in accordance with the law of election returns that had been carried out both before and after the election campaign. The *Metro* reporter was treated to a torrent of abuse from Mortakis, directed, he says, mainly against myself, but no information about the printing and financial payments made in connection with the election about which he was enquiring. The Honourable Member for Blyth then slapped a writ on Mike Chrisman. *Metro* responded by stating that they would defend the proceedings and the programme would go ahead. *Metro* News Editor, Kevin Rowntree said, 'We have been researching this programme for several months. Our advisers have told us that this material should be given to the Director of Public Prosecutions via the police. We should be handing it over within 24 hours. We still plan to broadcast the programme as soon as possible.' A *Metro* official later said that the writ was 'entirely separate' from their decision to contact the Director of Public Prosecutions. Following press reports on the matter, I wrote to the Director of Public Prosecutions on 9th September, 1975, drawing his attention to reports in *The Times* and *The Daily Express* and on *Metro Radio* about happenings in the Blyth Constituency during the October 1974 General Election, and indicating close interest in the investigations taking place. In the letter it was pointed out to the DPP that 'Following the General Election, reports were forwarded by my Agent, Councillor Mrs W. Yellowley JP, to the Clerk of the Crown in Chancery, the Home Office and the Speaker of the House of Commons. Complaints about Election spending and postal votes were also made to the Acting Returning Officer, Mr Peter Ferry, Chief Executive of Blyth Valley Council. *If the time and resources had been available to us then our election committee would have sought a petition to examine the campaign in the Blyth Constituency.*'

In his reply to me, some three weeks later, Mr P. R. Barnes, for the DPP, said that 'certain further enquiries are about to be made by the police regarding the election expenses of Mr John Ryman MP and it is hoped that it will be possible to reach a final decision by the end of October. He went on to say, 'If the officers of the Blyth Constituency ILP have any material information regarding offences, I suggest that they should communicate with Detective Chief Inspector McFadd, at the Police Station in Newcastle.' This I did on 2nd October, 1975, saying, 'The officers of our organization are available to meet you at a mutually convenient time. During next week I shall be on holiday in the Lake District but Councillor Mrs W. Yellowley JP will be available to make the necessary arrangements.' I had a 'phone call from McFadd before leaving for the Lakes; he had contacted Mrs Yellowley, but no evidence was sought from the ILP. Nor to the best of our knowledge has any evidence been taken from the other parties concerned in the October Election. I had also reminded Inspector McFadd that I had shown him my letter to the DPP of 9th September when he had visited two of our Party workers in the course of his investigations into the books of the printer. Detective Chief Inspector McFadd will be remembered from earlier in this book as having adopted a hostile attitude to Mr Alec Valentine of ITN on the occasion of a visit made to builder McCullough following my handing over to the Attorney General some papers and documents in connection with the sale of houses to police officers in County Durham. It was not only the police who bounced back into the picture of events arising from the October election. The next to appear was the Acting Returning Officer, Mr Peter Ferry.

On 20th March, 1975, Independent Labour Candidate Winnie Yellowley, had scored a remarkable victory in a Blyth Valley District Council by-election in the Waterloo Ward with a majority of close on 300 over Labour and Liberal Opposition. This was the seventh election fought by the Blyth Independent Labour Group, two General and five District Council by-elections, inside thirteen months, which showed a clear overall majority of votes in the ILP favour. Our Council Group now numbered four on Blyth Valley Council and one councillor in the Wansbeck District which covered the Bedlington end of the constituency.

On the eve of poll in the Waterloo Ward, I had accompanied our candidate on a round of the polling booths. As Mrs Yellowley was acting as her own agent, I was not there in an official capacity, but knowing most of the officials, had stepped into the polling booths in response to their greetings. In the Lynn Street polling station I was accosted by a voter, Mr R. R. Nuttall of 6 Lynn Street, Blyth, who demanded to know why I was in the polling station. I asked him if he was there in an official capacity, for Mr Nuttall was none other than the Chief Executive of the neighbouring District Council of Wansbeck and appears in at least three addresses in the telephone directory. Chief Executives are entitled to live where they wish, but when they have a choice of addresses from which to vote one would expect them to do so on their home territory. Perhaps votes are more important and carry more value in the Blyth Constituency than in neighbouring Morpeth.

As was to be expected, Ferry made a great song and dance about the issue. The Returning Officer who could not be contacted in the October election came to life in March 1975. He described my act of talking to the presiding Officer at Lynn Street 'as a distinct and serious breach of rules governing election procedures'. In his letter to Mrs Yellowley, he went on to state: 'This action placed the Presiding Officer in a difficult position in view of the fact that Mr Milne is a publicly known personality and known to be strongly associated with you, and few Presiding Officers would consider challenging his authority to be in the station, and it was quite wrong to take advantage of this.' Ferry interviewed Mrs Yellowley on the visit, but refused either to have me present at the meeting or to see me to discuss the issue. In very heavy-handed fashion he stated his intention of keeping the matter on file. We heard of no further protest from Mr Nuttall, who no doubt had been rather surprised at seeing me at the polling station, but I am sure it is of interest to Wansbeck Council and its electors that in a time of acute housing shortage, the Chief Executive can be listed in three homes. If modernisation grants were given by Blyth Valley Council to the Chief Executive of a neighbouring authority, it certainly strengthens the case made by so many, that an examination should be made of the procedures in this field. In fact Tony Crosland has just appointed Ferry to such a committee. Its findings should be of interest. Mr Peter Ferry has not been so precise or forthcoming in other matters connected with elections. His memory is not too clear on the fate of the missing packet of late-arrived postal votes handed over to a clerk in his office on 2nd December, 1974.

On this issue, following discussions with the officials of the Crown Office and letters to Mr Ferry, no progress has been made at the time of writing. I approached him for an interview in connection with the postal ballot and other election details because of material I was preparing for a book on the February and October Elections. I was also interested in having access to the file on myself which Ferry claimed he had at the Council offices, but it was not to be. His reply was, 'Without knowing what matters you wish to discuss and check I cannot decide upon the granting of an interview. Let me know the details of the items you wish to talk about and I will certainly consider your request further.' This was from a returning officer whose retainer, salary and superannuation are paid from the Consolidated Fund controlled from the House of Commons.

When I wrote him for further details he lapsed into vagueness. 'This is the first occasion,' he said in his reply to me, 'on which you have referred to a specific date about the packets.' The specific date, which Ferry knew well, was 2nd December, 1974. He claimed that the packet containing postal votes were despatched by normal post and no proof of posting existed. 'I have ascertained from members of my staff that a small number of postal packets were returned during December 1974 and January 1975, the last remembered packet being during the latter part of January, 1975.' But in a letter I received from the Crown Office, in response to my appeal for further information, I was told: 'A further check has been made and as a result I am unable to confirm that the postal packet to which you refer (which was despatched from Blyth some months after the General Election of October 1974) was received in this office.' More important to us at Blyth was the point in the letter which said. 'In this particular case I have communicated with the Acting Returning Officer in Blyth who says that the documents to which you refer were posted to the Clerk of the Crown as late as February 1975.' It is a pity that Mr Ferry cannot be as precise on this matter as he was about my visit to the polling station on the occasion of meeting Mr Nuttall. Otherwise a great deal of mystery surrounding the conduct of elections in Blyth could have been avoided.

It certainly confirms the correctness of our approach to Selwyn Lloyd for a Speakers Conference on Electoral Reform and arising from the experiences of those around me at Blyth, we have a lot of evidence and information to offer. I was a member of the 1966 Speakers Conference headed by Speaker King. I certainly look forward to being a member of the next.

An indication of the special attitude towards normal democratic procedures in the North-East was provided in a report of 15th October, 1975 in the *Newcastle Journal*. 'Former councillor and Labour Party official William Lewis said his action of "Marking off" who had voted was done by all parties in the country. But the difference in his case was that he was a presiding officer, sworn to secrecy.' He told the magistrates, 'in any area in Birtley and Chester-le-Street the parties can get to know the number of people who voted because of their markers off.' Lewis later commented that 'The law on this needs tightening up.' It is comforting to know that we have an ally in the fight for electoral reform in the Chester-le-Street area. How many more will emerge is uncertain. The secretary of Chester-le-Street Labour Party said: 'The executive committee will probably discuss the matter but, clearly, it does not come into the category of offences for which the party might consider disciplinary action.'

After discussing the postal ballot issue further with my campaign committee, and acting on legal advice, I approached the Speaker and the Clerk of the Crown in Chancery for permission to examine the election documents deposited with the Crown Office following the October General Election. On Friday 28th November, 1975, accompanied by a barrister and four top officials from the Crown Office, I visited the Public Records Office at Hayes, Middlesex. All the documents were placed at our disposal. A minute and thorough search was made of the late-arrived postal ballot papers from every constituency in England. No sign of the packet, which had been seen in the office of the Acting Returning Officer for Blyth Constituency, Mr Peter Ferry, and been handed over to a clerk in his office on 2nd December, 1975, was found.

As the heavy gates guarding all the documents and ballot papers for the October Election 1974 swung behind us, we expressed our thanks to the Crown Office officials for their help and guidance in the case of the missing packet, and realised that a number of questions now needed to be asked. Could we

239

any longer afford, in any part of Britain, to leave the democratic process of the election of Members of Parliament to officials who are or have been involved in heated controversies between political parties and the candidates in elections, either local or parliamentary? In the case of the missing Blyth packets of postal votes, which might have determined the result in a 78 vote majority, one would have thought that special care would have been taken in the despatch of the documents to the Crown Office. It did not escape our attention that most of the documents we examined at the Public Record Office had been sent by registered post. At Blyth in this case, proof of posting does not exist and even dates are unobtainable in any form of posting book. And besides, why did it take the Returning Officer from December 1974 until February 1975 to return the postal ballot papers? In addition, the packets of ballot papers that we noticed and brought to the attention of the Returning officer contained *opened* envelopes. As was clearly pointed out to us by the Crown Office, the official instructions, issued to ARO and contained in Statutory Instruments 1974 No 648 The Representation of the People Regulations 1974, which came into operation on (appropriately) 1st April, clearly states:

57 (2) Where any covering envelopes are received by the Returning Officer after the close of the poll or any envelopes addressed to postal voters are returned as undelivered too late to be readdressed, or any spoilt ballot papers are returned too late to enable other postal ballot papers to be issued, he shall put them unopened into a separate packet, seal up such packet and forward it at a subsequent date in the manner described in paragraph (1) of this Regulation.

Preciseness of detailed instructions can go no further. As in the past, police activities now loomed large among the matters to be dealt with in the closing weeks of the year. Detective Chief Inspector McFadd has been mentioned in connection with the Ryman investigations. Although he failed to make contact with myself or officials of my organisation for an interview he telephoned me from his Market Street headquarters, saying that he was talking on a direct line, that the DPP had asked him to pass some information on to me, and could he have a talk. I told him, as I had done in my letter, that arrangements should be made with Councillor Mrs Yellowley and a meeting could take place when I returned from the Lakes.

Then followed, history repeating itself, an approach from Detective Superintendent Terence Light of the West Midlands Constabulary. He telephoned to say that he wished me to check for him some writing on the documents to be submitted to jury concerning the sale of houses by the builder McCullough to police officers in County Durham. Readers will recollect that earlier in this book I referred to a visit paid to me in the House of Commons by Superintendent Light following my handing over the documents, which had led to the case, to the Attorney General. I arranged to meet Light at my home, but following legal advice contacted my solicitor, and advised Light to make the arrangements with him. I then had to leave for Aberdeen because of the death of an aunt and wrote to Light telling him to contact my London solicitor.

When Light visited my home on 10th November, accompanied by another police officer, he showed me the document on which some pencilled details had been made. It was not my handwriting and I pointed out to the police officers that if they had wanted to check on my handwriting they could have done it in two ways, by comparison with the handwritten letter I had sent them from Aberdeen and with the statement signed and initialled by myself when they interviewed me at the House of Commons immediately after the Attorney General had received the documents. These documents had been reported as stolen and investigations had been conducted for over a year by the North-East police and had caused much unpleasantness before, during and after the October election. On many occasions complaints were made to the authorities about police harassment. It was assumed, and stated to me by the police that there was a clear line of demarcation between the inquiries made by Superintendent Light into the sale of the McCullough houses, and the investigations of the police into the supposed stealing of the documents. This was not how it seemed to me and the police, both from the West Midlands and the North-East, appeared to be working in conjunction. .

On 9th July, 1975, I had received confirmation in a letter from the Attorney General that the theft of the documents had been under police investigation for a year. This certainly underlined the vigilance of the police in their operations, certainly as far as the harassment of our people and myself at Blyth was concerned. Silkin's letter also underlines the manner in which trials and hearings were being drawn out. Reference was made by him on 9th July to the proceedings against McCullough, the police officers, Cunningham and other Councillors, but the Crown Court hearing did not take place until February 1976. Silkin's letter is worth repeating in full.

Royal Courts of Justice, 9th July 1975
Dear Eddie,
Thank you for your letter of 3rd July. I am very sorry to have taken so long to let you have a fuller answer to the complaints which you made concerning a visit to your home by two officers of the Northumbria Force on 15th December, 1974. The reason for the delay has been that I wanted to send you as full a reply as possible to the questions which you raised and this I could not do until certain material police investigations were complete and decisions taken with regard to them. This has been done and I am free to write to you.

As you will probably have seen in the Press, two sets of proceedings have been commenced against McCullough as a result of the very extensive investigations which has taken place into the affair. The first are against McCullough, Cunningham, Docking, Urwin and Allon. The second are against McCullough and the two police inspectors, Bains and Young.

It is not possible, of course, for me to comment on these proceedings, but they are related as you will readily appreciate to the police investigation into the documents which you passed to this Department. As you know, it was alleged that these documents had been stolen from McCullough's solicitors' office. Once this serious allegation had been made, it was incumbent on the police to investigate the allegation thoroughly; it was certainly not possible for them to ignore it with all the obvious consequences which such a course of action would entail, including possible allegations of a cover up or a 'Watergate'.

Moreover, if it had not been investigated, the suggestion was open to be made that some persons had stopped at nothing, even theft of documents, in order to 'get McCullough'.

Before initiating the investigations in respect of the letters, the police, very properly, consulted the Director of Public Prosecutions and myself and we were of the opinion that the police had no option but to investigate the case in the same way as any other allegation. This has been done and their report has been considered by the prosecution team of counsel, who came to the conclusion, with which I and the DPP wholeheartedly concur, that there can be no question of proceedings against anybody arising out of the alleged theft of the documents.

If, however you have any complaints about the conduct of the police in this matter, I suggest that you take them up with the Chief Constable of the Force concerned in accordance with the normal practice. So far as a Tribunal is concerned, the position is that police inquiries, to say nothing of prosecution, are still continuing, and it would be inappropriate to establish a Tribunal. In any event, the decision whether to establish a Tribunal under the 1921 Act is not mine.

Yours sincerely

Sam Silkin

The point about approaching the local police needs no comment. Complaints to them are confined to matters of rudeness and manner of interview. What I have been seeking all these years is the underlying purpose of the police interviews and harassment, and why certain basic civilities are not observed by the police, particularly in the North-East.

Not long after Superintendent Light's visit, I received a letter from the Deputy Chief Constable of the Durham Constabulary, intimating that he had received a copy of the letter I had sent to Light and indicating that if I had any complaints against the Durham police he would be glad to receive and deal with them. It is entirely wrong for such a link to exist, for the two sets of police investigations are supposed to be unrelated. In any case the Durham Police cannot deal with the type of inquiry I was pursuing with the Home Secretary. Nothing less than a fully independent inquiry into the conduct of the Durham police during the period of Andrew Cunningham's chairmanship will satisfy. In their own long-term interests the present Durham police leadership should be demanding the same course of action.

Substantial libel damages were awarded to me, as I have already stated, arising from my action against Willie Hamilton, following his statement that I had wrongly claimed election expenses during the by-election at Blyth in 1960. 'Get out of your shining armour,' was Hamilton's challenge to me at that time. I am grateful to him for providing me with the title of this book and some financial help to make up for my loss of Parliamentary salary. Hamilton was nevertheless the first MP to speak for Ryman in Blyth!

At a press conference in London last September, I said that in the event of the police failing to move on the evidence given to them and the DPP by *Metro Radio* about the alleged excessive election expenses of the Labour candidate in the October General Election, a private prosecution would be initiated by myself. Action was taken, but only at the last minute under threat of a private prosecution. The Case was adjourned to February, then to March, then to April and May, and at time of writing, has been sent for trial in Newcastle for September 1976. The outcome may yet be long delayed and meanwhile Blyth has no active MP. I wrote to the Attorney General on 13th January indicating surprise that the defence had asked for a delay in the proceedings, and that at the Magistrate's Court, a leading Labour Party figure, Councillor Gilbert Barker was in the chair. I indicated to the Attorney General that, along with many other people in the constituency, I was concerned at the delay in bringing the matter to trial. The MP and his agent seemed to have come in for unusually favourable treatment. The issuing of summonses was delayed for around a fortnight to suit the defendants' convenience and in the end Mortakis and Ryman called by appointment at police headquarters in Newcastle to collect them.

Following the arrest of McCullough, large housing contracts were given to the firm with which he was connected by both Blyth Valley and Wansbeck Councils, and the sums involved were in the region of four to six million pounds. I raised the matter at public meetings in the constituency and wrote to Tony Crosland to clarify the issue. In some quarters it was being rumoured that the firm had changed hands and that McCullough was no longer connected with it, while others alleged that the contracts were being used for other purposes. To many of us the first issue to be cleared was that while the McCullough firm could continue to trade and draw contracts from local councils, the residents and ratepayers could not comment on the activities of the firm in any way. In fact on the day of my London press conference about the election irregularities, Councillor George Adams, the Labour Leader of Blyth Valley Council, launched an attack on my speeches at Blyth and Bedlington about the McCullough issue, asking Wilson 'to set up a judicial inquiry into the skilled and deliberate use of smear techniques which have exploited public uncertainty following reports of corrupt practices in the North-East.' (*Whitley Guardian* 31.10.75). Adams also referred to 'the myth that a single source has been responsible for exposing corruption in the North, of opposition within the Labour Party, and which has been maintained by frequent repetition of falsehoods in circumstances that may be highly questionable.' Wilson refused the appeal. I was not surprised, as I did not think that Britain's Prime Minister and Labour's leader would risk a full scale inquiry into the North-East or its Labour Party. Much more powerful voices than Adams' had raised this demand in the past and been refused. With Short at his elbow Wilson could always find reasons for refusing to turn over the stones of the North-East to find out what lay underneath.

Two other events bring the current Blyth scene up to date. First there was the arrival in Blyth of a BBC *Tonight* team with interviewer David Taylor. They allowed allegations to be aired in the surroundings of the Blyth Labour Club by Mrs Monica McClean and Mr Bob Watson, a former member of the Blyth Police Force, that a large van load of food had been delivered by the Co-operative to our campaign headquarters during the

February 1974 General Election. What seemed to start off as a serious exercise to examine the Blyth situation in depth, turned into a farce, describing councillors as being afraid to have a dustbin from the council in case it was labelled 'corruption', and with Taylor wandering on the beach at Cresswell holding up a lump of sea coal. He was hopelessly out on his facts about the account for food spent in the February election, which amounted to £9.50p. He was even further at sea in his reference, which showed scanty research, that I had never mentioned Poulson till 1972 and only after encountering difficulties with Mortakis and the local Labour Party. The heady atmosphere of the Blyth Labour Club and the North-East's bracing beaches seem to have had a deteriorating effect on Taylor's objectivity.

Of course Taylor has just returned from an interview with the Chairman of Durham County Council whom he said he was visiting in connection with his forthcoming book on Poulson. One would not expect Councillor Fishburn to have much to tell Taylor about dealing with corruption in the North-East. But on the references to Poulson that Taylor showed in the programme, dealing with Blyth Town Centre re-development and the building of the swimming baths in the town a year later, he said that the Poulson-Dan Smith influence had been fought by myself and others from the middle sixties onwards. In fact our February Election eve-of-the-poll message carried the details, which had already been made public at the time of the discussions with the Ministry on the future of the Town Centre, of how Dan Smith and Poulson had met for the first time in Blyth.

If Taylor had been the investigatory reporter he claimed to be, there was much material around for him to deal with. I realise that because McCullough was facing trial last February, he could not include in the programme the houses built for the Chief Executive of Blyth Valley Council and for the Burgh Engineer of the former Council. He placed great stress on the report of the former Blyth Labour Party Chairman and Housing Chairman of the Burgh Council, Fred Smith, and on my alleged 'failure' to do anything for the Blyth Constituency since 1960. Again much material may have been lost to Taylor because of his inhibition about the cars or houses given as gifts by McCullough to leading dignitaries, owing to pending legal proceedings.

246

But the *Tonight* team's handling of the Mrs McClean allegations had a much more puzzling look to it. It was the result of a major switch in policy by those responsible for the programme. Whether the directive, as in so many aspects of these matters, came from higher up or not, only time and events will tell. It has only been on rare occasions in 40 years of public life, in one role or another, that I have had to make a serious complaint about the actions and the attitudes of the news media, be it press, radio or television, but I have never experienced anything quite like the actions of those responsible for the *Tonight* programme on Blyth.

There could be no excuse for the BBC team failing to get our side of the story, for they spent hours with a number of us going into detail. A playback of my more than 50 minutes interview with Taylor would make interesting reading, not so much for what the programme contained, but for what it left out. Despite their sub-judice difficulties arising from so many corruption trials awaiting hearing in the North-East, they managed to devote time and space to the Labour Agent Mortakis, himself awaiting trial along with Ryman on charges in connection with election expenses. In fact the question could be asked as to whether Ryman, as MP for Blyth which he still is at time of writing, was approached to take part, and if so what was his answer. The sayings of Blyth's fox hunting MP should surely have been a good subject for a programme on the 'Blyth Affair'.

The cameras went into action for the first time at a public meeting in Seaton Delaval organised by the Blyth Constituency ILP and arranged well before the programme was ever discussed. It was a packed meeting of the enthusiastic, old-time public meeting type, seldom seen these days. In dealing with Blyth Valley Council, I mentioned a promise made earlier by Councillor Adams at a Council meeting, that all Labour Councillors would be prepared to show their bank accounts when declaring their interests for the register to be prepared.

I produced my own bank statements, and documents related to the purchase of my house, with mortgage arrangements and payments. The following is an extract from the *Whitley Bay Guardian* report on the meeting (28.11.75).

247

He (Milne) challenged every member and official of Blyth Valley Council to produce his bank statements and his house purchase documents as he did himself at the meeting.

'I have to tell why it was necessary in the February and October elections of 1974, in a Labour stronghold like Blyth, for those who are gathered as the Independent Labour Party to take the stand we did.' During the years from 1960, when he first became MP for Blyth, the over-riding factor for him had always been what was best for the people he represented.

'Things emerged from the February 1974 election when a decision had to be made. People ask why we left the Labour Party. We did not leave the Labour Party; they left us.

It is the ordinary folk who give to this movement its greatness. That is the background of the battles that have gone on in this constituency for years. It is a fight for the soul of the Labour Movement.'

At question time I was asked by the Blyth CLP chairman, Councillor Collier, if I always told the truth, apparently an innocuous question; but the camera path was then prepared for Mrs Monica McClean, who was not called by the chairman, who had called a questioner from the other side of the hall. Mortakis then stepped in and directed the camera team elsewhere while preparing himself for questioning.

He was not called by the chairman but we were later informed by a member of the BBC team that this was the point arranged for Mrs McClean to bring in her accusations about the money spent on food by the Independent Labour campaign committee during the February 1974 Election.

Certainly Mrs McClean's allegations about food consumed at our Campaign headquarters in the February 1974 General Election was nothing new. It was the centre piece of an effort by the Labour Party to reverse the result of that election in favour of Ivor Richard. It concerned the delivery to our rooms of some sandwiches and cakes for workers on polling day, which was ordered by one of our officials, but personally paid for by the catering manager, who gave the food valued at £9.50 as a donation to our campaign funds, and the matter was dealt with by our treasurer in the election returns and donation list. Mrs McClean raised the matter at this time, and it was fully explained to her.

Following the public meeting at Seaton Dalaval, I asked for an interview with Harold Whitehead, the Chief Administrative Officer of the North Eastern Co-operative Society Ltd, because of reports reaching us that two security officers from the Co-operative headquarters at Gateshead had been examining items contained in our election accounts at the Blyth Co-operative catering department. Along with Mrs Yellowley, I had an interview with Mr Whitehead, who was accompanied by the Blyth Area Manager of the North Eastern Co-operative, on Thursday, 27th November, 1975, and we voiced our protests about the intervention by private security officers into complaints concerning our election accounts. Whitehead's defence of the Society's action was that they had received a complaint about a *large quantity of foodstuffs* delivered to our campaign headquarters on polling day in the February 1974 election, costing in the region of £100–£150 and possibly stolen. A complete examination of the matter had been made and, as we had claimed in February, the purchase amounted to only £9.50. This had been paid by the catering manager and a receipt was in the Society's files. Whether the police had been notified before the Co-operative security officers stepped in to examine the item concerning our election account, or whether the police had asked the Society to investigate following a complaint from Mr McClean will possibly never be known. One thing is certain: many people were out to discredit me and the force of my attack on local corruption, and they ranged from the hierarchy of the Labour Party to elements of the police. The desperation with which one small item that could throw a shadow on my integrity was picked up and distorted shows how frightened some of them must have been.

Mrs McClean and Bob Watson were quite pleased to conduct discussions and give interviews to the BBC team by arrangement with Mortakis at the Blyth Labour Club, but when Mike Chrisman of *Metro Radio* called to see them at Mrs McClean's home, by appointment for an interview, Chrisman's notes were snatched from him by Mrs McClean, shielded by Watson, torn up and destroyed. A letter from *Metro* seeking the return of the Chrisman notes has been ignored.

I considered the matter serious enough to ask for the intervention of the Home Secretary and to ask him to treat the matter as one of urgency, but so far have received no reply.

As for the Co-op, their unease is evident in the following press statement:

An allegation has been made that the outside catering department of the North Eastern Co-operative Society provided food on 28th February 1974 to the Independent Labour Party at Blyth, without payment. The society's internal investigations have shown an account for food was paid and no gift in kind was made by the Society.

Our investigations are confined to our internal procedures as a result of the allegation. This is standard procedure. As the allegation was made to the police we are co-operating with their inquiries. The fact that this is alleged to be connected with the election returns of a Parliamentary candidate is outside our jurisdiction and a matter for the police.

The placing of the responsibility for the investigations on to the police is contrary to the statements of Whitehead of the Co-op when we interviewed him and distorts the question of the gift in kind received from the Society's catering manager. It was never claimed by us that a gift in kind had been received from the Society. With the people responsible for Co-operative decisions in Blyth at the moment it would have been surprising for our organisation to receive any consideration from that quarter.

The press statement was not only misleading but bordered on the malicious, for in an interview with the *Journal*, a Co-operative spokesman refused to *give details about the value of the account, who had paid it, or the food provided.*

Information of that kind would have assisted us greatly in dispelling the flood of rumours being circulated from the Blyth Labour Club about the February Election purchases, but it was obvious that the Co-op chiefs and those around them were more disposed to assist rumours than dispel them. The press statement from the Co-operative also gave credence to the *Journal* headline on the subject: CO-OP DENIES GIFT TO MILNE.

Legal action has been taken against both Mrs McClean and Bob Watson who it is alleged had set himself up as a private investigator after his connections with the Police Force in Blyth had been severed. Adams stepped in again to inform the Council that it had been decided to give evidence to the Royal Commission on Standards of Conduct in Public Life, but only if I was prepared to give information to Mr Peter Ferry that could be transmitted to the Commission. I would very much like Adams to prepare material for scrutiny by the Salmon committee. Adams justified his attitude in a rather wordy and pompous letter to me and said that any information I provided would be used by the editor of the *Journal* 'as seemed to him to be appropriate and in the public interest'.

His reason for writing me was in response to an invitation to address our monthly meeting as guest speaker. He replied by saying 'I shall not be accepting your invitation because I would not wish to blur my loyalties to the Labour Party and to the men and women in it whose support and trust are the prime source of the political activity in which I am able to engage.' He then went on to attack what he described as my 'dependence on publicity'. I pointed out to Adams that no complaint had been made by him about the publicity given to my successor as MP for Blyth after the General Election and that references to publicity came ill from the Leader of a Council which spent thousands of pounds of ratepayers money on the upkeep of a Department devoted to publicity and press relations, also pointing out to the Labour Leader of Blyth Valley Council the example set for many of us by his own parents who had been connected with E. C. Morel in his Dundee days by saying 'The people to whom I owe loyalty in the Labour Movement are the generation represented by the standards and example set by your parents and others in public life. A standard which today's Labour leaders seem incapable or unwilling to follow.' Adams had claimed that it was the Blyth MP whose support encouraged him to approach Wilson for a judicial inquiry into the Blyth Affair.

So, amid the sound and fury of the merchants of cover-up

and their refusal to accept the evidence of what corruption and lowered standards of public life had had on us as a nation, it increasingly became apparent that many people were moving in our direction. In the Blyth Constituency, the ever increasing campaign by the Labour Party to have us labelled as cranks was having no effect. Our organisation continued to grow, the interview sessions conducted by our councillors drew large numbers of people to them, and our Independent Labour organisation prepared to fight a number of seats at the May 1976 District Council Elections. I was invited to an ever increasing number of functions and meetings both inside and outside the Blyth Constituency. David Taylor's comment, in the *Tonight* programme, intended to be derogatory, that I was acting as if I were still the MP, was not far off the mark. For that is how the people of South-East Northumberland regarded the situation created by Ryman, Mortakis and the crew gathered round them in the precincts of the Labour Club at Blyth. Blyth, which like Walsall South at time of writing, did not have a Member of Parliament active, and much as 'official Labour' tried to cover-up the situation, the ordinary folks of Blyth were not all that easily gulled or kidded.

The number one need on a national scale is still for a Poulson inquiry. Until we have a Tribunal set up under the 1921 Act the course of justice will never be headed in the right direction. The constant delays in setting the dates for trial hearings, with new charges constantly brought to light, make it appear as if the present century will have run its course before a clear picture emerges of the stultifying effects of corruption on our public life, and on our economy as well.

Unfortunately in putting forward reasons and cures for present day malaises both political leaders and church leaders hide their heads in the sands and ignore, in case they offend anyone, the basic underlying reasons for the situation. Dr Coggan made a statement: 'The truth is that in Britain we are without anchors. We are drifting,' and went on quite rightly, to point out, 'Stark materialism does not work. It does not deliver the goods.' But he failed to mention the channels of corruption into which we had drifted as a nation because society was geared to materialistic aims. He should have been directing his fire at the Levers and the Shorts, the Walkers and the Keith Josephs, the Maudlings and others who neglected their public duties in order to pursue their personal interests. He could have done a special sermon on Wilson, land reclamation, Milhench and the use of the Prime Minister's private office for the personal gain of his staff at the expense of the well-being of the community. It would have underlined his comment, again a perfectly correct one. *'We must adopt a different attitude to money and to materials and to machines.'* If the Archbishop wants to give a lead let him get out into the highways and byeways, find out the soundness of ordinary people even with all the sordidness and chaos around them and then devote his appeals for the next few months to the so-called leaders of the nation in all spheres.

On the other side of the coin, powerful voices have been raised in the press for an inquiry into Poulson: in a brilliant editorial on the 9th June 1975, *The Times* continued its campaign on this issue. In referring to the two main suggestions as to what form scrutiny of the Poulson issue should take, *The Times* had this to say:

Only a wide-ranging inquiry into the Poulson affair as a whole could disclose the pattern of corruption within public bodies. It should also concern itself with the conduct of contractors, whose part in those transactions has come under too little scrutiny. The task could be performed either by a Tribunal under the 1921 Act, as suggested by Mr Marnham in these columns previously, or as one of the first functions of the Central Anti-Corruption Agency proposed by Mr Muir Hunter in his article in *The Times* last July. The precise mechanism matters less than the appreciation by the Government that there is both an immediate and a long term job to be done: to examine those aspects of the Poulson affair which have still not been exposed to view and to devise new safeguards against further corruption in the future. The Government must not suppose that so long as there are signs of activity over the second task the first one will be forgotten.

There the question is posed in its stark necessity. And yet the

Government lumbers on ignoring the calls and the appeals and Maudling and others are able to sit in the House of Commons and make statements like 'Put up or shut up'.

Muir Hunter in a letter to *The Times* of 9th June 1975, said

It appeared at the trial of Mr Poulson and Mr Pottinger that a crucial Scottish Office file, containing Mr Pottinger's end of his 'personal' correspondence with Mr Poulson, must have been tampered with. Only the diligence of the trustee in bankruptcy in unearthing Mr Poulson's own file of those letters enabled their true relationship to be assessed. Has this tampering episode been investigated, I wonder, and with what result?

The Civil Service registry system for 'marking out' files is reputedly very efficient. Mr Poulson was often assisted by some of his civil and public service contacts by way of the drafting of them, with impeccable language and logic, of official letters which he (Poulson) was to write to them or to their superiors. Did such cogent missives (sometimes in fact missiles) never raise a sceptical eyebrow among their recipients and did any such scepticism ever lead to an inquiry?

There is—concluded Mr Muir Hunter—*'much outstanding material still to be quarried in the Poulson case.'*

The comments of *The Times* editor added weight to Muir Hunter's already powerful appeal for the setting up of a Central Anti-Corruption Agency.

Mr Muir Hunter's letter is important for three reasons. The first is that as council for the creditors in the bankruptcy hearings he is in an exceptionally good position to know if everything that matters has already emerged. If he is not satisfied then others should not readily assume that enough has been done. The second reason is that it is necessary to be certain that there is no cover-up in any Ministry. The power of the Civil Service is immense. Its high standards are one of the surest safeguards for the probity of British public life. But there may be a natural temptation in any service of pride and spirit to close ranks when it feels its reputation to be threatened. That is a danger that must always be guarded against because if the Civil Service ever comes to believe that the preservation of its own reputation was the first priority then its standards would be progressively eroded. The third reason why Mr Muir Hunter's letter is important is simply that the Poulson affair should not be considered closed if there is any reason to suppose that there are people still in positions of power and influence in the public service who turned a blind eye, or worse, to his activities.

When it is realised that in the top reaches of all the parties at the moment, and in the service of the State, there are many people who must have read and inwardly digested the articles and editorials and letters on this matter, and who have yet ignored the powerful unanswerable case they presented, then it is seen that the situation in Britain is worse than any of us appreciated.

These words will echo and re-echo. The truth will emerge and the country and the world will be the better for it. But men of goodwill must now no longer hug the sidelines and imagine that without them the problem will be tackled and solved. It is not enough for men and women to say that something must be done and the truth will emerge. It is not enough to applaud the editorials and the letters, the messages and the articles and the books. We must compel authority to tackle the problem of corruption in its midst. Or let those in authority get out and make way for those who can and will.

We should let Bernard Shaw have the last word on this subject:

'POWER DOES NOT CORRUPT MEN. FOOLS, HOW-EVER, IF THEY GET INTO POSITIONS OF POWER, CORRUPT POWER.'

Postscript

This book was written to attack corruption in public life and it gives the story of my life to date. It has been in carrying out my duties as an elected public servant that I have come across the matters discussed in the preceeding pages. Chapter 15 is a late addition and events continue to move forward.

My supporters and I decided to contest the local municipal elections in Blyth valley in May 1976. Polling day was May 6 and eleven out of thirteen candidates who presented themselves as Independent Labour were elected, including myself. Councillor Fred Smith, who has been frequently mentioned in this book, died on 2nd May, and the five seats to be polled in the ward must therefore wait until late June, but my supporters are contesting every seat and the strangle-hold of 'Official' Labour, as the party now defensively calls itself in Blyth, is ended. I hope that this is the beginning of a new awakening and awareness, not just in Blyth, but in the Labour strongholds of Britain where it has been so easy to take advantage of the unthinking loyalty of ordinary people who elect corrupt councillors, enriching themselves out of the public purse.

I hope this book will help to spread awareness and help others to think again, especially those who see Socialism as an ideal and a means to a better way of life for all. It is in danger of becoming a cloak instead, to enable the unscrupulous to exploit others in the name of an ideal to which they pay only lip-service. As Smillie would put it, 'Our job is to serve, not to rule.' I am still serving in order to make it more difficult for those who seek *only to rule* to do so, because they are the real threat to democracy in Britain.   May 1976

Index

258